Grass Roots Leaders

To Tony Dottino's children Michael and Karen,
Richard Israel's daughters Lana and Susie
and Tony Buzan's mom of 91 years Jean, a true Grass Roots Leader

Grass Roots Leaders

The BrainSmart Revolution in Business

TONY BUZAN, TONY DOTTINO AND
RICHARD ISRAEL

GOWER

Published by
Gower Publishing Limited
Gower House
Croft Road
Aldershot
Hampshire
GU11 3HR
England

Gower Publishing Company
Suite 420
101 Cherry Street
Burlington
VT 05401-4405
USA

British Library Cataloguing in Publication Data

Buzan, Tony
   Grass roots leaders: the BrainSmart revolution in business
   1. Leadership 2. Knowledge management 3. Organizational
   change
   I. Title II. Dottino, Tony III. Israel, Richard, 1942-
   658.4'092

   ISBN 13: 9780566088025

Library of Congress Cataloging-in-Publication Data

Buzan, Tony
   Grass roots leaders : the BrainSmart revolution in business / by Tony Buzan, Tony
Dottino and Richard Israel
      p. cm.
   Includes index.
   ISBN 978-0-566-08802-5 (alk. paper)
   1. Leadership. 2. Organizational change. I. Dottino, Tony. II. Israel, Richard,
1942- III. Title.

   HD57.7.B894 2007
   658.4'092--dc22

2007007396

Printed and bound in Great Britain by TJ International Ltd, Padstow, Cornwall

Reviews of *Grass Roots Leaders*

Businesses are proclaiming the need for employees to "work smarter", this book provides a practical roadmap in how to do that.

Larry Hupman, IT CONSULTANT—PLEXENT

Grass Roots Leader delivers the essence of a comprehensive quality program without the unnecessary overhead. It gets the people most impacted by change involved early and committed to achieving measurable results.

Ron Glickman, Senior Vice President,
Global Quality Processes and Integration, UTi

Do not confuse activity for results! This book spells out the difference between wasteful busy work and brain smart thinking that gets you to bottom line results."

Dick Tibbits, VP of People Florida Hospital and author of *Forgive To Live*

My vision for Celebration Health is that every employee will bring passion, energy and the benefit of their personal experience to work with them every day. In this way we will truly make a difference for our patients. This book provides the knowledge, skills and tools to make this a reality.

Monica Reed MD, CEO, Florida Hospital Celebration Hospital and author of *The Creation Health Breakthrough*

The concepts and practices in this book are transformative. They can turn your workforce into a powerhouse of innovation, excitement and achievement that delivers tangible results over and over again. Or we could say, "A transformative work that turns the corporation on it's head, giving the workforce the power to lead."

Marshall Tarley, Director of Leadership Development, ASCAP

The people closest to the work are in the best position to identify and implement improvement. This book provides the specifics how on how to make this happen at any organization

Al Homyk, Director, Quality Assurance and Operations Services, Con Edison Company of New York

This book provides pragmatic skills and tools to every level of the organization so everyone can think and act to prevent problems. ... (that is crucial in providing excellent patient care which is vital to our mission of being a global pacesetter.)

Brian Paradis, COO, Florida Hospital

Must reading for every leader. It addresses the most prevalent management challenges in a unique way, providing practical strategies and tools to engage employees. Grassroots Leaders creates an environment that sustains creativity, passion for the work, and leadership at all levels of the organization.

Anne Kelly, CEO/Director, Federal Consulting Group

I have been waiting 30 years for this book and it arrived at the very time I am designing an Executive MBA Course in Leadership for the University of Maryland University College. I will be using *Grass Roots Leaders* as a foundational reading because it is the only book I have encountered that treats leadership as a brain function, understands that we all must step up to the leadership challenge and presents a set of things we can learn and do that will make eveything we do as leaders better. About time Tony.

Stephen Lundin, Big Tuna PhD wrote the multimillion best-selling series of *FISH!* Books. His most recent book is titled, *Top Performer*.

Contents

List of Figures

Acknowledgments

We have many people to thank: our clients, our friends and our readers who have applied our skills and sent us feedback.

Without a publisher there's no book. Thanks to Gower for their continued support and to our editor, Jonathan Norman, for his help, encouragement and insightful feedback.

Thanks to Susan Ford Collins for co-authoring Chapters 3, 4 and 5 and lending her expertise on the structure and flow of this work.

To Evelyn Walker for creating Mind Map summaries at the end of each chapter and contributing valuable insights. To Michael Dottino for his continued support, advice and wisdom and his intellectual contributions. To John Schenkel for critiquing our process and keeping us focused.

Our biggest thank you goes to the people behind the stories appearing in every chapter, who gave permission to have their stories printed. These are the real heroes, the ones with the courage, determination and vision to take our advice and turn it into tangible, profitable results. We are proud of you, our true Grass Roots Leaders.

Tony Buzan, Tony Dottino and Richard Israel

Authors' Preface

It is always a challenge to write a book when more than one author is involved. And with the authors living in different parts of the world and in different time zones—Tony Buzan in England, Tony Dottino in New York and Richard Israel in Miami—the challenge was even greater. Our daily communication process via email, phone and occasional face to face meetings reminded us how important it is to check and recheck what the other party is thinking, saying and writing.

This book is the second in a series by the authors, the first being *The BrainSmart Leader* published by Gower in 1999. A great deal has happened since: new brain research, and information and technology explosion and unprecedented global expansion and competition. With all this in mind, our publisher suggested it was time for a new edition.

Tony Buzan's work has greatly influenced the other authors. He is acknowledged as the world's leading expert on mental literacy. He is a consultant to governments and an internationally-acclaimed speaker and author.

Tony Dottino integrated Buzan's mental literacy thinking into a new and exciting process innovation methodology found in the chapters *Building the Story* and *The 3 Day Miracle*.

Richard Israel has taken Buzan's Mind Mapping to sales organizations around the world. He and Buzan wrote the bestselling book on whole brain selling, *Brain$ell*, Gower 1999, now available in 20 languages.

Susan Ford Collins, Israel's business partner, spent 20 years studying outstanding individuals and discovered 10 Success and Leadership Skills they were all using. In their chapter, *Shifting Gears*, they present one of these skills. The other nine can be found in Susan's book, *The Joy of Success* (HarperCollins 2003).

As we proceeded, it soon became clear that with so much new information in mind, instead of writing an update, we needed to write a new book—*Grass Roots Leaders: The BrainSmart Revolution in Business*.

In today's highly competitive global market place, companies are daily challenged to increase productivity and control costs. To accomplish this they need to develop new and innovative ways to work. This book will assist readers in doing just this.

Introduction

WHY THE GRASS ROOTS REVOLUTION?

Simply, because its time has come.

There is much written about the incompetence and confusion dominant in much modern business. Such writing always has, hovering in the background, an element of self-righteousness and, more significantly, surprise.
The fact is, that with a wider and more insightful perspective, the current situation in business and education is both understandable and correctable.

Let's take a look at that "making sense" perspective:

It was not until a mere 10 000 years ago, in the nearly five-billion-year history of our planet, that modern mankind, which itself had existed for a mere 100 000 years, managed to get its first tentative foothold on civilization.

This marked the beginning of the first, great and longest Human Age, the **Agrarian Age**. The **Agrarian Age** lasted for 9 500 years. During this entire span of time, humankind was not even aware where the centre of its Multiple Intelligences, its brain, was located!

That discovery, spearheaded by Leonardo da Vinci and Michelangelo some mere 500 years ago, laid the foundation for a new revolution which is still in its embryonic stages. The 10-millenia-long **Agrarian Age** ended, with the help of Da Vinci's and Michelangelo's discoveries, and evolved, a mere 150 years ago, to the next great age: **The Industrial Revolution**. The Industrial Revolution transformed the physical and psychological topography of our planet, requiring order, structure and an education system and society that emphasized order, numbers and words.

Business structures and education systems reflected this advance and its needs.

After only 100 years, in the mid twentieth century, the Industrial Revolution gave birth to electronic communication, and created its own child: **The Information Age**. The Information Age was powerful and transformative, yet lasted less than 50 years. Why? Because with the proliferation of information technology, e-mail, the internet and the web, information, instead of becoming

1

the tool of the privileged few, became a "level playing field" on which any individual, Business Leader or Business Follower, would have equal opportunity and access to *any* desired information.

People began to realize that more than simple information, *knowledge* of that information was paramount for success and competitive advantage. **The Knowledge Age** had, at the end of the twentieth century, been created.

During the same time period, another revolution had been burgeoning: **The Brain Revolution.** In a brief period of just 15 years, humankind discovered more than 95 per cent of what it had ever discovered about the internal workings of the human brain. Virtually all discoveries were both startling and hopeful.

We discovered, for example, that:

- The human brain is much more powerful than we had thought. Our functions in the areas of creativity, memory and learning, can be improved by minimally 400 per cent. The human brain can, and *should*, improve with age.
- *Every* normal brain has the capacity for brilliance.
- The number of thoughts potentially available to the average human being is greater than the number of atoms in the known universe.
- The human brain *can* be trained and that old dog *can* learn new tricks! The refreshingly exciting truth is that the human brain has, as *New Scientist Magazine* recently proclaimed, "**No Limits**."
- At the beginning of the twenty-first century, the Knowledge Age was already fading. As the volume of global information about the brain accelerated exponentially, clarion calls began to be heard: *The Harvard Business Review* announced that there was a looming Creativity Crisis that was a greater threat than the combined threats of all international terrorism and all trade laws. The Governments of China, Singapore, Malaysia and Mexico invested massively in new national initiatives for the development of the thinking skills of their citizens. President Vicente Fox of Mexico declared, in front of 10 000 United Nations delegates, at the 5th United Nations Annual Conference on Creativity and Innovation, that the twentieth century was henceforth declared to be "A century for the development of Creativity and Innovation." The coming together of all these giant evolutionary changes has given rise to a new, and what I predict will be, a many-millennia-long Age.
- At the beginning of our twenty-first century, we have come to realize that information is not enough. More than information we need knowledge and its management. More than knowledge and its management, we need to be able to manage the knowledge manager. In other words, we need to be able to manage the human brain and its Multiple Intelligences.
- We have just entered the greatest age in the history of both the planet and the Human Race: **The Age of Human Intelligence.**

- In the **Age of Human Intelligence** *all* workers will become leaders. Each individual in the business and other communities will need, in order to survive, to be creative, flexible, adaptable, quick-thinking, able to absorb and assimilate information at incredibly high speeds, intelligent, alert, and committed to and practising the development of the Multiple Intelligences. This will require special focus on the creative, social, personal, physical, sensual and the ethical/spiritual.

We are about to see, from the workers of the world, a massive eruption of intelligence. We are about to experience a true Grass Roots Revolution where everyone in the world will be developing, manifesting and contributing their previously underestimated Intellectual Capital.

The old clarion calls of "Workers of the World Unite" will no longer be an inherently antagonistic clarion call. It will mark the dawn of a new Revolution in which each worker will multiply the power of his or her Multiple Intelligences by linking, intelligently, with all other workers.

Never before in the history of humankind has the releasing of such astonishing power been so imminent.

Those who make themselves aware of all this will be able to ride the crest of a wave that will take humanity into a future about which so many great leaders, idealists and visionaries have for so long dreamed.

Tony Buzan

CHAPTER 1

A New Breed of Leader

A GRASS ROOTS REVOLUTION: WHAT IS IT? WHY IS IT VITAL TODAY?

To succeed in the years ahead, today's highly competitive, fast-paced organizations must initiate a revolution.

This is an unusual revolution. Not one side against the other, but both sides against a common problem: outmoded approaches, longer working hours and constant stress. Against endless crisis-focused meetings and short-sighted solutions that result in long-term problems and disasters instead.

A revolution against ineffective, inefficient and unproductive habits we find ourselves using. Against keeping secrets and withholding information; against using our minds ineffectively and singly, not smartly and collectively. This revolution will forever transform the way we solve today's and tomorrow's problems.

It is time for everyone in today's organizations to stand up and shout, "Enough is enough! We must change the way we do business day-to-day. It is affecting us all and so we must align. It may be time to slow down to go faster!"

This book will show individuals at all levels of organizations how to initiate a top-down, bottom-up Grass Roots Revolution and present the skills that will be needed to get there.

A CLOSER LOOK AT WHERE WE ARE

In today's global economy, businesses are being asked to do more with less. But unless the system works proactively—unless they take action up front to prevent problems and anticipate changes—such frenetic activity frequently produces the opposite: errors increase, quality goes down, costs go up and customers become angrier or take their business elsewhere. And executives, managers and employees burn out.

Leaders spend 70 to 90 per cent of their time in meetings dealing with "the problem of the day." Spending 25 per cent of an organization's budget on fixing mistakes and managing crises is not unusual. This leaves little time, money and energy to plan and invest in the future.

CONNECTING TOP AND BOTTOM

Most CEOs believe they must know how to solve the problems they face day-to-day. But it's not true. The truth is, people in their organizations frequently know why these errors are occurring and how to fix them, but they are not being asked or empowered to put their ideas to work. And they don't know how to present their ideas in a way that lets them be heard.

The greatest leadership challenge of our time is connecting the executives at the top of organizations, who have the company goals and big picture, and the bottom line, Grass Roots people who have the technical skills and experience to get the job done.

Grass Roots people are front-line workers, supervisors and managers: those within your organization closest to your customers, vendors and support teams, closest to producing your products and delivering your services. Those closest to your problems and solutions.

In today's global marketplace, we must be able to access the knowledge and creativity of everyone in our organizations to continue succeeding. Heads of organizations know this, but they are not doing it—and the results are becoming more and more outrageous, conspicuous and expensive. Exposed to this daily, we become numb—until a devastating consequence smacks us in the face.

HURRICANE KATRINA

Before Katrina struck New Orleans, everyone knew a major hurricane could deal their city a devastating blow. University studies spelled out in precise detail what could happen and lobbied far and wide for immediate steps to be taken. On a visit Tony Dottino made to New Orleans, even his salty tour boat driver warned the tourist, "This whole damn place is below sea level and, when 'the big one' comes, the city will be flooded." Everyone laughed then, but no one is laughing now.

Nobody wanted the levees to break or the city to flood. Nobody wanted people to be isolated in their homes or trapped in the Domed Stadium. Nor to be forced to flee to other cities. Nor die. Then why did this happen?

Like so many businesses, the New Orleans, Louisiana and US governments knew how disastrous "the big one" could be, but they were paralyzed by the immensity of the challenge and short-term costs. They didn't ask what it would take to make the changes that would be needed. They didn't develop comprehensive emergency plans in case "worst came to worst." They didn't anticipate the communication and supply networks that would be needed. So mass confusion compounded the crisis. There were so many top-down, bottom-up communication disconnections that even people a few blocks away didn't know what was happening, what was needed, how soon or by whom. And neither did the leaders of government in their offices thousands of miles away.

The bottom line is: Grass Roots people knew what needed to be done to solve the problem, but they did not have the power to do it. And people at the top who had the power to solve the problem were not aligned and did not take appropriate action. So the disaster ensued. Today it is easy to see that the collaboration and $1–2 billion needed up front to prepare the city and its population—to solve the problem proactively—was a far better investment than having to come up with the hundreds of billions that will ultimately need to be spent to repair the damage to the city, and the lives of the people who called it home.

While reading about Katrina, some of you may have thought, "That's just government." But it's not. The same thing is happening in major corporations. Take BP for example.

Before the disastrous March 2005 explosion killed 15 workers and injured more than 170 others, there were eight incidents at the Texas City refinery that signaled grave problems. Two incidents involved fires. Everyone knew there were serious problems but they weren't fixed.

Here are the facts: (CCN Money.com, October 31, 2006) "Internal BP documents reveal the oil company's knowledge of 'significant safety problems at the Texas City refinery,' months or years before the March 2005 explosion. According to the US Chemical Safety Board, "the company was warned of potentially hazardous conditions at the plant, "and while it improved working conditions, "unsafe and antiquated equipment designs were left in place, and unacceptable deficiencies in preventative maintenance were tolerated."

A BP spokesman said, "We agree with the CSB in that we, too, believe that the March 23, 2005 explosion was a preventable tragedy. We are deeply sorry for what happened and the suffering caused by our mistakes."

Instead of solving the problem proactively, "BP has accepted full responsibility for the disaster at its plant and has settled more than 1 000 lawsuits related to claims made by those injured on site, family members of those who died, and by people who suffered shock. More than $1.6 billion was set aside by BP to resolve those claims, a BP spokesman told CNN. Federal investigators have already fined the company $21 million for more than 300 safety violations at the plant."

Was a decision made at the top that led to the death of those 15 workers? Was it short-sighted cost saving? If it was cost saving, exactly what did they save? And what more could they have saved if they had dealt with these problems proactively—solved them up front? How many business and societal disasters could be prevented if leadership had only sought and used the advice of the Grass Roots—the workers who are closest to delivering the solution? If everyone were able to contribute their knowledge and work as a team wouldn't it increase the ability to find the best solutions?

WHY IS DEVELOPING GRASS ROOTS LEADERS MORE IMPORTANT THAN EVER BEFORE?

In today's rapidly changing, highly competitive global marketplace, change is the only constant. The executive level of today's organizations is no longer in a position to know the best solutions to the problems that emerge day by day.

Jean Turcotte, Nurse Manager of 100 nurses in the Cardio Vascular Intensive Care Unit (CVICU) at Florida Hospital, says, "I believe as a leader one-day-removed from the front line, I am outdated." And he's right.

Your Grass Roots workers are the ones closest to the problems and the solutions. By tapping into their knowledge and experience, you and your organization can more effectively, efficiently and creatively solve not just the problems that come your way, but identify and meet the needs of your customers, marketplace and industry. By collaborating with the Grass Roots you can lead your company ahead in today's challenging marketplace.

For a few weeks or months after the disasters like these, we are all in outrage. "How could this have happened? We have to do something." Then as we get back into our daily grind, we become numb again.

What is the *real* reason these disasters keep happening? Because, as you will soon see, reactive organizations will continue making errors like these and ultimately drive them, or us, out of business—unless we make corrections.

Is your organization reactive? How about your vendors, shippers and customers?

What warning lights are you seeing or ignoring?

FIRST STEP DIAGNOSIS: TWO STYLES OF MANAGEMENT—REACTIVE AND PROACTIVE

Evaluating whether an organization is reactive or proactive is the first thing Tony Dottino does when he begins working with clients.

In crisis or reactive mode, everyone is working hard, putting in long hours, doing all they can, given company politics, and then coming back the next day to a full desk and inbox, more calls, problems and meetings. Poorly considered attempts at cost reduction lead to errors and added expenditures. Accelerating stress levels and increased health cost affect the bottom line. Creativity and innovation is squeezed out. And most expensive of all, experienced employees leave and take their (*your*) knowledge base with them!

In Dr Monica Reed's book, *The Creation Health Breakthrough* (Center Street, 2007), she refers to research that suggests you can work yourself to death, which is happening in Japan, Korea and the USA.

Can this condition be permanent? No, because another name for the reactive mode is "The Going Out of Business Strategy."

LET'S LOOK MORE CLOSELY AT REACTIVE MANAGEMENT

In this type of organization, errors, stress levels and turnover are high. Morale and profits are low. Employees are unhappy and want to go elsewhere. Why? Here are four factors that may be all too familiar to you.

Too little understanding and ownership of job and customer requirements

Reactive management is a one-way street. Requirements and orders come down from the top—from executives, managers, task forces or committees—the very people who are farthest from the work. Their orders are frequently unclear, their solutions off course.

Let's look at an example: In the face of increasing overtime costs, industrial engineers at a major hotel chain were asked to do a workflow analysis. Their goal was to increase the number of rooms each worker could clean during their shift and thereby cut overtime. But it didn't work.

Completing their study, the engineering team decided to change housekeeping's work practices so that vacuuming would be the last step instead of the first. They wrote up new procedures and distributed them to the housekeepers.

Ninety days later, the general manager was shocked to see that instead of decreasing, time-spent-per-room had increased by 20 per cent. And overtime had gone up as well. Why? Industrial engineering's efficiency analysis was done *without* involving the housekeepers. So they didn't realize that vacuuming the rooms last would stir up dust which resettled by the time supervisors came back to check. Finding dusty surfaces using "the finger test," supervisors were calling housekeeping to come back and clean again.

People try their best to hit the target. But when they aren't sure what the target is and they aren't included in the decision-making process, they are less likely to be committed to how well a decision is carried out. Or they carry out that decision to the letter of the law—to prove a point.

A reactive culture doesn't allow time for people to ask questions or conduct question and answer sessions. It makes saying "I don't understand" next to impossible so "wrong solutions" to problems continue driving up costs.

Wouldn't it be better to ask the people who do the work for their input and ideas *before* making changes? Wouldn't they have more ownership and commitment to carrying those changes through to your satisfaction and your customers' or clients'? Couldn't daily crises on both sides be avoided? If we are this ineffective with our internal customer requirements, how well are we doing with our external customer requirements?

Prioritizing by crisis

The reactive system establishes priorities according to who is on the phone, which manager needs something ASAP or which customer has an urgent problem. Constantly in crisis mode, there is little time or energy left to discover *the real reason* things aren't working properly.

Facing a budget crunch, a major transportation company needed to reduce costs so they told their mechanics, "Stretch out your preventative maintenance schedules." In the short term, the numbers looked great. But in the long term, they looked terrible.

Over the next few years, fully loaded trucks started breaking down on the road more and more frequently. Regional dispatchers had to pull crews off other jobs. If they didn't have an empty truck, they had to either unload theirs or drive back to the yard to get one. Next they had to unload the contents of the broken-down truck by hand and wait till the tow truck came.

When the mechanics started troubleshooting the problems, they discovered that saving a preventative maintenance cost of $150 had turned into a major engine or transmission expense which ran into the thousands. The costs now included labor, towing fees, taking people off other assignments, customer refunds and customer dissatisfaction problems which ended up in the millions, instead of saving them anything at all. If we could see "cause and effect" at the same time, how much smarter and profitable would our organizations be?

In a conversation over dinner after an executive session, Tony Dottino told the president of a major airline that he didn't like to fly. The more Tony was discovering about companies cutting back on preventive maintenance, the more concerned he was about the airlines doing the same. Little did Dottino know that Jack was a former maintenance manager so he was surprised when Jack abruptly leaned across the table and responded in a firm voice, "Tony, we would sooner close up our airline than cut back on preventative maintenance!"

In reactive organizations, we not only burn out our equipment but also our people. With so much time and energy spent putting out fires, there is little left for upgrading skills and exploring opportunities. Without new skill sets and approaches, these organizations are simply shortening the time it will take till they clearly realize, "We're moving in the direction to going out of business."

Reactive management keeps everyone in a constant state of stress and anxiety. Medical and brain science research shows that you cannot keep humans in a perpetual state of stress and expect them to produce their best. Prolonged periods of stress alter the chemical makeup of the human body, breaking down its immune system and eventually leading to death.

Does your company promote and reward individuals who put out fires, or those who prevent them? And, when your company faces a budget shortfall, do your executives and managers cut preventative, future-oriented expenses like maintenance and training? How might these decisions impact your organization's future, and yours?

Poor conformance tracking measures

In reactive organizations, metrics are frequently established top-down from the executive/manager point of view and not from that of the worker or customer.

Dottino Consulting had a client in Chicago in the food packaging industry that was trying to keep their shipping costs down, senior management decided, "No more split shipments. Hold all orders till we can fill them 100 per cent."

According to internal metrics, they were doing just fine: All the orders they were shipping were 100 per cent. But a new problem was being created on the loading docks at their distribution points. Partially-filled pallets of shrink-wrapped product were piling up. They were waiting for the rest of the order to be produced so they could be loaded on trailers and shipped to customers.

Who were their customers and how were they being impacted? Their customers were fast food chains and, at their locations, managers were seeing their packaging supplies dwindling. In crisis-mode, they were calling customer service. "A drink without a cup, french fries without a bag simply won't work. Send me whatever product you have and expedite that order!" And, they started looking for another provider even though this one had been reliable until now.

At this point, a man Dottino had worked with over the years was brought in as president. He couldn't understand why the internal metrics his managers were handing him seemed so good but they were losing customers and revenue. A seasoned guy in his early 60s, Tom had grown up in the business and always walked the floor, but now he was sitting in the corporate office and couldn't see the pallets piling up on loading docks at plant sites hundreds of miles away. And since he was the new president, nobody wanted to tell him.

Tom asked Tony to tell him what was going on—why this discrepancy? So Tony went out to several sites and set up teams to meet with customers to find out how *they* were measuring the company's performance. Conversations with the customers about their metrics and how they knew they were satisfying them provided the information Tom needed.

The manufacturer's satisfaction surveys were designed to line up with their internal metrics so, looking from that perspective, Tom's company was doing well: The vast majority of orders shipped were 100 per cent complete. But from the customers' perspective, the product they needed wasn't coming on time and they didn't care about 100 per cent shipments at all.

If Tom's company had been measuring against customer needs in the first place, they would have known split shipments were a customer priority because, for them, some product was better than none. With this information in mind, Tom and his managers quickly made corrections, the loading docks emptied and revenue losses stopped. Fortunately, in this case their customers continued doing business with them. But how much revenue has been lost because of incompatible metrics?

Have you asked your customers how they measure your performance? Do your internal performance measures align with your customers'? And, does your front-line worker have all this information?

Unknown costs of management decisions

Reactive management is frequently so busy responding to the crisis of the day that they don't stop to think about the long-term impact of the decisions being made. Katrina and BP are glaring examples of this, but smaller ones are just as deadly when repeated day after day.

Bob, an accounting manager in a large multinational firm was under constant pressure to close the books as near month end as possible. The firm's finances started slipping and the CEO asked Bob to do weekly forecasts too. Soon the whole month was a mad dash to get the latest numbers upstairs.

Desperate, Bob decided to eliminate all education. Even though a large number of changes in accounting procedures were occurring, day-to-day demands made it seem impossible to send his team anywhere. Even with everyone at their desks, errors were being overlooked. Estimates were being accepted, and no one was making time to plan the new accounting system that was scheduled to come on board in 6 months. "We'll worry about that 30 days out," was Bob's response whenever questioned.

Months later, the system was close to installation but accountants kept finding problems: account balances weren't reconciling, ledgers were incorrect and income statements weren't balancing.

Bottom line: The new system couldn't be installed on time and the date slipped a full year. The firm's external auditors questioned whether or not they could certify the company's finances, and the manager who had worked so hard to put out day-to-day fires was blamed for not bringing them up to the executives for help. He was replaced.

Up-front monetary costs are not the only thing at stake. Bad PR or loss of company credibility may cost an organization far more than time lost up front in communication and training. And, given today's short supply of skilled, educated workers, the cost of having experienced employees say "I've had enough!" and leaving is higher than ever.

There are numerous communication gaps in the reactive system, but the communication gap to the top can be the most expensive. No one wants to tell the boss he made a costly mistake. Unfortunately some mistakes are so bad that the whole world gets to see them.

Tony Dottino knows personally how hard it is to deliver bad news. He once told a CEO that his people were afraid to talk to him. A few weeks later Tony realized the CEO had stopped talking to him too. But no matter how hard it is, failures and problems must be clearly identified and understood.

WHAT SEEMS TO BE A COST MAY BE AN INVESTMENT

While Dottino was at IBM, he was stopped in the halls by the CFO of a manufacturing division. "Tony, the cost of Process Improvement is depleting my capital budget. Go find out what's happening." So he got in his car, drove to the manufacturing site and sat down with key managers. Here is what he heard.

For several months major customers had been more and more upset because their computer systems were shutting down unexpectedly and no one could work until the problem was fixed. Corrective action needed to be taken immediately. And it was. Manufacturing requested and received $10 million to purchase additional equipment to make more extensive and lengthy tests on all computers before shipping.

With more testing equipment in place, more errors were found. So manufacturing asked for another $20 million for still more testing equipment. This request triggered a crisis meeting. The line managers argued, "We need more equipment because the risk of shipping defective computers to customers still exists." The finance managers responded, "But there's no more money left in our capital budget." They all knew customers were screaming loudly, "We need equipment that works 24/7!"

By talking to people on site, Tony discovered that manufacturing had found faulty circuits when they installed the first batch of new equipment. But no one had communicated this discovery to engineering and no root-cause analysis had been conducted.

Every department was operating as an island. Every department had its own politics and budgets. It was an increasingly expensive game of "hide and seek." Some people were counting errors and some were finding errors but no one was passing on what they knew until he brought a new approach into play.

A cross-functional team from engineering, manufacturing, quality and customer service was created to fix the problem at its source. While looking at total costs in all departments, they realized they could afford to use a slightly more expensive material in the circuits and significantly lower testing costs and increase customer satisfaction—without ever buying that $20 million worth of additional equipment.

TOP 10 LISTS

The authors regularly ask executives and employees, "What business issues and challenges keep you awake at night?" In their book, *BrainSmart Leader* (Gower 1999), they published the Top 10 Lists for 1999. Since then the employee list has changed very little, but the executive list shows a far greater awareness of the need to move from reactive to proactive management.

Executives are reading a growing number of reports that CEOs lost their jobs because of the poor performance of their reactive organization. These lists are offered as a benchmark for you and your organization.

EXECUTIVE TOP 10 LIST

1. Constant competitive pressures force us to do more with less.
2. The workforce needs to be constantly energized and inspired to be creative.
3. A constant state of crisis needs to be stopped and followed with action plans.
4. Managers need to hold people accountable for their commitments.
5. Skills of workers and managers need to be upgraded to provide solutions that eradicate problems.
6. We must tap the knowledge base of our front-line people to create a thinking organization.
7. We must cut costs without sacrificing quality and commitments to our customers.
8. We must prevent information overload and share the knowledge we need to grow business and find new markets.
9. We must make next quarter's numbers and keep the investors and board members happy.
10. We must attract and retain skilled, educated talent.

The authors also work extensively with employees on the front line. Although executives say motivating employees takes major effort, they have found employees are passionate about sharing what they see as the organizational challenges as well as their ideas for solving them. Here is what front-line workers tell them:

FRONT-LINE EMPLOYEE TOP 10 LIST

1. Talk straight to us.
2. Listen to what we are saying, really listen!
3. Make yourselves available and stop going to so many meetings.
4. Give us real feedback that leads to improving our performance.
5. Invest in our education so we can be more productive.
6. Stop cutting budgets/expenses/headcount without understanding the long-term impact.
7. Stop changing priorities every month. Create a plan and stick with it.
8. Provide recognition and appreciation for a job well done.
9. Trust us to do the right thing.
10. Respect our experience and knowledge. We are professionals.

You might play a variety of roles in your organization, from executive to human resource manager to front-line worker, so you might find yourself agreeing with statements on both lists.

THIS GRAPH TELLS THE WHOLE STORY

Let's look at two graphs that put the comments from the Top 10 lists in perspective (Figure 1.1). The graphs show a reactive and a proactive organization. The proactive organization is growing financially while the reactive one is heading for financial trouble. If you had your pick, in which company would you want to work?

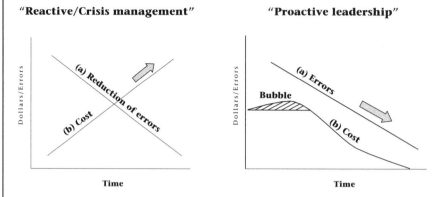

Figure 1.1   Where would you work?

The reactive system

On the reactive graph, to meet customers demands for better quality, service and effectiveness (line a), more money and resources (line b) are spent until a break-even point is reached and the lines cross. At this point, organizational conflict occurs: the finance team warns, "We can't afford to spend any more." And line operations counters, "But we need more money and longer schedules to keep up our quality and delivery." And constant debates and tradeoffs ensue.

The proactive system

On the proactive graph, something unique happens. After an initial increase in resources (line b: the bubble), both lines a and b begin moving down. Why? Because proactive organizations invest time and resources up front which enables them to meet and exceed their customers'/clients' needs and expectations now and in the future. They make time to communicate and solve problems at their source, to initiate preventative changes and gain buy-in from the people who complete the work. They invest in their people, tapping into existing experience and knowledge bases. Team members are enabled and empowered to learn from mistakes and to positively impact today's and tomorrow's success and profitability.

ASSESSING YOUR ORGANIZATION: A LOOK IN THE MIRROR

Take a few minutes to score your organization on the graph in Figure 1.2. (Be brutally honest. No one will see these assessments, but you.) Score your organization three times—from the executive, middle management and front-line worker perspectives.

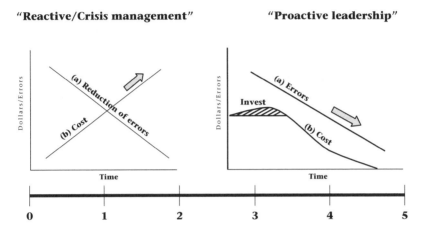

Figure 1.2   **Management versus leadership**

If all three scores are 4 or higher, your organization is moving in the proactive direction. But if your organization's scores are lower, pay close attention to the next paragraph.

At times it's our job to deliver bad news—and it's time for us to do that right now. Here's the blunt truth: *You cannot remain in the reactive management mode and expect to compete successfully in the future.* As you just saw, no matter how long or hard you work, your long-term results will continue trending downward. In a competitive global marketplace, this approach will put your organization's future at risk.

Today when a company evaluates its products, services, customers and competitors, it can no longer simply look within the borders of its country. China, India and South Korea are forcing us all to evaluate our costs, increase our quality and innovation. As technology improves and the global economy becomes more interconnected, additional players will enter the marketplace with a vigor and competitiveness never seen before.

Fast Company magazine recently screamed in bold letters on their front cover, "Change or Die: What if you were given the choice?" The truth is: You *do* have a choice.

PROACTIVE OR REACTIVE? WHICH ORGANIZATIONAL STYLE WILL YOU CHOOSE?

To the leader of reactive companies the authors say, "Stop trying to manage alone and reach out to your people." Proactive companies realize the surest way to flourish and prosper is to make the most of the knowledge, experience and creativity that *already exists* in their organizations, in their Grass Roots.

Your Grass Roots people know where resources are *not* being fully utilized. They have learned how to work around problems and respond to crises day by day. Their constant interactions with customers, internal and external, give them an edge in creating new ways to meet and exceed their needs and requirements. They have found ways to survive pressures and stresses and get things done despite poor systems and processes. Since they are front line, they can best anticipate and prevent problems from happening.

AN UNTAPPED RESOURCE: YOUR GRASS ROOTS PEOPLE'S KNOWLEDGE

Grass Roots Tip
Managers: Ask your employees, "Do you think your company executives care about you?" Why and why not?

Workers: Ask yourself, "Does your leadership understand the cost of reactive management, of not hearing and using what you know, your knowledge base?"

We believe that Grass Roots people's intellectual capital is the major untapped resource in organizations today. It is there for leaders to harvest as soon as they learn how. Grass Roots workers are waiting to be asked for their views, ideas and help. They need to be empowered to control their daily work activities and produce far greater results. And they need to know somebody cares.

INVEST IN YOUR FRONT LINE AND IMPROVE YOUR BOTTOM LINE

The results consistently reveal that empowering the creativity, ingenuity and willingness of the Grass Roots is the key to outpacing the competition and the optimal way to serve customers and move our businesses ahead. The authors believe a Grass Roots Revolution must be launched and supported now if an organization is to meet the constantly expanding expectations and demands of our customers.

Leaders and workers need to begin asking: "What tools and knowledge are needed to compete in the changing economy of our business? What technology is needed? What educational support will help us upgrade our organization's thinking and behavior, will make us a Thinking Organization?"

Although technology can facilitate change, the extensive use of information technology (IT) systems doesn't guarantee sustained success. If the implementation of an IT system (or any system, for that matter) was all it took to dramatically improve an organization's performance, what would stop your competitors from rapidly implementing the same?

Neither workers nor managers *alone* can solve today's business problems. It will take everyone being mobilized toward common objectives to create the foundation for an organization's future growth. The objective of writing this book is to give leaders and workers the critical skills and tools they need now.

WHAT WILL IT TAKE TO INITIATE A GRASS ROOTS REVOLUTION IN YOUR ORGANIZATION?

It will take at *least one person* inside your organization who commits to becoming proactive and who is willing to do whatever it takes to make that happen. It will take someone in your organization who realizes you cannot stay in reactive mode and survive. It will take tenacity, persistence and unyielding focus. Anne Kelly is just such a person.

COMMITTING AND GETTING OTHERS TO BUY-IN

Post 9/11, Anne Kelly attended a presentation Tony Dottino gave in Washington, DC on *Leadership through Grass Roots Innovation*. As the President of Federal Consulting Group, Anne was charged with finding the right training programs for government agencies, including a newly formed one at the US Department of Homeland Security. Suddenly on the front line in the "War on Terror," they urgently needed to transition from reactive to proactive.

As a senior leader and a consultant to senior leaders, Anne had been through years of TQM, Zero Based Budgeting, Six Sigma and Lean Manufacturing. So it was with a generous dose of skepticism and "initiative fatigue" that she listened as he talked. But she had to do something new for this agency, and do it now.

Anne's interest was piqued that day and in their meeting afterward. But before she was willing to put her name behind a program, she would need to verify it would be worth the time, money and energy her clients would need to invest. Anne reviewed Tony's literature, analyzed his data and spoke with his clients. Could Grass Roots leadership really bring about changes in the fundamental issues plaguing most managers today? And, most of all, could it be sustainable?

Anne knew seismic breakthroughs couldn't be guaranteed. But, as she told Tony later, his enthusiasm was infectious and helped keep her mind open.

Armed with the validation she needed, Anne decided to present Grass Roots Innovation to senior leaders at the Department of Homeland Security. She would need to gain their buy-in and support before anything could happen, and she knew getting it would take time. These things always do. She suggested to these leaders that Grass Roots Innovation was a potential opportunity to have "a real win" in an area in which they could use one. She explained the methodology, shared feedback from organizations who had success with it and suggested criteria she felt would lead to a successful intervention. Intense discussions over several months led to the identification of a suitable pilot location. It would be Station 11.

STATION 11

Station 11 was about as problematic, dismal and underperforming as any place Anne had ever been asked to turn around. Daily crises, stressed managers, low morale, antiquated equipment, exploding workload with no increase in staff, no budget for more equipment, inefficient processes—in short, a staff in need of new skills and new enthusiasm. Everything about Station 11 provided a prime opportunity to test the Grass Roots skills and methodology.

The division chief at Station 11 was optimistic that a Grass Roots Revolution could bring about the necessary improvements. He knew the challenges he faced were monumental and that the only way Station 11 could be successful in its mission was to tap the knowledge and experience of the men and women on the front line, the Grass Roots of his organization.

Several factors were working in the chief's favor: Station 11 employees were dedicated to the mission, passionate about wanting to improve and willing to learn new skills. With funding beginning to come in, the division needed to ensure these new skills would be applied where they were most needed and would show the most measurable results.

At Ground Zero

Station 11 is one of a number of facilities throughout the nation that process, detain, house and deport illegal aliens. Because of developments in international affairs, its workload had exploded with no increase in staff. The systems for getting things done had atrophied over time and rarely delivered the intended results.

Anne knew she would be under pressure to produce results immediately, but she knew it would take a long-term commitment to optimize their investment.

First, she would need to build a shared belief that the new approach would produce real and permanent results. Bottom line—the Grass Roots Revolution would work.

What did success mean to them and what does it mean to you?

The process began by learning what the DC headquarters executives defined as their SUCCESSFUL OUTCOME. The results they were looking for sounded simple enough—improved morale, increased productivity and increased efficiencies that would lead to deporting illegal aliens faster without adding cost. A very large order! To meet it, skills would need to be taught that you will learn in the chapters to come.

CONCLUSION

Even the most seasoned, talented executive team cannot be all-knowing and all-powerful. To be successful in today's environment, new skills and perspectives must be developed. There is an answer, and although it's simple, it's not easy. The required combination of new skills and perspective is what is called a *Grass Roots Revolution*.

What skills will you and your organization need? These are the skills you will be learning in the rest of this book. Numerous case studies are included so you will not only learn the skills but also know how and when to apply them, and so you will be able to use them immediately.

GRASS ROOTS REVOLUTION ACTIVITIES

1   What are your Top 10 challenges, the issues that keep you awake at night? Are they on either the Executive or Worker list?
2   List at least three problems you believe need to be solved proactively in your organization. What departments would be included? Who would be on each team?
3   Are you willing to be the Anne Kelly of your organization?
4   Who else's buy-in and support will you need to get your Grass Roots Revolution underway? Remember, it only takes one person and that person could be you.

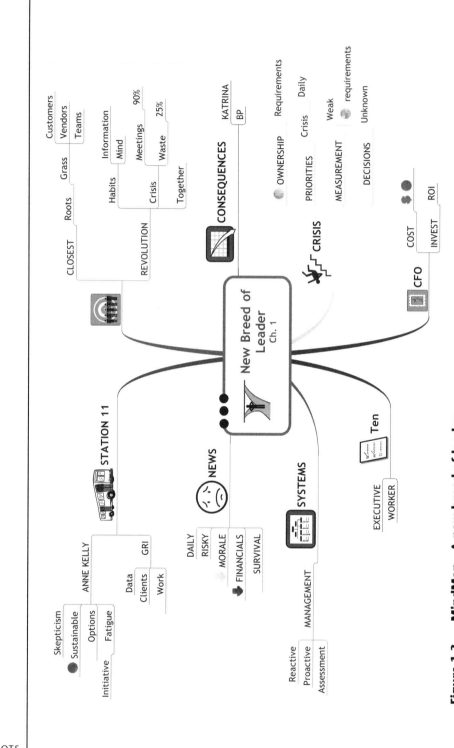

Figure 1.3   MindMap—A new breed of leader

CHAPTER 2

A Proactive Approach to Change

This chapter will describe the proactive system in detail and explain how you can use it in your everyday actions. The chapter will update thinking about employees—instead of costs to be eliminated, they become assets to be nurtured. The initial steps in moving from reactive to proactive are defined. Critical questions lead to new possibilities for your organization's success. Finally we share with you the initial plans developed for Anne Kelly and Station 11.

THE PROACTIVE SYSTEM

The proactive management system offers a more effective, efficient and creative approach to handling day-to-day work actions within the culture of an organization. An organization's culture is the sum total of the way its people think, feel and work in their day-to-day activities, the way they adapt to the needs of the marketplace and fellow employees.

Like the reactive system, the proactive system, has four components.

Establishing ownership of requirements

Before Grass Roots teams begin working, they need to thoroughly understand what is expected of them. It is essential to make time to clarify an assignment, and to properly assess the skills, resources and support that will be needed for a successful result. Effective two-way communication between workers and management brings focus to what needs to get done, by whom and by when. When employees own the requirements they become responsible and accountable for all the steps needed to meet their commitments on time.

Manager of Grass Roots team: *Are you clear on what I'm asking you to do?*

Worker: *Not exactly. Do you mean that ...?*

Manager of Grass Roots team: *Yes. And we need to get it done by ...*

Worker: *All right, but to do it in that timeframe, I'm going to need some extra ...*

Manager of Grass Roots team: *I will see that you get them.*

The dots (...) above, of course, refer to the specifics of whatever is under discussion in a particular situation.

Note that in the conversation, understanding is continually refined until there is consensus among all involved about the requirements. The dialogue is crisp, clear and focused, and although it is brief it is not hurried. It is vital that everyone be committed to finding holes and blind spots up front.

Once you are clear on the requirements, you can walk away as the manager and expect that the time you invested in clarifying the target will be repaid by work results of a staff that knows what it has to do. That is being a leader who operates in a proactive mode.

A senior finance executive at IBM was asking for a detailed headcount analysis from a resource manager. The executive wanted to make sure that appropriate resources were being deployed in a new market. This was a critical area for the company in meeting its revenue goals. The manager asked him if he would like to get the report 2 days sooner than requested. Since this market was critical to meeting the year's profit targets he was delighted at this possibility. There was only one small catch—since the report was not part of the normal monthly schedule, the manager asked for 15 minutes of the executive's time to better define the requirements of what he needed.

The manager took out a piece of paper and they drafted a pro forma report. They drew out a matrix of the report showing the column headings and the various total lines: percentage details, geography totals, line item specifics, year to year comparisons, totals by geography and percentage of this headcount versus total.

Grass Roots Tip
In short, once an assignment is given, always confirm the requirements by repeating back what is expected. Sounds simple, doesn't it? It is, once it has been integrated into your culture. But the process of getting there, although not difficult, requires persistence and dedication.

When they were finished, the manager left with full clarity about the preferred report format and content and, even more importantly, an understanding of how the report would be used. The manager was then able to use the draft to articulate the same details to his Grass Roots team. The manager's team needed to request data from a number of divisional and country contact points. But with a clear understanding of the target and a pro forma to use, they could spell out more specifically what was needed and obtain the necessary information in one cycle. Because they understood the context of how the information was to be used, clarifying questions about the information request were easily answered. Fewer back and forth efforts at rework, fewer time lags caused by a series of questions and answers to more clearly define requirements—simply a smooth process of meeting the boss's request.

The bottom line was that the senior executive received his report as promised with no revisions needed. An incremental workload request was completed early, with no disruption to the schedule for the normal month-end reporting cycle.

Prevention of problems

In a proactive leadership team, the qeustion asked by everyone from executive to Grass Roots worker is:

How do we prevent problems from appearing in the work outputs or deliverables?

The focus is on the prevention of unproductive work and the discovery of problems at the point of origin. To achieve this, the communication between all levels focuses on the needs of the next department (process customer) as well as the ultimate customer. Everyone invests time to ensure the targets are hit, dead center.

Several changes must occur in the organization for a proactive mind set to take hold.

The first change is that the skill sets must be developed so that front-line workers are capable of identifying and addressing potential problems in their piece of the process. They must also have the communication skills to clearly articulate, both upstream and downstream, the requirements of each person in the process.

This requires an upfront investment, where training and time are committed with the expectation of improved performance later.

The second change requires a shift in mindset. The organization must view improvement as not just a learning experience, but an opportunity to get smarter and more profitable.

No matter how sophisticated skills training becomes, it can never cover 100 per cent of potential situations that occur in day-to-day work activities. This means that training should be focused on critical thinking and interpersonal skills (assessment analysis, providing feedback, communications and so on) as well as technical skills. Front-line workers are not viewed as robots but as the best resource to gather intelligence. Their analytical skills make it possible to identify and resolve the issue, and the communication skills make it possible to share learning throughout the team.

An organization operating under the proactive system uses the old analogy, give someone a fish, feed them for a day; teach someone to fish, feed them for a lifetime. You are training a Grass Roots team to fish, so they are capable of feeding themselves even in unfamiliar territory.

Grass Roots Tip
A leader should ask his staff, "Is there anything else you need to know about the outcome, additional help required or ambiguity about the communication? Is there anything else you need to know to ensure compliance with our agreed-upon requirements?" This becomes a moment of truth, because once the Grass Roots team has been given a clearly defined set of requirements and the opportunity to clarify them, they then own the accountability to meet them. It is critical that the organization's culture encourages active communications to take place before requirements are finalized.

A PROACTIVE APPROACH TO CHANGE

When this is successful, every worker is able to recognize problems in the making. At this point, they have to be empowered to take action to resolve them as quickly as possible.

The proactive leader provides time for the Grass Roots people to create work flows that run smoothly. When problems occur, analyze why, invest the time to trace the root causes back to the source, and then adjust the process. The goal is to make sure that errors aren't repeated!

To assess whether your organization operates in a proactive system, here are a few questions to consider:

- When we make budget reductions, do we take away preventative investments? Preventative investments are those that are focused on preventing errors before they occur, such as preventative maintenance or planning meetings to discuss what needs to be done to make sure everyone is able to meet the customer requirements.
- Do our employees lack thinking and/or communication skills which will help them perform more efficiently?
- When we provide training, are we transferring skills, or are we teaching employees how to follow a policies and procedures manual?
- Do we give our team time to work on the causes of repetitive problems?

Nursing team

A nursing team was challenged to find time to analyze a recurring problem they had with patient monitors going off incorrectly. Because a monitor going off always had the potential of signaling a life-threatening situation, every monitor alert required immediate attention. The many false alarms caused constant interruption of the nurses's work, high levels of overtime and incredible stress.

BrainSmart Leaders, who know how to inspire employees to produce leading-edge results, decided to make an investment in providing time for a team of nurses to analyze and discover the source and solution for the frequent false alarms. The team created a mind map (see Chapter 4) of all the issues, frequency of interruptions, people they would have to contact (upstream and downstream in the workflow), and possible solutions. Eventually, they were able to derive an action plan, which they piloted.

They identified the correct engineer for providing assistance, and he was able to immediately visit the unit floor and fix the problem. Because he had never been told about the problem, he had no idea that his assistance was even needed. Though it took the team a number of calls to find the right person they now have a best friend in a critical department to help them with future engineering requests.

This small seed proved to be so rich that a whole garden grew; this one process improvement was implemented across the whole unit and led to a significant reduction in overtime. The metrics developed by the nurses showed a dramatic reduction in false readings, which provided better patient care with fewer hours devoted to unnecessary interruptions. Afterwards the team was asked how long they had been doing it the old way—"YEARS," was the answer. By having the skills to trace the problem back to its source, they identified what actions needed to be taken. By possessing the skills to clearly define and communicate requirements, they were able to articulate what their learnings were to the subject matter experts and leaders of the hospital. Just ask the Grass Roots people to generate ideas, and give them some time.

Measurements which lead to error-free standards

To prevent errors, workers at the Grass Roots level must clearly define standards of performance, and they must have metrics that measure how close performance is to those standards. Since those standards are in effect commitments made about products or services produced, feedback of performance against standards really measures meeting the commitments made to customers, both internal and external.

Metrics—numerical data—are instruments or other gauges of performance that give the person doing the work this feedback. It tells workers "how well" they are doing, and, if it is necessary, they can be used to make immediate corrections. Errors can then be caught as they occur, and the workers can make immediate changes in their workflow. Ultimately they can reduce all errors. The ultimate goal, of course, is to prevent all future errors.

It's vital that every person or team has feedback upon which to identify failures and build on successes. Equally critical is the quality and timeliness of the information necessary to making timely adjustments to what is being produced.

Covering up

If you were to cover the speedometer as you were driving, a very valuable metric would be lost. You would not know exactly how fast your car was traveling, or whether you were exceeding the speed limit. That lack of feedback would increase your risk of getting a speeding ticket. If you have the speedometer, however, that risk is much lower. If you see a trooper sitting on the side of the road, you quickly glance at your speedometer, and if you see that you are doing 15 mph over the speed limit, you quickly hit the brakes.

Leaders of Grass Roots teams ensure that their workers receive timely feedback regarding their performance, so they can make immediate adjustments.

Grass Roots Tip
As teams are assembled, ensure that all the players affected are included before making decisions. It is less costly to get their views before changes are made rather than afterwards. Customers and suppliers who have not been included in the effort may be more resistant to any changes that are proposed.

When making cost reductions, create a short analysis to document the impact the cuts will have on longer-term results. Establish a reward and recognition process for workers who are making investments in preventing the same problems from being repeated.

Know the costs of decisions

Do our Grass Roots workers have metrics or instant measurements that let them know if it's time to hit the accelerator or the brake?

Have we been able to link their work activities to specific metrics?

Have we taken the time to link their performance measures to those of leadership?

Does everyone see the value of the measurements to their own performance as well as to the organization's goals?

The last aspect of a proactive management system is to know the cost of decisions. All the players involved—the managers requesting the resources, the executives allocating the resources and the workers doing the work—must know the impact of how resources are prioritized. They have to be aware of the effect on productivity, service, cost and morale. Most importantly, they have to know what the consequence of this decision will be to the customer.

No leader wants to make decisions that will lead to higher expenses, unhappy employees and upset customers. One of the most challenging behaviors for proactive leaders is to take the time to think through the consequences of their actions. Because being quick and nimble is prized so highly in a rapidly changing competitive environment, the temptation is to react to any new threat as quickly as possible. In this environment, decisions are very often made today without the full impact being known until some future period, sometimes years away. A proactive leadership team is constantly making an effort to understand the ultimate results of their decisions, both short and long term, so lessons can be learned and applied to future decisions.

WHO and WHY?

A great example of this aspect of proactive leadership was shared during a Grass Roots presentation being given to a Vice President of a utility company. The employees had put together an analysis which questioned a decision that had recently been made. Their analysis showed that the decision was causing the company to spend an additional $1million on equipment. As they presented their findings to him, they were a bit anxious in anticipating his reaction. Their research, however, was rock solid, and the financial impact was clear.

Their presentation concluded with a presentation of solutions for the $1million issue, and the Vice President supported their plans. He told them to do it and report back on the results. He congratulated the team on a job well done and then asked a question which resulted in the room going silent,

> *Who made the decision to spend an extra $1million?*

Everyone in the room knew the answer except for the Vice President himself. Finally, after an awkward silence, the team leader stood up to respond. With a bit of nervousness and soft voice he spoke,

> *Jim, it was you.*

Jim couldn't believe it. His managers reminded him of the history which led to his original decision. The Vice President spoke to the goals of what he was working towards and why the decision had seemed logical to him. He then asked two more room disquieting questions:

If I was making such a stupid decision, why didn't someone tell me? Does anyone think I sit in my office trying to think of ways for the company to waste its resources?

After more silence and heads looking down at the conference table, he closed the rather tense session. His parting words to the team were to emphasize how important it is for the people closest to the work to understand, and if necessary question, the logic behind decisions that impact their workflow. Even when those decisions come from their executives they should be questioned for clarity.

IS A GRASS ROOTS REVOLUTION BASED ON SOLID PRINCIPLES, OR IS IT JUST THE LATEST FLAVOR OF THE MONTH?

The approach that we have found creates the best results is a pragmatic combination of leading-edge science with time-tested business principles. Although the structure of our work is sensible, changing mindsets is hard work. Frustrated executives have shared with us, "If what we needed to do to fix our problems was simple, don't you think we would have already done it?"

SO HOW DO YOU MAKE TRANSITION FROM REACTIVE TO PROACTIVE?

It is time to invest in upgrading skills and tools of the Grass Roots to improve the bottom line. We believe a high percentage of people closest to the work have the experience, knowledge and ideas to meet even the toughest challenges. Our results consistently reveal that it is their creativity, ingenuity and willingness to change that is the key to outpacing the competition and the optimal way of serving customers. A company's Grass Roots successes can be accumulated and their sum will consistently exceed challenging business goals.

When an organization starts such an effort, it needs to simultaneously upgrade the analytical, problem-solving, communication and teamwork skills of their workforce.

New communication, planning, creativity and team management skills are necessary to facilitate this cultural transformation. Managers need to ask and address, "What tools and knowledge are needed to compete in the changing economies of our business? What educational support will help us leverage and upgrade existing fundamentals of our organization's thinking and behavior?"

Grass Roots Tips
When current budgets are being reduced, have the finance team meet with the Grass Roots workers to reach a balanced understanding of potential cost impacts that may result in the future.
As resource decisions are made, verify that all costs are considered for the departments being impacted. At times it might be helpful to track the impact of decisions 1 year later, not for purposes of laying blame, but for learning valuable lessons about the decision-making process.

A PROACTIVE APPROACH TO CHANGE

A CHANGE IN PERSPECTIVE WILL CHANGE THE SYSTEM

Salary and benefits costs typically show up on a company's financial statements as an expense. In many instances, it is the largest expense on the profit and loss statement. Because pressure exists on so many businesses to improve operating margins, a common management focus is to reduce expenses. Logically, reducing the largest expense line item seems like a reasonable place to start. As a result, downsizings and other reductions in employee-related expenses become the first answer for improved financial performance.

But what if employees truly were viewed in a matter consistent with what is written in so many annual reports—as "the company's most valuable asset—its intellectual capital?" Would that change how executives handle the pressure for improving profits and growing markets?

To begin, expenses are almost never viewed as beneficial to the business, and reducing an expense is almost always considered a good thing. Asset size, however, is neutral, and what is critical is the return on the asset (or investment). If the company views payroll and employee development costs as an asset, how would it change the way decisions are made? Certainly the size of the asset is crucial when looking at the overall risk and returns to be realized.

The focus would no longer be on achieving a continuous reduction but on the relationship between *changes in investment and changes in results*. Employees would be expected to link their performance to business or operational metrics of the company. Incremental costs incurred to develop employee skills would be acceptable provided that they drive tangible results that can be measured and shown to provide an adequate return. Similar to a capital project, additional spending will be approved when it demonstrates improved productivity or top-line growth. Just like a shareholder, management should expect to see a return on investment, one that can be clearly quantified and linked to the overall health of the organization.

Leaders find new ways to inspire staff to discover their natural creativity, freely express ideas and demonstrate passion for their business. They guide their workforce so they feel valued and part of a team, and build upon the group's own synergy. Day-to-day knowledge of employees is utilized and environments created that foster open communication channels. Everyone feels comfortable enough to talk about their challenges and is encouraged to share their suggested solutions.

The focus is on how to get a tangible return from human assets and grow intellectual capital.

STATION 11—A KEY DECISION?

This became a critical decision for the senior team in Washington, DC—"Invest in building the skills of the detention and deportation officers and with their knowledge of the operation it would generate of plethora of ideas on how to improve the camp's operations."

Proactive investment provides big return

The authors had the opportunity of working with Bob Hughes while he was senior manager of two different IBM accounting functions. The messages he delivered to his staff and leadership principles he valued are timeless.

Bob Hughes faced the biggest challenge of his career. He was a manager who was responsible for consolidating IBM's corporate travel and relocation expense accounting into one nationalized, central operation in Endicott, New York State. Prior to this centralization, the accounting departments were found scattered throughout the USA, requiring too many staff and generating too much expense.

The plant was on the verge of being downsized because of budget pressures, and workers were being laid off due to a fall in workload. Bob was charged with retraining as many employees as possible to work in his newly created, centralized travel and relocation expense accounting division.

Bob had in front of him a blank sheet of paper—no existing structure or employees—and a very small budget. To his new workers, he wasn't exactly offering paradise: their offices would be temporary structures in an off-site parking lot littered with surplus furniture. With his enthusiasm, Bob convinced four people to move from their comfortable offices in Southbury, Connecticut, to work in the parking lot in Endicott—a distance of more than 200 miles.

None of the other 70 workers he hired, other than four managers with accounting backgrounds, knew a thing about expense accounting. Some were warehouse workers, some were secretaries and others were cafeteria or maintenance workers. Bob's challenge was to forge this diverse group of individuals into a close knit team dedicated to becoming the best accounting organization in the USA.

Under his leadership, Bob's team achieved his goal, and over a 5-year period of time won two prestigious CFO Reach Awards (Chief Financial Officers for best accounting practices in the USA) and the Hackett Best Practices Award (the same as CFO).

A PROACTIVE
APPROACH TO
CHANGE

"The only thing I looked for in the people I hired was attitude," said Bob. "If they had the right attitude, I figured I could teach them three principles that would guarantee success."

Those three principles were:

1   Control
2   Challenge
3   Connect

Control

Bob taught his workers that they controlled everything that happened in their careers: who they worked for, how much money they made and whether or not they came to work. He emphasized that continuing their education would give them more control over their future: the more new skills they learned, the more choices they would have regarding jobs and salary.

Bob backed up his words with action, and made education a priority. He started classes in accounting, and gave team members 2 weeks of classroom teaching, followed by 2 weeks to apply the training in the work environment. He then scheduled 2 more weeks in the classroom, each time bringing everyone a little more up to speed. Each new class expanded the subject by building upon the previous material—it truly was "learning as you go." The momentum generated by this continual cycle of education and application was like a snowball rolling down a mountain, continuing to gain size and speed.

> *Because of Bob's belief that the knowledge of the front-line people was his most valuable asset, he resisted pressure to minimize the cost of training: "Whenever a budget cut came, I said, 'We need to invest more, not less, in education.'"*

Bob explained.

> *I did whatever I could to make up the savings someplace else. I kept raising the level of the lowest common denominator. By raising the level of each individual's knowledge, even if only by small amounts, the improvement became exponential. You take 74 people with this increase in knowledge, and the results become phenomenal.*

Challenge

Bob wanted his people to see their new responsibilities as a challenge—a challenge to put a smile on their customers' faces. "The single focus, minute-to-minute, hour-to-hour, was to ask, 'Are we working towards our goal and delighting our customers?'" said Bob.

With this as the guiding principle, he did not need to supervise his 74 employees closely. Whenever any doubt crept in about what they should be doing, all they had to do was remind themselves of their goal, and they would find their way back on track. This was true whether their job was to open the mail or to deal with a problem by telephone.

Connect

The staff had to form bonds with one another and see themselves as one big unit that would benefit by the sum total of each person's small successes. Frequent pats on the back were an integral part of Bob's success formula, delivered to everyone when they achieved small or large successes. "We came up with ways to recognize those who had done well. We held celebrations that had elements of being both special and tied in some way to the business," Bob explained. When Bob's team expanded into Canada, for example, they celebrated with French vanilla coffee and French pastries.

Learning to succeed!

Bob could have spent his time talking down to people, rattling off the principles of the organization in rote terms and micro-managing everything they did. But Bob knew that he needed to take advantage of the brainpower of everyone on his team, from the least to the most skilled person. He needed extraordinary results from a very diverse group of people—and he needed them fast. This called for extraordinary efforts to unlock people's imaginations and build confidence. It wouldn't take a miracle, but it would take an unconventional approach.

Like juggling.

Juggling?

What in the world does juggling have to do with accounting? Everything, when it is used as a metaphor for learning how to adapt to change.

"I knew I had to do something unique with my people if I wanted them to become leaders and change agents," he explained. "I wanted them to understand the importance of continuous learning, and that they had unlimited capability. Most people see juggling as difficult. If I could show them that they could master juggling, it would encourage them to try other new challenges."

Bob knew that people learn better when they are having fun and when they participate actively. He also knew that anyone who has even a small amount of success in juggling will see themselves in a new light.

"In half an hour everyone had learned to juggle," Bob recalled. "It was powerful seeing that many people doing something they perceived as difficult or impossible, and being successful at it."

Bob let everyone keep the training balls they had used as a constant reminder of their achievement.

Through the metrics he kept, Bob was able to demonstrate a strong ROI (return on investment) on his people investments. The average cost per transaction dropped by more than 50 per cent and the changes his team was able to implement in both departments over this time saved IBM millions of dollars. Eventually he received a CFO (Chief Financial Officers) award for best practice in the United States, a CEO award for management excellence and a key assignment in the IBM Global Services Division.

> *To more accurately measure the return on investment (in employees), change the measurements.*

Once you view employees as valued assets and enable them to acquire new skills and tools there is one more question to answer. What else is necessary for a Grass Roots Revolution to succeed?

An old expression says, "What you measure is what you get." Organizations tend to focus on improving performance in areas where metrics are available and distributed. What's wrong with that?

In theory, nothing, but it has to be the right metric. The brain is a success-driven mechanism that seeks feedback to evaluate progress. Providing accurate feedback through metrics is essential for success.

The essence of an effective metric is that is measures the right thing, at the right place, at the right time. The feedback it provides is immediate and actionable. The person or team receiving the feedback makes adjustments in performance. The workers closest to doing the actual work have the greatest ability to make use of this type of feedback but may need additional skills and tools so that they can be effective.

A critical factor for driving a successful Grass Roots Revolution is the collaboration of executive and front-line employees to develop a series of measurements that align all parts of the organization. Those measurements will probably be different at the front line than they will at the top; they will look different in accounting than they look in human resources. Yet they all must fit together to achieve common organizational goals.

WHY DOESN'T EVERYONE MOVE TO A PROACTIVE SYSTEM?

What causes executives, managers and Grass Roots people to opt for the reactive state if the proactive approach produces such better outcomes? *Because in order to move into a proactive system, there is an investment which must first be made.*

As with any investment, you invest *today* with an expected return *tomorrow*. There's the rub. Many times employees have the right intention and promise their leaders, "Spend this today and tomorrow we will realize the benefit." Then a crisis erupts, focus is dispersed and the promise of a better tomorrow is never realized. How many people would invest in a bank that states, "Trust us with your money and maybe we will give you a return tomorrow." Can you take someone's word to the bank, or is there a shortage of trust?

To successfully make the leap from reactive to proactive, Grass Roots workers must make commitments to their managers that once they receive the tools, education and support they need, there will be an ROI. Leaders must trust that the Grass Roots of the organization will deliver on their commitments. In turn, leaders commit to providing the tools and support, and must resist the temptation to jump back into reactive mode at the first sign of difficulty. In short, there must be a strong belief in the words spoken by all levels of the organization that proactive actions are real and going to be sustained, even when the waters get a bit rough.

If the transition from reactive to proactive is so fraught with difficulties, how should it begin? Does it need to be a massive organization wide effort, complete with kick-off meetings and pep rallies? We have found that the opposite is actually best—that the journey of a thousand miles begins with a single step.

Our approach to making the transformation from reactive to proactive begins with taking small actions that require small investments but offer real returns. The success of the small projects demonstrates that the skills transferred to the Grass Roots have real value toward improving business metrics. It strengthens the foundation of trust and instills confidence. After several consecutive successes, momentum becomes sufficient to keep the improvements self-generating. Repetition and momentum are essential: without both, the effort does not become self-sustaining.

Because the proactive system requires trust, patience, resources and discipline, it is easy to slip back into old habits. When crises happen regularly, the focus can easily shift back from thriving to surviving.

INVESTING FOR THE FUTURE

In the proactive system, there is an initial bubble of an investment. After a short period, both the costs and errors go down because the errors are corrected as they occur. Eventually errors are prevented from occurring at all. That offers a great long-term return and is an extremely cost-effective way of doing business.

What you have done is solved problems at the source. The bubble of higher costs is actually an investment that will pay off in a short time. You have reduced the waste and your costs will be reduced as your errors drop and your productivity increases. Unit cost will be lower and you will be able to produce more, with better quality, and for less money. A return on your investment creates an annuity that pays off over and over again.

FIRST STEP IN DEVELOPING THE PLAN

Anne's next steps

A key challenge in making the changeover from a reactive to a proactive leadership system is to identify the people in both leadership and at the Grass Roots level who look at both the future and current operations. They are passionate about the organization's success. Proactive leadership invests in these employees to bring them the skills and tools that yield the highest benefits.

Once Grass Roots leaders have been identified, they need leadership support, encouragement, coaching and recognition. In addition to outstanding financial returns, there is an emergence of leaders that will drive the organization toward a better long-term competitive position. As a senior executive commented to us, "The Grass Roots teams have made my job so much easier. They are so eager to share their ideas and are willing to implement them. All they want is a thank you and off they go again to their next project. My family sees the difference in my mood every night and they love it. Why didn't we implement this before?"

SHHHHH—NOW IS THE TIME TO SHARE A SECRET

First, a bit of history. Tony Dottino had an outstanding opportunity during the 1980s while he was working at the IBM Quality Institute. He was the leader of a team that put together the Best Practice document given to former President Ronald Reagan. This document eventually became known as the Malcolm Baldrige criteria for outstanding company performance. The elements of a reactive versus proactive management system, along with some work Tony was doing on process management, were used as the framework for the standard. If you have had any experience with this award you now know the rest of the story.

You may already be creating a bit of your own history. The authors would welcome the opportunity to help you through your journey. Let's continue along the way, sharing the critical ingredients that produce leading edge results.

So let's begin our journey in developing a Grass Roots Revolution. It is time for introspection into how leaders tap into this endless field of information and knowledge.

EVOLUTION OF A GRASS ROOTS REVOLUTION—THE FLORIDA HOSPITAL STORY

How does a Grass Roots Revolution get started? Must it begin with the Board of Trustees? Is it a blind leap of faith? Can a revolution in one part of the organization impact the whole?

As Paul Brantley, Assistant Vice President for Leadership Development began his journey to mobilize Grass Roots power at Florida Hospital, these were the questions he wanted answered.

Health care organizations are some of the most reactive and crisis-driven organizations you will find anywhere. The environment of the hospital is anything but stable. Hospitals battle normal organizational politics, legal challenges, physician issues and regulatory review, to say nothing of financial stress and strain. Add to this mix a segmented workforce in which the primary patient care employees—nurses—struggle to communicate with those who impact their day-to-day world—physicians, administrators and other power brokers.

In addition to the factors mentioned above, Florida Hospital, in the Orlando Metropolitan area, has experienced precipitous growth over the decade leading up to its centennial in 2008. The hospital is one of America's busiest, with nearly 2000 beds and a work force of 16000 employees distributed over seven distinct campuses and numerous other clinics and agencies.

Neither the governing board nor executive hospital administration had ever heard of a "Grass Roots Revolution." Moreover, given the fatigue of previously responding to numerous improvement projects, hospital administration was extremely wary of embracing yet another initiative.

Beginnings

Against this inauspicious backdrop, Paul Brantley thought of a plan—introduce the Grass Roots Revolution as a pilot project. The Hospital's smallest campus in a nearby suburb offered to become a test site. The first 3-day Grass Roots Workshop (see Chapter 11) was a resounding success.

- The campus' emergency ambulance service came up with a plan to reduce its on-location ER wait time by 70 per cent with a potential savings exceeding $100000 per year.

- The campus' radiology unit decreased waiting time and increased satisfaction of clients in the waiting area itself.
- A nursing department began using Grass Roots tools as its way of solving work-site problems. The veteran Director of Nurses—wary of numerous prior improvement projects—exclaimed, "Finally! A way of working that makes sense!"

The initial unexpected success immediately attracted the attention of Nursing Administration at the main campus. Directors of the hospital's 4000 nurses thought that using the Grass Roots approach was an ideal tool for helping nurses organize practice councils to solve unit problems. This idea helped propagate the Grass Roots Revolution to other campuses.

Within 4 months, the success of the incipient revolution was sufficient to attract the attention of the hospital's Chief Operating Officer. He decided to expand the educational efforts and the results continued materializing across campuses. Among those results were:

- reduction of errors in EKG documentation by 25 per cent, saving double-checking and reworking;
- increase in patient satisfaction scores in some units;
- changes in ordering patient supplies on one campus that resulted in a projected $150000 annual savings;
- reduction in the time needed to educate parents from 86 to 22 minutes by using mind maps;
- decrease in food waste on patient trays by nearly 90 per cent on another campus.

For the longer term, one of the CEO's key objectives would be to keep front-line nurses energized.

Challenges

Like any revolution, the Grass Roots movement was met with numerous roadblocks. One challenge involved the difficulty of sequestering busy hospital professionals away from their pulsating work places for a 3-day retreat. Finding and compensating substitutes to backfill employees was tough during a time of nursing shortage and escalating financial challenges.

Moreover, it became evident that busy practitioners would often dislike the paperwork needed to document results. Nurses, whose roles revolve around patient care, were generally ill-prepared to deal with tracking the measurements needed to validate group results.

The greatest challenge to the Grass Roots Revolution lay in the disconnect between the front-line workers and their leaders. In every case, front-line participants left the 3-day workshop inspired and ready to change the world. This unbridled Grass Roots enthusiasm was soon met with the realities of busyness, lack of resources, and bureaucratic hurdles. Without sustained manager support, even the best front-line intentions grind to a halt.

Changes

Energy from the front line was building at the time the Florida Hospital's executive team experienced a change in executive assignments. The former COO was promoted to CEO and the former CFO was given the position. The new COO decided to hold open meetings to feel the pulse of the employees. The first 3 weeks were spent visiting campus employees and managers.

He wanted to learn more about the results of the Grass Roots work projects and see if it was energizing the front-line employees. A message that was repeated again and again was the value and enthusiasm that had built around the successes of the Grass Roots workers.

When invited to actually attend a Grass Roots workshop, the Chief Operating Officer was intrigued by the passion of the people for improving the organization rather than feathering their own nests. He began to see a way to effect wider and wider organizational change through the power of the Grass Roots Revolution.

But how? In what way could he connect the power and passion of the Grass Roots with his top priorities for the organization? A top priority for many hospitals is improving the emergency department. Florida Hospital had set an ambitious goal to reduce the time it takes to see and treat patients who come for help. An intervention was needed that would call for total staff involvement. What strategy did the COO choose? The Grass Roots Revolution.

1   Cascade Down

Hospital campus executives, who had assumed more passive roles in the past, were challenged to take responsibility for their Grass Roots initiatives within their borders. They were charged with insuring that their campus priorities were communicated downward along with the accompanying metrics that served as work targets. They were also given more freedom from HQ control. In turn, they were to become more active agents accountable for the Grass Roots outcomes within their territories.

Middle managers, along with their counterparts above and below them in the hierarchy, were charged with taking hospital priorities and determining the sequence of processes needed to reach the metrics and the activities required to accomplish each process.

Grass Roots employees would take a given activity (specific enough to reside at the work unit level) and determine the individual tasks needed to effectively accomplish each activity along with timelines and an action plan for completion.

A prioritization matrix was created to serve as a dashboard to establish project priorities and track accomplishment. It served as an accountability tool for the entire organizational staff.

Finally, Grass Roots teams would be given a challenge that hospitals across the country are facing. If there was going to be a Revolution, it would be focused on the Emergency Departments and the Nurse Practice Councils for all campuses.

2   Cascade Up

Grass Roots participants—those closest to the work—would become the prime stakeholders of organizational change, with power to act in their zones of influence at the unit (department) level. The organization chart would be turned upside down and the front-line workers would be on top and the executive team would support them.

You will be able to see the early results of this work as you read the Jean Turcotte story in Chapter 8 and the Nurse Practice Council Story in Chapter 11.

RECOMMENDATIONS

Here are a few suggestions that Paul Brantley would pass along to an organization that is building a Grass Roots Revolution:

- You don't have to start the revolution from the top. It doesn't have to begin as a large-scale planned change effort. Find your people who have a passion for making a difference.
- For a revolution to be sustained throughout the organization, however, top leadership must eventually champion the change. The executive level needs to actively participate in the presentation portion of the workshop (Chapter 12) and signal strong support.
- For a revolution to become a way of life, a part of the organization's culture, the front line, middle management, and executive levels must all own the change as co-partners.
- Middle managers must communicate clear direction of key organizational goals.

SUMMARY

The evolution of a Grass Roots Revolution at Florida Hospital has been anything but simple and predictable. It emerged from a pack of management initiatives at the hospital as a unique way to energize the front line and make them passionate for improving their places of work. In the words of one employee, "I never before realized that I could make a difference in this big place. I'm so excited that this organization really does care about my views!"

Dr Brantley concludes, "At its basic core, a Grass Roots Revolution is not about flow charts, processes and schematics. It's about hope, respect and voice. It's about making leaders—people who influence others—out of every person in the organization."

"Do all this," asserts Brantley, "and watch miracles happen!"

WHAT'S NEXT

Whether you are a leader at the top or the bottom of your organization or a Grass Roots employee, understanding how and when to use *all three* success and leadership gears is essential. Your continued success will depend on it, as well as your ability to create and innovate so that you and your company can continue to compete and lead in the competitive global marketplace.

CONCLUSION

The most important investment an organization can make is in developing its Grass Roots employees, in making them skillful workers and leaders.

A strong Grass Roots team will get to the heart of the matter. By bringing in the workers who are closest to the job, you get the purity of direct communication from the source. You get to listen to the perspective of what's really going on and you discover that brilliance and innovative solutions occur everywhere. Maybe it's on the next floor, in the next department, the person you see in the cafeteria everyday, or the person at the water cooler taking a break. Sometimes it's the person in the next building. These Grass Roots people are vital to your organization's success, now and in the years to come.

The goal is to build a level of trust and confidence within the whole organization, so everyone communicates freely in passionate conversations about the issues that need to be addressed.

ACTIVITIES

1   For each element of the reactive and proactive management systems, ask your Grass Roots people for their evaluation on where they believe the organization is strongest and areas where it needs to improve.

2   Follow up on the exercise in Activity 1 by having a senior executive advise them why the organization needs to be more proactive.

3   Arrange for a third session and solicit Grass Roots ideas to commence a transition to a more proactive team.

4   Identify the skills they need and establish development plans for them.

5   Finally, have your Grass Roots team read the Bob Hughes story and solicit their thinking and ideas from it.

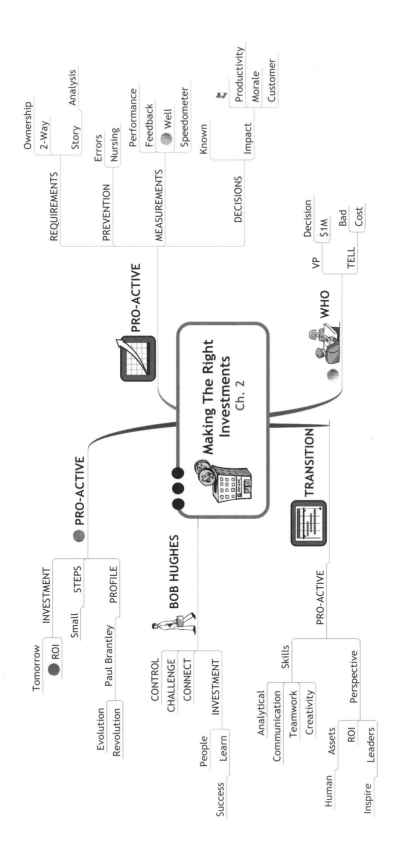

Figure 2.1   Mind Map—Making the right investments

Shifting Gears: Breakthrough Understanding ... Success and Leadership have Gears

OVERVIEW: TO BE PROACTIVE YOU MUST KNOW HOW AND WHEN TO USE ALL THREE

To be a proactive leader, you must understand that Grass Roots workers and customers are constantly shifting their thinking and behaviors through three gear-like phases. Being able to recognize which gear a person is in and knowing how to respond will make you far more able to succeed and lead others to success. Today, using one or two gears is no longer enough. To move your career and business ahead, you must be able to use all three at the right time.

THE THREE GEARS OF SUCCESS AND LEADERSHIP: WHY IS UNDERSTANDING THEM MORE IMPORTANT TO YOU THAN EVER BEFORE?

What else will it take for you, and your organization, to shift from reactive to proactive? And what could prevent this shift from happening? Understanding this up front will make the change far easier. Let's take a closer look.

In Susan Ford Collins and Richard Israel's book *Shifting Gears: How You Can Succeed and Lead in the New Workplace,* they overviewed the Grass Roots shift that has been occurring in the workforce—the growing division between traditional and emergent workers.

Traditional workers expect to be told what to do and when to do it; they depend on the company to direct their career path; they are dependent and reactive; and they believe that, by remaining loyal and traditional, their jobs will be secure. But more and more traditional workers found themselves out of step and out of jobs.

During the sharp business downturn of the 1990s, corporate employees were forced to take control of their own careers. With their jobs in constant threat, instead of depending on their bosses to direct them, they began assuming responsibility. They realized that they needed to upgrade their skill set and develop their own career path. They might be out of a job soon and have to repackage themselves or become entrepreneurial. They realized something else: unlike their parents, they weren't going to work for the same employer their whole lives. These workers are called emergent workers. These workers are the ones who are developing into Grass Roots leaders and bringing about the Grass Roots Revolution.

For more, go to http://www.spherion.com and search for "emergent worker."

Alone, they had to ask themselves this question: what will it take to create a new job or business? And they discovered it required three things: 1) the time and energy needed to upgrade their skill set and acquire new skills; 2) the self-confidence and ability to be productive and competitive; and 3) the creativity to generate new ideas, angles or approaches.

Grass Roots Tip
Is your company traditional or emergent? How about your clients?
Are you traditional or emergent?

These workers realized they had an edge: they knew the products and services they were making and selling as well as their competitor's products and services. They knew their customers better than anyone else, what they were asking for and complaining about, where breakdowns and inefficiencies were occurring, what needed to be improved to gain more market share and profitability. They knew far more than their bosses, who lacked the daily input and contacts that they had at the Grass Roots level—they realized they needed to move beyond the old familiar corporate approaches.

Successful emergent workers were beginning to understand what Susan had been observing for years—success and leadership have gears. As a researcher at the National Institutes of Health in the US she began asking, "What makes some people far more successful than others? Are there Success Skills?" During the next 20 years, she shadowed outstanding individuals and teams in all fields and discovered 10 skills they were all using consistently. These are the skills she teaches in *The Joy of Success: Ten Essential Skills for Getting the Success You Want* (HarperCollins 2003). One of these skills is *shifting gears at the right time*.

Susan says: "When we learn to drive a manual shift car, we are taught how to shift into 1st gear to move the car ahead slowly without stalling or lurching; how to shift into 2nd to accelerate to move ahead more quickly and efficiently; and how to shift up into 3rd gear to travel to the destinations we have in mind. Our teachers in the seat beside us remind us which gear is needed when and how to shift into it."

Today most of us drive cars with automatic transmissions and we leave gear-shifting to our car's engineers and manufacturers. Their standards for performance generally work for us, but for high-performance drivers, this level is not enough. They want to be able to shift gears for themselves so they can achieve more effectiveness, efficiency and creativity as they drive.

But as we prepare to reach the business destinations we have in mind, we are not given the same depth of instruction. In fact, until now, you may not have been told that success and leadership also have gears—three gears—each of which you must know precisely how and when to use in order to support yourself, and others, in becoming more successful.

What are the three gears of success and leadership? How can you recognize when each one is needed and when each one is misused? In this chapter, Susan and Richard provide answers.

1ST GEAR SUCCESS: BECOMING EFFECTIVE

1st gear is for learning new skills and information, for using new tools and technologies, for grasping the basics of new jobs, experiences and relationships. For keeping your skill set up to date. In our time of accelerating change, this gear is more important that ever.

But, as adults, most of us avoid 1st gear like the plague. We avoid slowing down to read manuals and follow instructions step by step. We tell ourselves we're too busy to set aside the time needed to master the basics of new skills and technologies. Why? Because, as kids, we spent most of our time in 1st gear—being told what to do, how and when to do it. Our parents and teachers didn't understand these gears either and so, according to their needs, they attempted to gear us up before we were ready or they held us back too long. So, as adults, we resist gearing down into this mindset again.

To succeed in 1st gear, you must be willing and able to follow the Beginners Rules and Limits your leader/coaches/trainers prescribe for you, to use their experience, feedback and corrections. Then, when you are performing safely, effectively, self-confidently, consistently, your leader is responsible for sensing when to shift you into the more independent and more accountable 2nd Gear of Success. Or if he or she fails to, you must shift yourself.

2ND GEAR SUCCESS: PRODUCING AND COMPETING

The mantra of 2nd gear is more-better-faster-cheaper. Instead of sticking to Beginner's Rules, you now begin developing shortcuts, dropping out steps and streamlining the methods and limits you've been taught. In 2nd gear you work to produce more in less time at higher quality with fewer people, to be more productive and competitive, to put out fires and meet projections and deadlines. You become more and more efficient. When your performance drops or your safety is threatened, your leader steps in and gears you down into 1st gear again.

Grass Roots Tip
To continue succeeding, you must be willing and able to regularly shift into 1st gear to master the basics of new jobs, situations and skills. And you must be able to recognize the stalls and lurches in learning that mean you are trying to gear up into productivity too soon.

1st Gear Success: becoming effective

You need to shift into 1st gear whenever:
   you learn new skills and information;
   you learn how to use new tools and technologies.;
   you find yourself in new places, relationships or experiences;
   life circumstances change drastically or unexpectedly.

In 1st gear, you feel like a kid again:
   dependent and needy;
   your emotions swing: safe/unsafe, excited/scared, trusting/distrusting,
   certain/uncertain, eager/about to quit;
   you know you don't know. Or think you know but you don't;
   you need others to tell you what, where, how and when;
   you must stick to Beginner's Rules and Limits to succeed.

**The following words signal when you or someone else is in the
1st Gear of Success:**
   right/wrong, good/bad, should/shouldn't, can/can't, have to/must,
   always/never, possible/impossible, rules, limits, safe/unsafe, certain/
   uncertain, excited/anxious, eager/scared, trusting/distrusting, following,
   leader, questioning, trying, succeeding/failing, retrying, controlling,
   values, morality, integrity, praise/punishment, supervision, correction,
   effective, consistent, competent, test, permit, allow, dependent, under
   control/overcontrol, fear driven, needy, unsure, rule driven, bureaucratic,
   rigid, unbending, limited, resentful, angry, hostile, withdrawn, helpless,
   reclusive, anti-social.

**These words give you a feel for what is most desirable—and most
destructive—about the 1st Gear of Success, depending on how
skillfully you use it.**

Most people in today's workplace are stuck in 2nd gear: quantity vs quality.
Deadlines and profit margins. Perks, prizes and bonuses. No matter how much
you do, you're pressed to do more—using the methods and systems you know.

3RD GEAR SUCCESS: CREATING AND INNOVATING

The shift to 3rd gear comes when accumulated experiences and observations
suddenly morph into invention and discovery. When an idea wakes you in the
night or pops in mind while you're walking down a hall, showering or driving.
"Aha! There's another way to do this—a different way, an easier way"—and
you're charged by your realization. Or "Wait a minute! I just thought of a new
system, product or service!" (Interesting to note, most creative ideas occur away
from your desk, when you're defocused and relaxed.)

2nd Gear Success: producing and competing

- In 2nd gear the pace and expectations accelerate, the more work you do, the more work you're given. The more quality you produce, the more quality is expected.
- Instead of following Beginner's Rules, you begin taking shortcuts.
- Trying no longer counts; now you're expected to be efficient, to produce and compete.

You're working independently but still dependent.

- Your leaders are no longer there to give immediate feedback and answer questions.
- Now their charts and numbers signal when you're on or off track.
- Their quotas and projections motivate or depress you. Their bonuses and perks encourage or discourage you.
- Your leaders regularly evaluate your productivity and spell out next steps.

The following words signal when you or someone else is in the 2nd Gear of Success:

more/better/faster/cheaper, win/lose, quantity/quality, goals, evaluations, perks, bonuses, promotions, demotions, firings, timeframes, budgets, measures, deadlines, pressures, planning, projections, marketing, global competition, power, politics, anger, spin control, wealth, investments, mortgages, credit cards, debt, retirement plans, stock prices, interest rates, points, profits, buyouts, layoffs, takeovers, stress, exhaustion, vacations, workouts, health issues, weight loss or gain, caffeine, ulcers, stress, tranquilizers, high blood pressure, greed, corruption, depression, drugs, collapse, imprisonment, humiliation, death.

These words give you a feel for what is most desirable—and most destructive—about 2nd gear ... depending on how skillfully you use it.

Grass Roots Tip
Today's overuse of 2nd gear means we have little or no time and energy leftover for keeping our skill sets up to date and innovating the next level of products, services and procedures. Bottom line, this overuse prevents us from transitioning from reactive to proactive.

"This exciting moment is the **Shifting Point** to 3rd gear—if you recognize and utilize it. But most people miss it." says Susan. "Why? Because the shift from 1st gear to 2nd gear is usually decided for you by others—trainers, coaches and managers. They announce it; they issue diplomas and licenses; they celebrate it with you and your family. But the shift to 3rd gear is one you must make yourself. No one will be there to shift you, to prompt you or prod you. You must notice and respond, allowing the power and passion of your idea to guide you and your team through the long process of implementation. 3rd-gear insights move your life, your business and industry ahead—if you are alert, if you are willing and able to use them."

Grass Roots Tip
Next time you
have a creative
idea, be sure to
take it all the
way through
to completion,
profitability and
enjoyment ...
before someone
else does.

To operate in 3rd gear, you need to have the self-confidence to hold your dream despite daily work pressures and the doubts and negativities of those around you. "What in the world are you thinking?" "You don't have the time, money, skill, experience, resources—or whatever—to do that." "Trust me my friend, that will never work." Their arguments will be powerful and convincing, sometimes more convincing than your dream at this point in its development!

If you don't take action, your idea will fade from your mind—until you see on TV or read in the paper or online that someone turned "your idea" into a profitable product or system. Until you realize you missed an opportunity to change your business, life and world. Until you realize that amazon.com, ebay and the computer on your desktop, and everything else you use and value, began as a 3rd gear insight.

If you don't know what you want—in detail—you'll probably get what someone else wants. Possibly someone who wants you to shift back into 1st or 2nd gear with them. Or who wants you to complete their dream and not your own.

3rd Gear Success: creating and innovating

To operate in 3rd gear:
- you will need the self-confidence to hold your dream for as long as it takes;
- you will need the personal power to take the necessary steps despite your day-to-day pressures and workload;
- you will need to believe in your outcome despite the disagreement of people around you ... that's not right, that won't work, you don't have the time, skill, money, experience ... to do that, what are you thinking?
- If you fail to act, "your idea" will fade from your mind until you hear about someone who responded to their hunch and invented Teflon, Post-It Notes. Or someone who let go of a job they didn't want and created one they did.

In 3rd gear, you realize that "everything is connected to everything else:"
- everything you see, hear or feel offers clues to what you're creating;
- even a conversation in an elevator can trigger your next realization and step;
- traffic jams, delays and obstacles become inspirational;
- in 3rd gear, you realize what a fertile mind you have;
- having birthed a new idea, you must now become a leader—a champion and spokesperson, a nurturer and protector, an implementer and team builder, a production and marketing director, a politician and coach.

The 3rd Gear of Success is alive and inspiring:

- in it you will discover your passion and mission;
- your idea may offer you the opportunity you've been longing for—the opportunity to change your life, your business and world;
- will you seize this opportunity—or will you let it pass?
- the path to your dream is not a well-marked highway;
- the way to proceed now is to focus on your dream and let it guide you there.

The following words signal when you or someone else is in the 3rd Gear of Success:
Aha, insight, realization, innovation, imagination, dreaming, creating, planning, intending, communicating, collaborating, co-dreaming, co-creating, detailing, team-building, open, listening, flexible, responsive, inclusive, cooperating, sensing, trusting, intuiting, embracing chance, serendipity, synchronicity, coincidence, putting two and two together, out of the blue, whole, holographic, magic, inner guidance, inner knower, co-creating with a Higher Power, in a dream world, too far out there, space head, hopeless dreamer, full of hair-brained schemes, can't pay the bills, a drain, an outcast.

These words give you a feel for what is most desirable—and most destructive—about the 3rd Gear of Success, depending on how skillfully you use it.

LEADERSHIP HAS THREE GEARS TOO

"To improve your performance and your organization's, you need to recognize which Success Gear individuals and teams are operating in *and* be willing and able to shift your leadership approach. To fail to do this will block their success and produce short- and long-term pain and disruptions in your business, economy and society," Susan says.

"Why is this Gear-Shifting Recognition more important than ever before? Today, many leaders are overusing 2nd gear, constantly expecting those they lead to do more-better-faster-cheaper instead of shifting up and down as conditions require. They constantly race and rev in the name of productivity and profit. And they train, promote, perk and bonus their employees to stay stuck in 2nd gear with them—at great cost."

Grass Roots Tip
The more you can see, hear, feel and prelive what you have in mind, the greater the probability you will experience those results—positive or negative. Therefore, dream and don't dread. Let detailed ideas guide you to the realities you want at work, in your team and business.

A year in the life of a top sales rep
Susan Ford Collins and Richard Israel

It was a peak moment. Bob McMillan had just returned from Pharmco's national sales convention where he had been appointed to the President's Council and asked to speak on how to be a successful sales rep. Because of his consistent high performance, he had won every mixer, toaster, bonus and trip, even one that plopped him and his wife Ellen down, via helicopter, on top of a volcano high above the clouds in Hawaii.

Bob and Ellen finally felt secure enough to start a family. They received the long-awaited call from Ellen's doctor: she was pregnant. Elated, they took the steps they had been planning: they bought a larger home and a mini-van.

But a few weeks after the conference, Pharmco lost the contract with SMB, a major healthcare provider. The loss was over profit margins and had nothing to do with how well, exceptionally well, Bob had been servicing their account. But instead of backing the loss out of Bob's next year's numbers, knowing it would eliminate one quarter of his income, management tagged the usual 6 per cent annual increase onto his sales quota and told him to make up the difference however and wherever he could.

Bob was staggered. Now just to make his numbers, he would have to produce a 31 per cent increase! Six per cent was a stretch but 31 per cent was outrageous—a goal he couldn't imagine reaching. He tried talking to his boss and director and proposed alternative approaches, but they accused him of having a bad attitude and reaffirmed their goal. Bad attitude! That really stung. Bob had always been seen as "positive and resilient." In fact, those were the words his bosses had included in past appraisals.

The next 12 months were tough. Bob had felt valued and heard when he was exceeding expectations. His manager's and director's doors were always open. But now he felt he would have to survive on his own. Bob sensed he was rapidly becoming upper management's personalized message that "no matter who you are or how well you've done in the past, you will have to increase your business 6 per cent each year just to stay around."

Each morning Bob pumped himself up and called on new accounts. He was bringing in business at a respectable rate, but the threat of not making 31 per cent kept him up at night. A few months ago, Bob and Ellen were sure they could handle the expenses a baby would bring, but now, whenever they sat down to pay bills, they worried. A nervous Ellen asked, "What if your paycheck stops coming and all these expenses don't? Our mortgage and credit card companies won't care about the loss of your SMB account! The first and fifteenth will still roll around."

"How long can we last on my income and our savings?" she wondered. "What will happen if you lose your job *and* your health insurance?" They both knew that her company's health plan wouldn't provide adequate coverage for the baby. Their long-trusted assumptions of job security and 6 per cent growth were feeling like empty promises.

Bob's relationship with his boss, Howard, continued to decline. Howard kept delaying his annual appraisal and when they finally did meet, instead of reaffirming his confidence in Bob and pointing out his progress, Howard was critical and clearly seemed worried. "You just aren't making enough calls. You aren't bringing in enough clients. What's your plan, Bob?" A few months later, his boss's feedback started to feel threatening. "Bob, unless you pick up the pace and get the job done, we'll be forced to find someone else who can."

A year passed and it was time for the convention again, but this year Bob didn't walk away with all of the prizes; in fact, he didn't take home any. His directors who had introduced him around last year seemed uncomfortable even talking to him. Did they know something he didn't? Was there a message they weren't telling him yet?

He couldn't wait for this convention to end! His mind kept making excruciating comparisons between this and previous years. And most devastating of all, this year's winner only exceeded his plan by 10 per cent. On the way to the airport, he passed his director, Rick, in the hall. Rick didn't look up. Bob was in a daze all the way to the airport. When his flight was finally called, he gathered up his garment bag and laptop and headed down the ramp to the plane.

What've you done for me lately?

Until last year Bob was accelerating along in 2nd gear, building his business and making money for Pharmco and his family. When Pharmco lost the SMB account, it hit Bob like an oncoming truck. Wham! He was in shock but his leaders acted as though nothing had happened. They didn't shift back into 1st gear to offer him the advice, care and support he needed. They didn't offer him the time, experience, and expertise that would have helped him. Instead, they continued racing and revving in 2nd, struggling to reach their goals and satisfy their own bosses.

Like good drivers, they should have stopped to see if Bob needed help. They should have made time to support him in rapidly becoming productive and competitive again. And, if they had been truly interested in their company's success, they should have considered the enormous cost of having Bob take the knowledge and experience he'd gained at Pharmco into the open arms and minds of a competitor. But they didn't. And he did.

If your leaders fail to shift, the resulting mis-gear-match is expensive. It not only retards your growth and enthusiasm but costs your company time and money—if you're let go or you decide to move to another company. Someone else will have to be interviewed, hired, trained and sensitively led in 1st gear again. Whether you are learning to use a new tool or technology, or you're gearing down because of an obstacle or setback, your leaders need to be able to recognize when you're in the 1st Gear of Success and adjust their expectations and behaviors to shift into the 1st Gear of Leadership along with you.

What would 3-gear proactive leaders have done?

What would more skillful leaders have done when they heard about the loss of the SMB account? As soon as they found out, they would have immediately asked Bob to sit down with them. Let's imagine sitting in on the beginning of this meeting. "Bob, we've just learned that we've lost the SMB account due to pricing, and we know this is going to profoundly affect you and Ellen. That's why we've asked you to come in and think this through with us." "SMB? Whew, it sure will. What happened?," a stunned Bob asked. "We simply couldn't make the price point they insisted on. These things happen from time to time, but we don't want it to hurt you. We would like to help you lay out a new plan and rethink your goals for the upcoming year," his managers said encouragingly.

This kind of support would have been great, but it didn't happen. If they had immediately geared back with Bob, if they had looked at next year's goals with him and guided him to them, he would have felt that Pharmco's leaders were there for him, and he would have reached his goals and taken home some awards. And even if he hadn't, he would have felt good about his company and been a far more motivated and loyal employee in the future! But instead they lost Bob to a competitor who gave him the support he needed and made him number one in their company (with an inside track on all the moves Pharmco would probably make). Unfortunately, millions of valuable employees are being lost in just this way because company leaders fail to understand this crucial shift from the 2nd Gear Success back into 1st.

His managers should have asked Bob what he needed from them. They should have set interim goals so he could begin having successes again, successes they could acknowledge to lift his spirits. In situations like these, your company should be your support system. After all, you spend more of your waking hours at work than any place else!

Your company chose you from a group of competitive candidates. They trained you in the skills they felt you would need and supervised you as you learned how to implement them. They cheered and encouraged you during startup. But will they gear down to match your needs now?

If his leaders had supported Bob in these unexpected circumstances, his wife Ellen would have felt better about Pharmco too. She would have had confidence that the situation would work out successfully and his leaders would be there for him. Instead she told him how unfairly he was being treated and encouraged him to move on to another company—which he did.

Some leaders chronically overuse 1st gear, drowning their teams in a sea of red tape, restrictive rules and regulations. In the name of control and loyalty, they fail to feed their employees the information and opportunities they need. They limit their independence and prevent them from thinking for themselves and their organization. They demotivate their people and retard the development of their products, services and systems. Other leaders are so stuck in 3rd gear that they can't gear down to effectively communicate their ideas so their teams can move them into production.

Marvin on Monday mornings
Susan Ford Collins and Richard Israel

The chairs squeaked as the staff in the state office of Jobs and Benefits sat waiting uncomfortably for the Monday morning meeting to begin. Four seats were empty when their office manager Marvin started, "OK, the first item on our agenda is lateness. Please note, this meeting was scheduled for 9:00 and people are still missing at 9:15. This is wrong, people. This is wrong." Their faces never moved. They were sick and tired of hearing the same ole, same ole, and they knew none of them would be there except for the paycheck.

Running Jobs and Benefits should have been simple. There was a clear set of rules and regulations to follow so everything would run smoothly. But something deeply-rooted in his staff's psyche was blocking that and it could be summed up in one word—resentment. They resented that they were earning $1 250 a month while their peers in the private sector were earning two to three times more. They were tired of driving old cars, wearing old clothes and counting every penny. They were sick of threats from "the powers that be in the state capital" to cut their budgets once again. They hated the endless rules and procedures that governed their every move.

"We must start and end on time. Coming late and leaving early is grounds for dismissal." But they all knew Marvin was powerless to enforce what he was saying so his words fell on deaf ears. "People, clean up after yourselves when you use the kitchen. Also, someone has been eating Margo's lunch. No, this isn't funny. Margo left her sandwiches in the refrigerator twice last week and somebody ate them." Chuckles could be heard in the room followed by this suggestion, "Margo, next time, how about putting some poison in your sandwich so you can catch that rat." And Marvin continued, "If you are using your car for official business we must have accurate paperwork in order to reimburse you." "What do you mean if we are using our cars? Are you suggesting state-owned vehicles are available to us?" Chuck blurted out, and more laughter ensued.

Grass Roots Tip
Your team's success is your success too— your success as a leader. If your team is not succeeding, what changes do you need to make in your leadership?

The 1st Gear of Leadership: instruct, correct and praise

As a leader, you must shift into 1st gear when:
- you have new employees or students who need to become effective in new situations relationships, methods or skills;
- people are upset, disoriented or confused;
- they lack the skills and self-confidence to act alone.

Individuals in 1st gear expect you to:
- teach the Beginner's Rules needed to perform safely and correctly— effectively;
- develop a learning plan and support them through it step by step.
- give them the confidence to try new ways;
- listen to their questions and willingly provide answers/instruction;
- explain, correct and acknowledge till they can perform safely, correctly, consistently;
- if you have a stand-in, make sure they have the necessary skills. Give and receive progress reports—lead them together;
- test, graduate and celebrate;
- shift them into 2nd gear and explain changes in expectations and leadership;

If progress is slow, find out:
- if they are in too many 1st gear situations at once—a new position, a new company, a new city, a new marriage, a new home, a new child, a new school system;
- if this person, or someone close, is coping with illness or pain, death or serious loss;
- if this person is eating, resting and exercising in a healthy way;
- if this person has a solid physical, emotional and educational foundation in place.

Someone is unable to succeed in 1st gear:
- when they can't or won't imagine succeeding in this area;
- when they refuse to listen and follow through;
- when they lack the skills, knowledge and aptitude to do this task or job;
- when they were not allowed to ask questions or make mistakes without punishment;
- when they have such low self-confidence that, *without major intervention*, they simply cannot safely move ahead in this direction.

The same complaints were heard week after week and never a mention of doing a good job. Just stick to the rules, do your work and keep your nose clean. "Please people, park your cars in the back and leave the front spaces for clients. And once again, I shouldn't have to tell you there's no, NO smoking in the offices. If you have to smoke, go out back and only one cigarette please. Last week I found people outside who don't even smoke. If you're a smoker, sign up on the Smoking List so I know who you are," Marvin added to more snickers.

"Now, here's an urgent matter. People, I have the numbers from the capital for last month's performance, and they're not good. Placements were down and the number of visits to prospective employees was down too," Marvin charged. "What's going on people, what's going on with you?"

"But, Marvin, how can we compete with recruiters in the private sector? They're impeccably dressed with company cars, leather briefcases and laptops, and we look like a bunch of hobos nobody takes seriously," Dan, the most outspoken member of the team, blurted out. "If they paid us a decent salary we could dress sharper and feel better about ourselves. But instead, we're the working poor." "Dan, you know the rule. We do not discuss salaries at these meetings," warned Marvin. "As a state agency, we don't charge employers for finding jobs. Providing this free service should be our incentive." There was a stony silence in the room. No one bothered to answer. What's the use?, they concluded. "Please people, we must improve our performance," Marvin whined.

Grass Roots Tip
As you lead, be sure to help your team gear up and down as circumstances require.

The meeting ended. Some associates wandered back to their desks while others headed to the kitchen to refill their oversized coffee cups. Doris, who'd been with the department for 15 years, went to speak with Dan in his cubicle. "Have you read this article in *The Daily News*?" she asked and she laid the paper on his desk. "Nope," replied Dan. "Then you definitely should. It's from an insider who says the state is planning to close our division next year," explained Doris. "Oh really, and where will the unemployed masses go for help?" he volleyed back. "The article says Lockheed Martin does what we do in other states and they're having talks at the capital," Doris replied. Dan scanned the article quickly. "This is scary," he concluded, "Very scary. Well, you know the story. We need updated computers, new fax machines, more phone lines and furniture. But there's no budget for upgrades and so we keep slipping farther and farther behind the times," Doris asserted.

"Dan, why don't we start a recruiting business of our own? Between us we have the knowledge and experience we need and we know all the local employers." Dan thought for a moment and responded wistfully, "You're right, Doris, you know. But it takes capital in a capitalistic system and we don't have any."

"Perhaps we should be pushing harder for change," Doris mused and Dan cut in, "If we had decent leadership that might make a difference. But enough already. You and I could spend the rest of our lives debating this issue. I've got calls to make," Dan said ending the conversation.

Days, weeks and months dragged by with nothing much to report. Oh yes, there was increased absenteeism. People showed up with fake doctors's certificates. Someone stole the audiovisual equipment from the training room but a police investigation led nowhere. And at the end of the year Marvin ruled no alcohol would be allowed at the holiday party because things had gotten unruly last year. And somebody told him to go screw himself.

Soon after New Years, an article appeared in *The Daily News* announcing that a private company had won the bid to take over Jobs and Benefits as of March 1st. And months later, it was over—no more department, no more Marvin and no more squeaky chairs on Monday mornings.

Train him or replace him: he's stuck in 1st gear

Here's a leader who is clearly stuck in 1st gear. And who's trying to keep his staff stuck there with him. He's bureaucratic and unbending. He wastes his time and that of his staff member's on his constant attempts at control without providing the 2nd and 3rd Gear Leadership that would empower them and him. And we know just how his team feels. We've seen corporate bosses, teachers and parents behave the same way. And even say the same things. That's why you probably laughed as you read this story. Because it's true.

What can you do when you find yourself in a situation like this? All too frequently the only solution is to build your self-confidence in other areas of your life, look for something that suits you better and move on. Over time the marketplace will eliminate organizations stuck in 1st gear. Take the Post Office, for example. Little by little their customer base has been nibbled away by FedEx, UPS, DHL and e-mail. But now they're gearing up and implementing creative changes.

How many departments around the world are caught in this gear-shifting dilemma? Some leaders and organizations don't allow their employees to shift into 2nd gear productivity or 3rd gear creativity. Instead they starve their confidence and enthusiasm by a steady diet of restrictive rules and regulations, backward systems and inadequate pay.

And, sad to say, early on those employees shifted themselves into 2nd gear hoping to get additional rewards for their productivity. And, yes, they shifted themselves into 3rd gear to devise creative solutions. But when their attempts were not rewarded, were laughed at and even punished, they moved on to more rewarding and fulfilling positions in other companies. Or they gave up and stayed for the paycheck. They comply and do the minimum, poking fun at their bosses and "the system" to keep themselves sane and functional. But on TV we regularly see stories about usually-quiet, hardworking, rule-following people who can't take the limits of 1st gear any more and go ballistic, turning their anger against co-workers and themselves.

Dan said leaders above Marvin knew he was the problem and didn't do anything about it. That's how it usually is. What could they have done to turn this organization around? If we want individuals to operate in 2nd and 3rd, then we have to make sure they have leaders who reward them not just for sticking to 1st gear rules but for 2nd and 3rd gear behaviors, for being productive and competitive, creative and innovative as well. Marvin should be retrained and then reevaluated on his ability to succeed and lead in all three gears. And, if he will not or can not, his managers need to let him go and find someone else who can and will. *Organizations—government, corporate or community—cannot afford to lose their viability because a leader is stuck in one gear, whether that gear is 1st, 2nd or 3rd.*

The first step is awareness. One of the greatest challenges we face globally is that managers and leaders aren't aware of these gear-shifting errors. In order to meet the needs of today's marketplace, we'll have to find ways to teach these Success and Leadership Gears to everyone who lacks them—or continue paying the price.

Leader profile: Christine Martindale

Around Miami International Airport, there are 200 or so flower wholesalers. Each day they fly fresh-cut flowers in from Columbia and Ecuador. Once these flowers clear customs, they are trucked into industrial coolers to be stored until their sales teams can sell them to wholesalers around the country. Cut flowers are perishable so, as the day fades, importers adjust prices to clear their inventory. Prices go down steadily unless other factors intervene.

After working for a leading wholesaler to learn the business, in 1980 Christine Martindale decided to start her own company, *Esprit Miami*. Christine had very limited start-up capital and business training, but with vision and determination she entered this highly competitive field and started developing a sales force. They were all up before dawn, hitting the phones and building their client base. Christine had early setbacks, "I was honest and I expected that my customers would pay me. I had a lot of people who didn't pay the first year. In that year, I lost four times my entire investment," Christine recalls. So she reached out to experts and engaged the services of a credit agency that kept tabs on her clients's credit histories. Then she could refocus on sales.

In 1985, Richard began working with Christine to enhance the skills of her sales team. By then, her sales were exceeding $7 million and she had over 300 active accounts. Christine had learned to sense when she needed to shift into 1st gear to patiently explain how each job had to be done and when to shift to 2nd to motivate her team to clear the day's inventory.

With 200 plus importers, the 2nd gear competition was brutal. Christine realized it would be important for her to find ways to distinguish *Esprit Miami* from the rest of the pack. One day she woke up thinking about "designer flowers." They would be the perfect accessory to fashion clothing in stores. This would be her competitive edge.

The 2nd Gear of Leadership: measure, evaluate and reward

What sort of leadership do your followers need in 2nd gear?

- Shift them to 2nd gear when they are ready. Or if they aren't ready but show promise, retrain them and re-decide.
- Spell out specific details and timeframes of their job, what you will be measuring and how.
- Provide timely feedback, charts and graphs.
- Sit down face to face to appraise on a regular basis and stay available in between.
- Offer incentives—perks, bonuses, promotions and raises.
- Allow them more freedom as they assume more responsibility.
- Monitor the effectiveness and efficiency of their short cuts.
- Listen carefully to their suggestions for product, process and system improvements.
- Gear them back to 1st gear if they make serious errors, production drops below standards or serious errors or breaches of values occur.

What do you need to do at this point in the success process? You need to:

- provide corrective actions they need to take;
- fill in skills and information they are lacking;
- acknowledge their progress as they relearn;
- continue building and rebuilding their self-confidence.

As a 2nd Gear Leader you must decide:

- what rewards do you have in place?
- are you rewarding 2nd gear more-better-faster-cheaper behaviors disproportionately?
- if these rewards will result in errors, stress, burnout and breaches of integrity and mission?
- if you are rewarding people for overusing 2nd gear? What will that cost you long term?
- if you are also rewarding 1st gear and 3rd gear successes?

Christine quickly shifted into 3rd gear and sought advice from a fashion forecast company. Fashion colors had to be decided well in advance so factories would have sufficient time to manufacture the clothing. With these understandings in hand, she flew to her South American suppliers. It was a big gamble for these farms to grow "designer colors" but Christine was persuasive and promised to purchase their full production.

Next season *Esprit Miami* was the only wholesaler offering "designer flowers." With no competition, Christine set her prices and put her company on the map. The other 200 importers were stuck in 2nd gear fighting it out on price.

But Christine was able to shift into 3rd gear with stunning success. It shows that creative thinking is the ultimate marketing tool. Looking back, Christine said, "I realized that I was in a competitive business. If I could get some small advantage just to give me an edge, then I would have a chance."

She let her dream guide her

Christine's leadership skills speak for themselves. She was a three-gear, proactive leader capable of shifting into whichever gear was needed at the time. Once she had her 1st gear foundation in place, instead of pushing longer and harder in a highly competitive marketplace and burning her people out, she implemented a new idea—one that was solidly grounded in 2nd gear understandings. She knew her South American growers wouldn't be interested in planting experimental "designer flowers" unless she committed to purchasing their whole crop. The guaranteed sale made it safe for them to engage in her dream. No, Christine didn't know how to pull this off—all by herself. She reached out to experts to provide the specialized information she needed on advanced selling skills, fashion colors for the upcoming season, and how to accurately assess her customers' ability to pay.

One of the primary skills of creative leaders is their ability to generate such a detailed, well-formed dream that they can "live" in that dream until they can bring it into reality, and they can bring others into that dream with them. Instead of focusing their attention on fears or what might go wrong, they commit to their outcome. They give people around them the opportunity to make this magical leap of faith with them. No, the realization of a dream doesn't just happen—poof! It takes systems and information, powerful co-dreamers, consistent focused hard work and the ability, moment by moment, to shift up and down into whichever gear is needed.

Most people don't realize that there are three Success and Leadership Gears, so they habitually use the one or two that are familiar to them. Like drivers who don't have all the gears working in their transmission, they are unable to move ahead smoothly and efficiently. And they do the same things the same way— day after day—even though they aren't getting the results they want.

We are in the midst of a paradigm shift. Our old logic and systems are not able to keep up with the changes we're confronting—not just in our towns and cities but all over the world. Because of the internet, overnight deliveries, modems, computers and interconnected systems, an idea created anywhere in the world can be an idea you can quickly use and profit from if you are willing. But will you stay open to new ideas? Will you stay open to finding the expertise you need? And will you have the courage to reach out and grasp it—wherever it is? The courage to keep learning and changing?

Despite all the changes, certain foundational values never change: integrity, cooperation, full communication and trust. Without a solid 1st gear foundation in place, our more-better-fast-cheaper structure is subject to collapse and disaster. But with that foundation in place, we can work together to solve any problem that confronts us. Above all, we are creators, and to move beyond our current limits we must regularly engage—and trust—our creativity and the creativity of everyone around us.

3rd gear leadership at IBM

For 72 hours last summer, we invited all 319000 IBMers around the world to engage in an open "values jam" on our global intranet. IBMers by the tens of thousands weighed in. Some of what they wrote was painful to read, because they pointed out all the bureaucratic and dysfunctional things that get in the way of serving clients, working as a team or implementing new ideas. But we were resolute in keeping the dialog free-flowing and candid. In the end, IBMers determined that our actions will be driven by these values:

- *Dedication to every client's success.*
- *Innovation that matters, for our company and for the world.*
- *Trust and personal responsibility in all relationships.*

Samuel J. Palmisano, Chairman, President and CEO, IBM

CONCLUSION: YOU MUST USE ALL THREE GEARS— AT THE RIGHT TIME.

"Most people don't realize that success and leadership have gears. Like gears in a car, you must know how and when to shift up and down to optimize your results. If you use the wrong gear at the wrong time, no matter how hard you work or how many hours you put in, you will be unable to advance in the years ahead," says Susan.

Three-gear, Grass Roots Leaders are able to use all three success and leadership gears—at the right time. Whereas reactive leaders fail to shift up and down appropriately and become more and more frustrated and out of sync.

Three-gear, Grass Roots Leaders are able to sense precisely when each gear is needed. They are able to quickly and flexibly shift up, and down, to realize the outcomes they choose effectively, efficiently and creatively. They know when to lead by instructing, correcting and praising; when to lead by measuring, evaluating and rewarding; and when to lead by co-dreaming and co-creating.

"Three-gear, Grass Roots Leaders are proactive," Richard emphasizes.

The 3rd Gear of Leadership: co-dreaming and co-creating

When is 3rd Gear Leadership needed?
- when someone is presenting a new idea or concept;
- when they need you to experience what it looks, sounds and feels like in detail and precisely what it will do and contribute;
- when they need you to add details and additional perspective and experience;
- when they need you to understand that if this idea isn't it, the next one may be;
- when someone needs you to remember that what was impossible yesterday may be possible now.

What do you need to be aware of in the 3rd Gear of Leadership?
- many brilliant ideas go neglected or, worse, are brutally stomped out at the start;
- to succeed in business, we will need to be able to shift into 3rd Gear Leadership to continue innovating and leading;
- the timing of the shift to 3rd gear is subtle. It can't be predicted or planned;
- it may seem to happen at the "wrong time" but its timing is always perfect—in retrospect.

What does someone in 3rd gear need from you?
- give them the time and freedom to develop their ideas;
- let them collaborate with others in your organization who have expertise;
- ask questions to clarify what it looks, sounds and feels like, what it will do specifically;
- hold the details of their dream for them when they get discouraged or overwhelmed, when they are tempted to give up;
- point out successes they are having along the way.

As a 3rd Gear Leader, ask yourself and others;
- what trends are emerging? What is happening globally that will impact your supplies, workforce and economy?
- what complaints do you regularly receive? What are your products/services unable to do? What is missing in your facility or plant?
- what are your vendors and customers asking for? What services are your competitors offering that you're not?
- who is creating new methods and systems that could be useful to you?
- what education/training will you and your team need to compete and lead in the future?

WHAT'S NEXT?

What skills will you need to become a proactive, three gear leader? These are the skills you will be learning in the rest of this book. In the next chapter, Susan and Richard teach you Mind Mapping, a powerful tool for detailing new ideas and projects.

Mind Mapping will make you a more successful and persuasive presenter. It will help you create the support and alignment you'll need to implement your ideas successfully and profitably. Mind Mapping will improve your memory and greatly expand your knowledge base. By using Mind Mapping, you will not only be able to more fully use the information and experience you have, but also utilize more fully the information you read in books and articles and hear in meetings, talks and conferences.

For additional information on the Three Gears of Success and Leadership, read:

Shifting Gears: How You Can Succeed and Lead in the NEW Workplace, Susan Ford Collins and Richard Israel (The Technology of Success Publishing USA 2005).

The Joy of Success: 10 Essential Skills for Getting the Success YOU Want, Susan Ford Collins (HarperCollins Publishers USA 2003). *The Joy of Success* is also available is Chinese, Polish, French and Indonesian.

Our Children Are Watching: 10 Skills for Leading the Next Generation to Success, Susan Ford Collins (Barrytown USA 1995).

ACTIVITIES

1   What new skill have you promised yourself to learn but haven't? What is stopping you? What time, energy or capability considerations do you have about learning it? What fears will you have to overcome?

2   Think of someone you report to. Which gears does this person use? Which one do they overuse? Underuse?

3   Keep a one-day log on which gears of success and leadership you and your co-workers/customers are using and when.

4   Teach the three gears to someone you work with.

5   Think about your career. Identify times when you were in the 1st, 2nd and 3rd gears of success and leadership.

6   Which leaders that you've had failed to shift into the leadership gear you needed at the time? What was the result to you and to your leader?

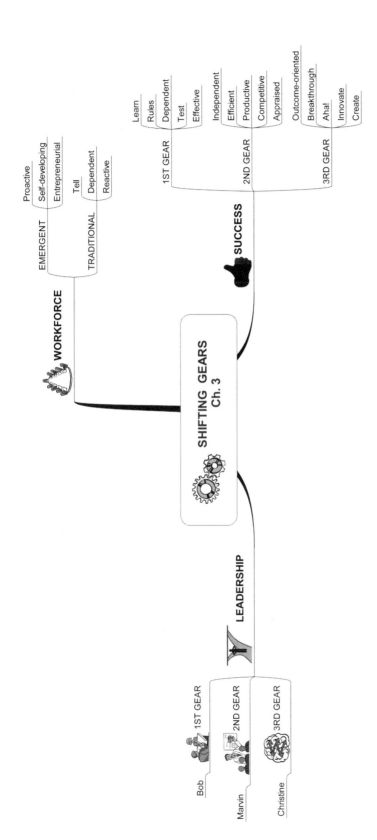

Figure 3.1　Mind Map—shifting gears

CHAPTER 4

Creativity at the Grass Roots: The Power of Mind Mapping

OVERVIEW

The truth is, everyone is creative. But not everyone knows what to do with their creative ideas—how to give them form, how to attract support and resources, how to carry them through to implementation and profitability. Mind Mapping is a revolutionary brain tool invented by Tony Buzan that will help you optimize solutions and breakthrough ideas you generate day by day.

Mind Mapping will make you a more successful and persuasive presenter. Mind Mapping will improve your memory and greatly expand your knowledge base. By using Mind Mapping, you will not only be able to more fully use the information and experience you have, but also more fully utilize the information you read, see and hear.

THE CREATIVE BRAIN

Have you ever wondered why the human brain is called *"the Creative Brain?"* It's simple. We are constantly creating ideas, thoughts, impressions, insights, judgments, realizations, associations—it's how our brain works, whether we realize it or not.

But here's a bigger question: have you ever wondered why most of our creative ideas, even brilliant ones, never make it to fruition? Why potentially life- and process-improving ideas are ignored or not pursued? Or why some individuals and teams are far more able to move their creative ideas to realities and profit centers, new processes, products and services, new businesses and industries? Here's the bigger answer.

We have Creativity Filters on—Whether we Realize it or Not

What are these *Creativity Filters* and where do they come from? Creativity Filters are the overriding judgments we make moment to moment; the questions we ask ourselves, consciously and unconsciously, as we decide which thoughts to put into action and which ones to shelve or ignore.

Richard Israel's business partner Susan Ford Collins discovered Creativity Filters while facilitating workshops around the world. She asked participants to list the reasons why they felt their creative ideas had not come to fruition. Workshop after workshop, whether in the US, India or China, the same list emerged. Next she began exploring why and when these filters had developed, and how you and your team can move beyond unnecessary filters that block innovation and advancement, personally and organizationally. She discovered they were linked to the three Gears of Success and Leadership presented in the previous chapter.

FILTERING QUESTIONS IN EACH GEAR

In 1st gear, the filtering questions you have been taught to ask are: is this safe? Can I or can't I do this? Is this right or wrong? Should I or shouldn't I do this? Is it possible or impossible?

When you are learning a new skill, you aren't experienced enough to safely get creative, whether a new computer program or how to scuba dive. In 1st gear, it's time to listen and follow instructions, to do as your leader/coach/trainer says, gain approval and use feedback. Why do we take people off the job and put them in training rooms? Because you have to slow down to master 1st gear and you simply can't do that when you are pushing to complete all the work on your plate, attending meetings, handling e-mails and calls (when your 2nd gear productivity filters are on.)

In 2nd gear, you have learned to use a different set of filters when creative new ideas pop up: will this idea make me more productive and competitive right now? Will it raise my quantity/quality measures? Will it improve my evaluation and help me earn a raise, perk or bonus?

Have you ever had a boss who tried to get you and your team to use a new tool or computer program when you were pressing to make a deadline? If so, what happened? Chances are everyone slowed down at first. Then, with 2nd gear filter questions in mind, they reverted to familiar methods and behaviors to complete their work on time. And gave up on learning the new skill.

Susan says, "In 1st gear, your leader, trainer or teacher filters your thinking and actions for you. In 2nd gear, your bosses, supervisors or managers do it for you. But in 3rd gear, you are the one who filters your creativity, the one who must decide whether your idea has value. But will you be able to get past your 1st and 2nd gear filters?

Unfortunately, you have probably been taught little or nothing about the questions *you* need to ask *yourself* when you are in 3rd gear: can I pre-experience this idea in detail and imagine it producing a positive change in my life, job or industry? Will I make time to explore this idea in detail, to organize and prepare it so I can present it to those who can support, finance or collaborate with me?

You never know when a 1st gear learner will ask a question that will shine light on a useless or outdated method that you and your team are using without questioning. Or when someone pressing ahead in 2nd gear stumbles on a shortcut that can be shared with everyone on the team to make it more productive and competitive.

There's a time and place for everything

When you use the wrong Creativity Filter at the wrong time your idea dies on the vine. Why? Because your 1st gear Filters—your fear of inability or disapproval—blocks you. Or your 2nd gear Filters—your need to be productive and competitive short term—blocks you. So you fail to sell your new idea up and move your career, business or industry ahead long term.

In 3rd gear, you must not only understand your Filters and but others' as well. After all, you can't complete a great idea alone. You will need to bring others on board. It will be up to you to help them pre-experience your idea at work.

MIND MAPPING: HOW TO GIVE YOUR CREATIVE IDEAS FORM

What tools will you need to get the support, money and team you will need? When you have a creative thought, what is the best way to record it so you can communicate and develop it further?

When Tony Buzan was teaching in England in the 1970s, his students asked him for help. They told him, "Everyone always tells us what to learn but no one ever tells us how to learn it." Little did his students know that their questions would propel Buzan to make a profound breakthrough, Mind Mapping.

Buzan was well-prepared for the challenge. While a student at the University of British Columbia, he studied the brain. "My research covered the work of Professor Roger Sperry of California, who was subsequently awarded a Nobel Prize for his work in the brain's cerebral hemispheres."

How does the brain store, process and recall information? Sperry discovered that the cortex is divided into two sides or hemispheres. These hemispheres cooperate and coordinate. *The right hemisphere* processes rhythm, spatial awareness, gestalt (wholeness), imagination, daydreaming, color and

Grass Roots Tip
When you lead at work or at home, you need to keep your 3rd gear Creativity Filter on at all times. To explore the future value of your ideas and others.

Grass Roots Tip
Creative ideas will be laughed at by almost everyone up front. Why? Because an idea is impossible until someone has done it! "Resistance to the Revolutionary" is something you need to expect! And prepare for.

dimension. *The left hemisphere* processes an equally powerful but different group of mental skills: words, logic, numbers, sequence, linearity, analysis and lists.

At the same time Buzan decided to study the note-taking approaches of "great brains" like Leonardo da Vinci. He observed that, without exception, they used images, pictures, arrows and other connective devices, while those who did less well in academic studies made only linear notes. In other word, "the great brains" used both sides of their brains to learn and remember. Buzan began to use their approach and thus began the evolution of Mind Mapping, a major new tool for optimizing how we use our brains to create, plan and develop ideas.

HOW TO MIND MAP

Viewing a Mind Map is like looking down on a tree. As you explore this Mind Map, notice the central image which represents the main idea of the map. It contains pictures, colors and symbols that can be easily remembered. Now notice the branches attached to the central image and how each branches again to include more information and detail. Take a moment now to notice the keywords written above the branches in easy-to-read letters. What else do you see? Go over it one more time. Now close your eyes and recall this Mind Map.

Chances are you can remember almost every detail. Why? Because Mind Maps are brain friendly.

Like the notes of "the great brains," Mind Maps give your brain what both sides need—rhythm, spatial awareness, gestalt (wholeness), imagination, daydreaming, color as well as words, logic, numbers, sequence, linearity and analysis. They give your brain what it takes to be "great."

OK, let's slow down to draw your first Mind Map.

1 Choose a project of yours you would like to Mind Map and follow these instructions.
2 Place a large sheet of white paper on a table or desk plus three or more colored pencils or pens.
3 If appropriate, collect the materials, research, articles and additional information you will need to refer to while drawing your Mind Map.
4 Position your paper horizontally in front of you.
5 Draw your central image in the middle. Use color, shape, rhythm and so on to make your central image brain-friendly.
6 Add branches to represent your main ideas and topics.
7 Print a keyword or words along the length of each branch.
8 Continue branching out and adding keywords, pictures and colors.
9 When you have finished, go back over your Mind Map and add other thoughts that come to mind.

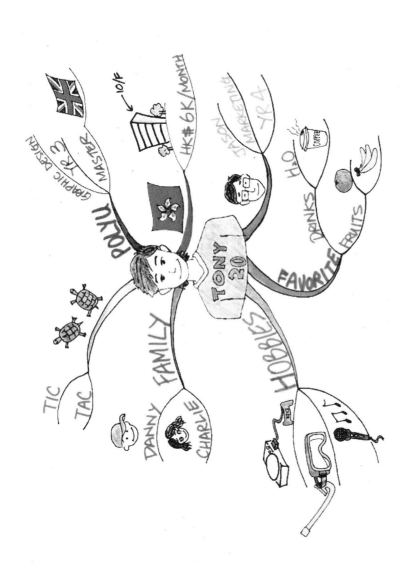

Figure 4.1   A Mind Map of Tony, a 20 year old student in Hong Kong © Quicksilver, Hong Kong

CREATIVITY AT THE
GRASS ROOTS:
THE POWER OF
MIND MAPPING

10 After 24 hours, review your Mind Map, make additional connections, add more thoughts and details.

The impact of Mind Mapping has gone far beyond Tony Buzan's classroom and the lives of his early students. Richard Israel and Buzan co-authored numerous books and have spoken to audiences around the world. Today Mind Mapping is also available in software form.

Mind Maps are popular in Silicon Valley

Grass Roots Tip
Draw a Mind Map of your current life: your projects, hobbies, activities, family.

David Kelley, founder of IDEO and the Hasso Plattner Institute of Design at Stanford, uses Mind Maps to foster creativity.

When I want to do something analytical, I make a list. When I'm trying to come up with ideas or strategies, I make a Mind Map.

Mind Maps are organic and allow free association. They are great for asking questions and revealing connections between seemingly unrelated ideas. I start in the center with the issue or problems I'm working on and then as I move farther away I get better and better ideas as I force myself to follow the branches on the map and in my mind. The coolest thing is that you allow yourself to follow your inner thoughts, which is different than making a list where you are trying to complete and deal with data.

(*Business Week*, September 2006).

Grass Roots Leaders get creative ideas while eating!

Apple Computers is renowned for its innovation and creativity. Senior Vice-President for Industrial Design at Apple, Jonathan Ive says, "Many Apple products were dreamed up while eating pizza in the small kitchen at the team's design studio." Creativity happens anytime and anyplace. A fleeting glance at a passing car, a whiff of baking bread, or the sound of a jet overhead can start an association of creative ideas. The key is remaining alert—alert to the value of your thinking and others. Alert to the need to give them form—the form of a Mind Map."

You too can benefit from using Mind Maps

A Mind Map records the details of creative ideas. Like a road map, a Mind Map:

1 gives a quick, one-page overview of a large subject-area showing the flow and connections;
2 encourages daydreaming, problem-solving and the pursuit of creative pathways;
3 enables you to plan strategies and make decisions;
4 lets you and others know where you are going and where you have been;
5 allows you to be highly efficient;
6 is enjoyable to look at, read, think about and remember;

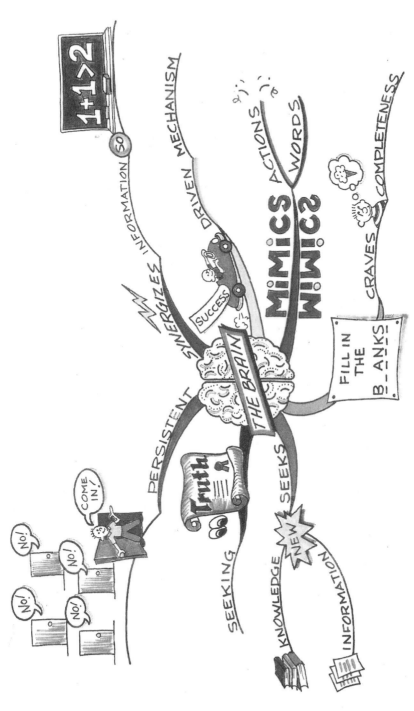

Figure 4.2 Mind Map—Brain Principles (see Chapter 6, © Dru Fuller)

CREATIVITY AT THE
GRASS ROOTS:
THE POWER OF
MIND MAPPING

Grass Roots Tip
How to Become a Master Mind Mapper
Set a goal: I am going to create 50 Mind Maps in the next 2 months. Mind Map the evening news, your favorite TV show, meetings you chair or attend, your favorite magazine or topic in the newspaper. Practice, practice, practice.

7   helps you share your ideas effectively to gain support;

8   works the way the brain works, by linking, associating and connecting thoughts and ideas.

PUTTING MIND MAPS TO WORK

Richard and Susan's clients have discovered numerous applications for Mind Maps.

The radio world: planning sales presentations

Dennis Collins is one of the US's most successful radio executives. He started his career at the Grass Roots as a radio announcer but soon moved to COX Broadcasting to become a media representative. During 12 years there he worked his way up the ranks and became an outstanding manager. Dennis's success was based on his ability to pull others up with him. He trained thousands of record-breaking salespeople and helped develop the careers of dozens of Grass Roots leaders. Today he is Senior Vice President/General Manager of Lincoln Financial's 101.5 LITE FM, MAJIC 102.7 and AM 790 WAXY.

Dennis and his team created LITE FM and MAJIC. These stations are consistently top performers in ratings, revenues and profits in the competitive South Florida radio market. LITE FM is the number one listen-at-work station and MAJIC is South Florida's number one oldies station.

Dennis and his team have been extremely successful in using Mind Maps. Each executive has a Mind Map of the Corporate Vision on the wall. Over the years Dennis had had Richard teach all of his salespeople how to Mind Map their sales presentations. His team uses Mind Maps to guide their presentations of radio costs and benefits compared to other media. The Mind Map is left behind so their presentation will be remembered and accurately shared for decision making. Contact information is placed on the bottom of the Map for follow up and follow through. And what impact has this approach produced?

On October 13, 1999, *The New York Sunday Times* wrote an article on brain power in business in which Dennis was quoted as saying that "Sales at WMXJ, a Miami radio station were 10 per cent ahead of a year earlier, after the station worked on Mind Maps with Richard Israel."

See *Brain Sell*, Tony Buzan and Richard Israel (Gower 1995), for a full description of how you can use Mind Maps to increase sales in your organization.

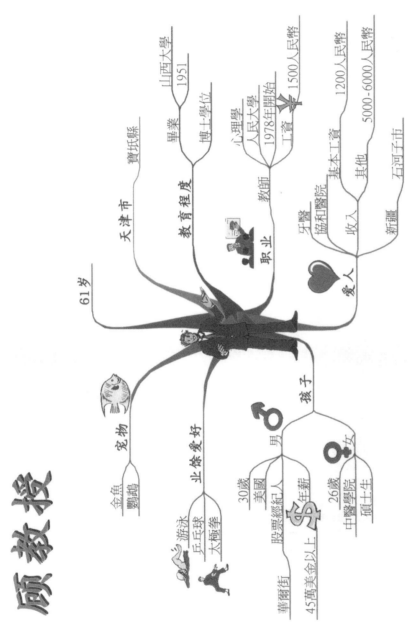

Figure 4.3   Mind Maps work in any language © Quicksilver, Hong Kong

Group Mind Mapping elicits creative ideas from the Grass Roots up

When you have a problem or a creative project in your organization, create a large Mind Map and tape it to the wall in a shared work area. Invite team members to add their ideas, pictures and branches. Group Mind Mapping is a powerful way to tap the knowledge base of the whole group and gain buy-in to the final solution and implementation. Many businesses have solved profit-robbing problems using this approach.

Grass Roots Tip
Draw a Mind Map of a project that is important for you to complete—personal or professional—a trip or house renovation or new career direction.

Vincent Liuzza Jr, President of CuCos Mexican Restaurantes in Louisiana faced a major problem: customers were being robbed as they returned to their cars after dinner. He had hired security services and lit the area, but the problem persisted. Vincent decided to draw a Mind Map of the problem and potential solutions and post it in the hall so it was visible to everyone from top management to dishwasher. Day by day, team members added their ideas and approaches. And, no, the solution didn't come from the top. It came from the Grass Roots. A busboy saw the map and added his creative solution: "Why not walk our customers to their cars?"

No one else had imagined this approach and it worked. The security issue was quickly resolved. Customers liked the personal attention and brought their friends to enjoy Mexican cuisine at CuCos more and more frequently. And profitability returned.

Mind Maps will help you find funding

To take business to the next level, Greg Horn, former CEO of General Nutrition Centers (GNC), decided to repackage the vitamins they were selling to meet specific needs of their customers—such as formulas for men to build body mass, or for women to lose weight. This not only pleased their customers but increased their profit margin. Greg's idea took GNC from $400 million to $1.5 billion in revenues. The number of stores grew form 937 to 5 866.

After selling GNC, Greg had been dreaming again but was struggling to find the best way to present his new idea. It was at this point that he attended Susan Ford Collins and Richard Israel's *Managing Information Overload* seminar (see next chapter) and learned how to Mind Map.

Greg Horn wrote:

> *For 2 years, I have been working on a business model to reinvent the way the food business systematically creates innovative and commercially viable new products. The resulting business has a simple objective, but a fairly complicated execution requiring the orchestration of a complex array of resources and talents. Keeping the message simple and easy to grasp was a challenge.*

The Monday following Susan and Richard's Friday seminar, I had the presentation for funding the second and final round of investment. Over the weekend, I scrapped my long PowerPoint presentation, bought the Mind Mapping software online, and put the entire business on one page. I then flew to California and used that one page as my only "prop" to describe the business to the investment decision-makers.

The story has a happy ending. We closed on $15 million in financing 2 weeks later, from strategic investors such as Nestle, Unilever, Bayer, ADM, AM Todd and others. Clearly, your techniques represent a powerful tool not just for retaining information, but also for efficiently communicating complex concepts.

Mind Mapping the 9/11 clean up

Con Edison, the major utility company for New York City, provides electric, gas and steam services to more than three million customers. On September 11th immediately following the collapse of the World Trade Center towers, Con Edison's Environment, Health and Safety (EH&S) Department put together a team of company experts to identify and develop plans for addressing environmental and safety issues employees working in the disaster area would face. Industrial Hygiene experts were brought in from outside.

Asbestos was identified as the primary concern. Bulk samples and air samples were taken and personal air monitoring was conducted. Con Edison's ChemLab was placed on a 24/7 schedule to gather and interpret numerous measurements of air, dust, carbon monoxide, combustible gas, hydrogen sulfide, oxygen, noise and volatile organic compounds at various work locations. Information was shared with government agencies. EHS Bulletins, Guidance and Communications were issued to field workers. Showers and vehicle wash-down facilities were set up. Medical vans were moved into the area. Respirators and protective equipment were procured. Numerous safety tours and inspections were conducted. By late September 11th, an extensive sampling, testing and monitoring effort was underway.

Con Ed used Mind Mapping software to develop the action plan and to manage the enormous volume of data and documentation this cataclysmic event generated. Real-time data was displayed on a large high-definition plasma monitor to facilitate accurate decision-making, updating and follow through. The Mind Mapping and strategic planning was led by Al Homyk, Director of Compliance.

Mind Map your next career

In 1994, Dilip Mukerjea flew from his home in Singapore to England to learn to be a Buzan trainer and attended a workshop in which Richard explained his Expert Strategy. First, pick a topic that interests you, an area in which you would like to become an expert. Then identify read and Mind Map two books a week on that topic. Review your Mind Maps frequently to optimize memory

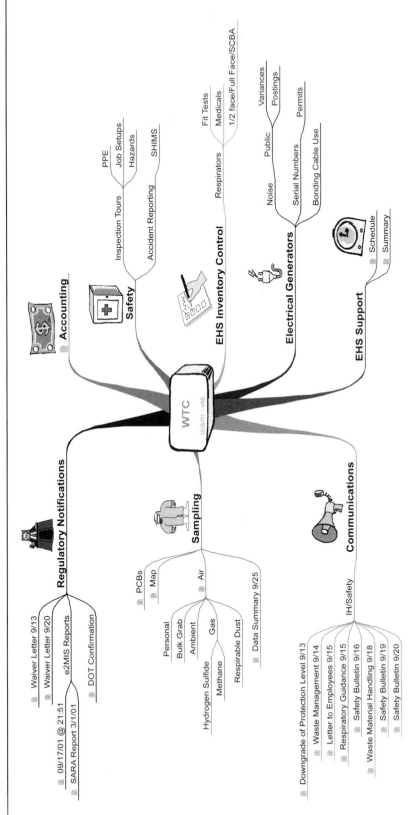

Figure 4.4   Mind Map—World Trade Center Mind Map by Al Homyk © Con Edison

and retention. By the end of 1 year, you will have digested the expertise of 100 books and know more about your topic than almost anyone else in the world.

With all that knowledge in mind, you will be an expert in that field, whether ice-cream making or Mind Mapping, and you can begin speaking and writing on the topic and move into a new career and income stream.

Dilip was excited and immediately told Richard he was going to do it! Dilip was a full time ship's engineer which meant he was at sea for months at a time and away from his wife and child. Richard's Expert Strategy was exactly the tool Dilip needed to make a career change. What else would it take? What skills would he need? First, he learned to speed read so he could optimize his study time. During those months at sea, he read his 100 books and created and learned his 100 Mind Maps.

Wanting to illustrate his maps in a more powerful way and to incorporate them into books he would write as an expert, he began studying art with Betty Edwards, author of *Learn to Draw: Drawing on the Right Side of the Brain.*

Two years later, in 1996, Dilip wrote his first book on "brain skills for the 21st century," *Superbrain.* Today Dilip's books, *Superbrain, Brainfinity, Braindancing, Surfing the Intellect, Building Brainpower, Brain Symphony,* and *Unleashing Genius,* are bestsellers in Southeast Asia. Tony Buzan has called Dilip "phenomenally creative and easily one of the World's Top 10 Master Mind Mappers."

It all began with a dream and the Expert Strategy thoroughly applied.

Busy executive earns his MBA thanks to Mind Mapping

Mike was a 50-year-old marketing executive at the Mandarin Oriental Hotel Group who spent much of his time traveling around the world visiting the many hotels in this prestigious chain. Mike was a family man with a wife and two children he loved dearly but rarely got to spend time with them in his Hong Kong home. He was caught in the usual bind: he wanted to go back to school to advance his career but he didn't have time. So he enrolled in an MBA correspondence program. With everything on his plate, he found it tough going. His old approach to learning wasn't good enough to get him through. But he was committed.

A friend of Richard's heard about his academic struggle and introduced him to Richard's work. They had four 1-hour sessions on "Learning How to Relearn." He drew Mind Maps for all his courses and taped them up on his wall so he could regularly review them. Here is the letter Richard received 6 months later.

Grass Roots Tip
Mind Map a decision that you need to make in the near future.

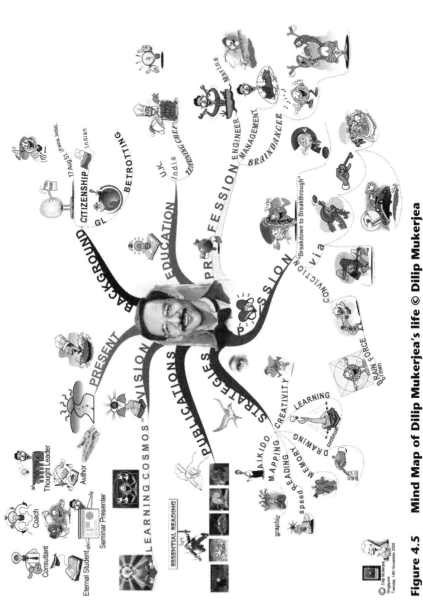

Figure 4.5   Mind Map of Dilip Mukerjea's life © Dilip Mukerjea

Michael H. Hobson
Senior Vice President, Sales & Marketing
Mandarin Oriental Hotel Group
December 29, 2003

*Thank you Richard and, by the way, thanks to you in part I passed my exams
and graduated with an MBA this past summer. The Mind Mapping was a great
way to learn, especially just prior to exams whereby I had the material up on my
walls for weeks!*
    All the best to you and your family. Michael

Teaching MBA students the latest information-processing skills

Today Susan and Richard are having the same experience Buzan had in the
early 1970s. Graduate students are constantly telling them, "Our professors tell
us what to learn and by when but they fail to teach us how to learn the assigned
material." We heard this frequently as members of a high level executive
network called The Strategic Forum which meets at the Huizenga School of
Business at Nova University in Florida. Each month top business leaders are
invited to speak and MBA students sit around the outside of the room to learn
first hand from these business geniuses.

During one of these sessions, we introduced Mind Mapping to them and the
students. The students asked us to facilitate our *Managing Information Overload*
seminar in its entirety for them. These students will be tomorrow's business
leaders and learning this updated information now will make a vital difference
in their ability to advance in our competitive, global marketplace in the future.
Learning and using these skills will not only allow them to keep up with what
is going on but will enable them to pass on these skills to their Grass Roots
workers and make them powerful leaders as well.

Giving what he didn't get

Another Strategic Forum member is Blas Moros. Blas was the man who, as a
Director at Microsoft in the very beginning, delivered the Microsoft concept to
Latin America and Southeast Asia. He and his wife Karin attended the workshop
as well. At the end, they rushed up to Susan and Richard excited. "It was a great
session! I only wished I had learned this 30 years ago! But better now than
never!"

Today Blas is on his second career, creating a new business that aligns with his
passion for exotic cars. The Collexium is a private club that enables members
to drive some of the most luxurious cars in the world, without having to buy
them. Go to his website www.collexium.com to get a feel for the experience he
offers. Richard and I were invited to the opening of his showroom—Ferraris,
Maseratis, Aston Martins, Lamborghinis, Bentleys, and Lotuses. But most

Grass Roots Tip
Mind Map a
talk you need
to make or an
article you want
to write.

exciting of all, the opening experience was just like the Mind Map he had
drawn and shared with us a few days after the workshop.

To pass these skills on, Blas brought his entire team to our next Managing
Information Overload workshop. He wanted to make sure he gave his team the
skills he had never learned. He wants them to use Mind Mapping and other
updated information skills as together they build his next successful venture,
not Microsoft this time but a business he dreamed and created himself.

From British Airways to the classroom

Mind Mapping is needed not just in graduate school but in elementary and
high school, and informed business leaders are taking it there. Jim Kalinowski,
Regional Marketing Manager for the British Airways USA, used it to produce
higher levels of results for his company, but he didn't stop there. Jim knew Mind
Mapping would help school children to learn and remember the information
assigned more easily. So he stepped up into leadership and reached out to teach
a teacher, his younger brother Don, who taught history in a local school. Jim
laid out a sheet of paper, drew a central image and labeled it "US Wars." Which
wars should we include? Don quickly came up with names and key images for
each US war. In a matter of minutes they had a detailed Mind Map. The pictures
and colors they used had made the Mind Map memorable and interesting.

Don started drawing Mind Maps for his history class. To motivate his students,
he promised that if they drew Mind Maps of each chapter he would exempt
them from homework review questions. His idea hit home and his students' test
scores improved significantly. Don also uses Mind Mapping to create lessons
plans that can be easily Mind Mapped by his students. Like MBA students, they
find Mind Maps particularly valuable when they prepare for exams.

Summary: MIND MAPS have many applications.

- Think creatively
- Think, teach, study
- Make presentations
- Organize meetings and follow-through
- Make decisions
- Record your ideas and others'
- Enhance memory
- Brainstorm creative solutions
- Problem-solve
- Clarify ideas
- Record information like a diary
- Self-analysis
- Family study
- Management
- Empower yourself and your team

See *The Mind Map Book*, Tony Buzan (BBC Books 2003) for a full description on Mind Maps' applications.

Leadership profile: David Hill

David Hill, an Information Technology specialist at Con Edison, borrowed *The Mind Map Book* from his company library and something clicked. Mind Mapping immediately made sense to him and he began practicing his Mind Mapping skills. The results were so powerful that he committed to bringing Mind Mapping to the rest of Con Edison, all the way up to the CEO.

David's wish to make his dream come true came sooner than he predicted. Attending a seminar in New York City, he met Tony Dottino, Richard Israel and Tony Buzan. David brought Tony Dottino into Con Edison to conduct Mapping Workshops for over 500 employees. Soon Mind Maps were being used in meetings and presentations. At the time, Eugene R. McGrath was the chairman and CEO of Con Edison. But the opportunity to get the chief executive onboard came in an unexpected way.

David's co-worker Lisa Frigrand, a Project Specialist, had been working on a project for the CEO for some time. She had developed a solution she was sure would work but she was not sure how to present it. The Con Edison's Leadership team came to her rescue and recommended she attend a Mind Mapping workshop. With her new skill in hand, she set out once again, this time with David's help. They created a Mind Map to communicate her ideas and their efforts paid off. "Lisa, great job. This is the way I think," said her CEO. Soon he and other members of the executive team were using Mind Maps to create and share projects and solutions.

So here's the moral to this story: if at first you don't succeed, get a new skill and try, try, try again. David discovered Mind Mapping worked well for him and he committed to making it available to everyone in his company. But how? He didn't need to know up front. The needed methods soon presented themselves in unusual ways; a meeting attended, experts met, and a first-hand connection to the CEO. Through David's persistence, he not only succeeded in reaching his own goal but he was also able to help hundreds of other Grass Roots workers/ leaders at Con Edison reach their goals as well. Thanks to David, Mind Mapping is in everyday use at Con Edison.

CONCLUSION: USING YOUR BRAIN TO ITS CREATIVE BEST

Knowing that you have Creativity Filters, and when they are and are not appropriate, is a powerful tool. Now you will be able to move past excuses that block the creativity of most individuals and teams: 1st gear excuses like "I can't" or "That's impossible!," as well as 2nd gear excuses like "I don't have time," "I'm too busy." Susan and Richard found that "the real reason creative ideas don't come to fruition *isn't* because they're bad ideas but because their creators lacked skills. They didn't make time to think their ideas through, to Mind Map and share their Mind Maps to gain their input, buy-in, support and funding."

We all have a Creative Brain, but not all of us use it to full advantage. By studying the note-taking skills of "the great brains" Tony Buzan was able to help us make all *our* brains great. In the midst of the Grass Roots Revolution, we must schedule time to slow down and gear down to acquire new skills.

Most of us didn't have teachers who knew as much about the brain as Buzan did or who were as interested in teaching us the latest information. This book is your opportunity to learn these skills. Your opportunity to increase your memory and ability to use and communicate information and ideas. To gain support and bring your ideas to realization and profitability.

Grass Roots Tip
Mind Map a summary of this chapter for future reference. Post it where you will see if regularly—your refrigerator door or over your computer.

WHAT'S NEXT?

Now that you know how to Mind Map, it's time to deal with the vast quantities of information that come across your desk every day. How can you move from information overload to having an ever-expanding knowledge base? How can you read more quickly and retain far more of what you read? How can you get more out of the meetings you attend, the e-mails you send and receive? The conversations you have?

In the next chapter Susan and Richard will help you update your information processing skills to meet today's rapidly accelerating global information flow.

ACTIVITY

1   What are the Creativity Filters that prevent you from realizing your creative potential? What Creativity Filters does your leader have in mind? What Creativity Filters does your organization use consciously and unconsciously?
2   What creative project of yours failed because you didn't know how to develop and communicate it?
3   Mind Map your favorite TV or radio show. When the next episode begins, you can add to your previous map or start a new one.
4   Mind Map your favorite section of the daily newspapers—sports, weather, local news.
5   Create a Mind Map of your job description!
6   Create Mind Maps of your customers (internal or external) and update them regularly.

7   Mind Map meetings you attend. Take a drawing pad and colored pencils with you so you are ready to give that information form and make it memorable.

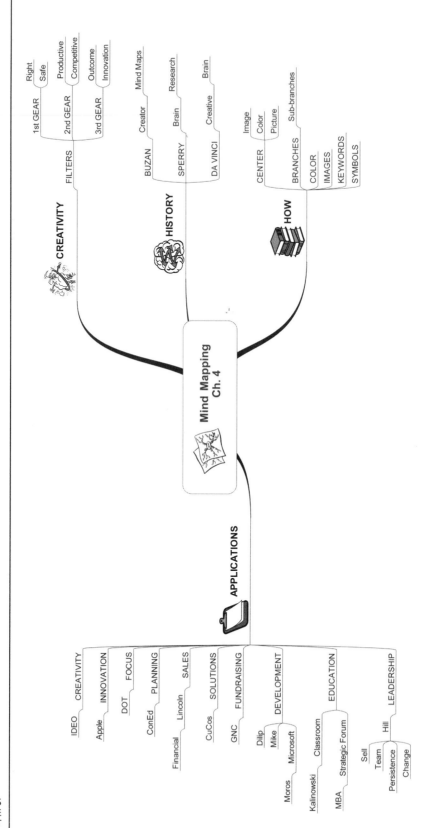

Figure 4.6   Mind Map—creativity at the Grass Roots

CHAPTER 5

Managing Information Overload: Getting More Done in Less Time

OVERVIEW: MORE INFORMATION THAN EVER BEFORE

Tell the truth: Are you are struggling to keep up with the e-mail, calls, meetings and written material on your plate? Are you constantly being interrupted and forced to shift your attention and lose your focus? Do your company's best-laid plans change just when you've gotten underway? Is your current reading speed too slow to get you through all the written stuff you need to understand and follow up? Most business people honestly tell us—YES.

Then welcome to Information Overload and the stress it's bringing to today's workplace. And if you think the overload is bad now, just wait! Bill Gates says it's going to get worse. Much worse. "Business is going to change more in the next 10 years than it has in the last 50."

Are YOU and your organization ready? Susan Ford Collins and Richard Israel have found that like most organizations today, your answer is probably NO. If so, this chapter will teach you how to update your Information Skill Set and to free yourself, and your team, from the stress and struggle of undigested information bombarding you from all sides. This chapter will help you move more from a reactive, crisis driven, to proactive, outcome-oriented environment. It will enable you to move from Information Overload to an ever-expanding Knowledge Base.

WHAT HIDDEN INEFFICIENCIES ARE HOLDING YOU BACK?

Now that you understand all three gears of success and leadership, let's analyze what else might prevent you, and your organization, from achieving the goals and outcomes you have in mind for your business and life. What may be costing you time, money, and profitability? Are there hidden inefficiencies you may not have noticed until now? First, let's examine the 1st gear areas that have fallen behind. These areas may be putting your business at risk, the risk Marvin and his team faced—the risk of obsolescence.

NEW TIMES, NEW REQUIREMENTS

Instead of making our lives easier, technological innovations like the internet, e-mail, Google, cell phones and Palm Pilots, have generated a glut of information almost none of us can handle.

You may carefully budget time and money to upgrade equipment and technical skills, but are you as carefully budgeting time and money to update the skills you and your people use 80 per cent of the time—the backbone of your business—your human information processing skills? Chances are you're not.

Grass Roots Tips
Make a list of your stresses. Analyze the causes.

Many of today's business leaders are so paralyzed and fatigued, so caught up in putting out fires that many haven't noticed what's happening to them. Most business people are still relying on skills they learned in school. But chances are your teachers had absolutely no idea what today's information flows would be like. Or how to prepare you to succeed and lead in a 24/7 information-based, global economy.

Today we are bombarded by information—mail (electronic, voice and snail), phone calls (wired, portable and cell), messages (voice, memo and text), meetings, journals, newsletters, manuals, reports, books and e-books, TV, movies, advertisers. Like a frog in a pot of slowly heating water, we are now nearing the boiling point—the point where "what you're not noticing" could do you in!

To reiterate, according Bill Gates, "Business is going to change more in the next 10 years than it has in the last 50." So if you're pressed already, you need to do something now—something in 1st gear.

Whether you realize it or not, Information Overload costs you Big Money because it:

- paralyzes your analytical capacity;
- increases anxiety and self-doubt;
- results in a tendency to blame others;
- produces a lack of critical thinking and creativity;
- increases errors and accidents;
- makes you and your team less productive;
- throws your life, and your family's, out of balance;
- increases absenteeism and healthcare costs.

HIDDEN COSTS: HEALTH, STRESS AND ERRORS

As with any disease, the first step to cure is diagnosis. Dr Nikolai Bezroukov of the UN Sustainable Development Networking Program states:

You have Pseudo-Attention Deficit Disorder if:

- *you find your mind wandering from tasks that are uninteresting or difficult;*
- *you say things without thinking and regret having said them later;*
- *you make quick decisions without thinking enough about their possible bad results;*
- *you have a quick temper, a short fuse;*
- *you have trouble planning in what order to do a series of tasks or activities and are time starved;*
- *you have a hard time waiting your turn in group activities;*
- *you usually work on more than one project at a time and fail to finish many of them.*

From the Information Age, we have moved into the Knowledge Age. So now, instead of struggling to get information, we are faced with a new challenge: what skills do we need to convert the glut of information that is available to us—the piles of stuff on our desks and in our computers, the hours of meetings that chew up huge chunks of our day—into the knowledge we need to skillfully run our businesses and lives? But here is the rub.

BUSY PEOPLE CAN'T LEARN

"It's true," says Susan. "They're stuck in 2nd gear, doing more–better–faster. So instead of slowing down long enough to master 1st gear—to follow instructions exactly, to learn as much as they can from trainers and manuals, to practice the new skills until they can perform them safely and effectively consistently—they put in a little effort and then rush back to their desks."

"Re-plugged into 2nd gear goals and expectations, they quickly become frustrated because they can't get up to speed with their incompletely-learned new skills. To meet deadlines and make quotas, to get bonuses and pay raises, they revert to old familiar methods and approaches. And the problem gets worse. (This is the heart of the reactive, going out of business approach at work again.)

"Your challenge is to reward yourself and your team not just for 2nd gear behaviors but 1st gear behaviors as well. OK, let's gear down and get started."

HOW TO GET MORE FROM READING IN LESS TIME

Reading requires your brain to convert linear information into a multi-sensory form it can receive, store and retrieve. And it does this rapidly—even though you've probably been taught otherwise. To prove this point, read the following note:

> I cdnuolt blveiee taht I cluod aulaclty uesdnatnrd waht I was rdanieg The phaonmneal pweor of the hmuan mind. Aoccdrnig to rscheearch taem at Cmabrigde Uinervtisy, it deosn't mttaer in waht oredr the ltteers in a wrod are, the olny iprmoatnt tihng is taht the frist and lsat ltteer be in the rghit pclae. The rset can be a taotl mses and you can sitll raed it wouthit a porbelm. Tihs is bcuseae the huamn mnid deos not raed ervey lteter by istlef, but the wrod as a wlohe. Such a cdonition is arppoiately cllaed Typoglycemia.
>   Amzanig huh? Yaeh and yuo awlyas thought slpeling was ipmorantt!

Yes, your brain is capable of doing much more work much more quickly when you know how.

What is your current reading speed?

"Most people know their weight but very few know their reading speed. How many words per minute are you reading? This information will become more and more important to you, and your organization, in the months and years ahead," says Richard.

Grass Roots Tip
Know your current reading speed in words per minute.

Before Susan and Richard teach you more, let's take a few minutes to evaluate your starting point so you can assess your progress and improvement along the way. And so you can reinforce the time and effort you are investing.

Make sure you have a pencil or pen as well as a watch with a second hand or timer for this exercise. When you are ready, set the timer for **3 minutes** and read the following story *at your normal pace*.

Mighty Mike: What a Difference a Leader Makes
Susan Ford Collins and Richard Israel

Phil Johnson was frustrated and worried: frustrated that in his mid 50s with a Masters from a top University and 30 years in PR, he found himself unwanted and redundant and worried that last year he had sent out 150 resumes which resulted in five interviews but no job.

His funds were drying up. If it wasn't for his wife Audrey's position as a loan officer, they would have exhausted their savings months ago. "What can I do?" was the question that plagued Phil day and night. Interviewers kept telling him he was too old for a full time corporate ➔position. But, with 7 years to go until Social Security and Medicare would kick in, he had to find something—and hopefully something with benefits.

Several months ago he had joined a support group looking for guidance. But it was his wife, Audrey, who reminded Phil that he loved working on cars, that he had more skill than their mechanic and, if he followed his passion, perhaps he could find a job in that industry. "What would I do with cars?" he charged back. "Sell 'em," Audrey concluded. "In good times or bad, people still need to buy cars."

The ➔thought of being "a car salesman" was his biggest barrier up front. He and Audrey discussed his feelings at length. "What would my family say if they knew I was selling cars? My poor mother would die—or cry." "Cry about what?" Audrey fired back. "Cry because you're out making a living? Put your ego aside and go find a job selling cars. We both know you can do it and God knows we need the money."

It took less than 20 minutes for Phil to skim the classified section of their local paper and circle six ads that all ➔said the same thing: "Experienced Car Salesman Wanted. Write your own check. Work your own hours. Commission only." For a few minutes Audrey and Phil sat in the warm glow of believing they'd found an answer and money would soon be coming in again.

Phil's background in PR provided the keywords he planned to use in the interview. When his interviewer asked him, "Why do you want to sell cars?" he would reply honestly, "Because I'm hungry to make money." Walking onto a neighborhood car lot, he quickly spotted a sign that read, "We sell NEW reconditioned cars." And his ➔"hungry to make money" pitch hit its mark. The sales manager Mighty Mike's eyes immediately sparked and he shouted, "You're hired."

Mighty Mike was true to his name, all 280 pounds of him. His huge frame shook as he wise-cracked "Give me five and his salesmen slapped their hands against his extended giant paw. At their early Monday morning motivational session, all seven salesmen sat around with drooped shoulders and freshly ironed shirts, sipping sweetened black coffee from chipped enameled mugs. "New day, new man," said Mighty Mike pulling Phil to his feet. "Give him five," he roared and they ➔all went through the motions. Mighty Mike said they were on the "up system" which meant you had to wait your turn to walk up to a customer.

"What do we think when a customer tells you 'just looking?'" And they all answered in unison, "They're going to buy, buy, buy." "Give me five," shouted Mighty Mike jumping to his feet. Walking out of the sales office with one hand on Phil's shoulder and the other stroking his glossy silk tie, Mighty Mike chanted, "You're going to do just great here, yes sir, just great." As they ended their conversation ➜with the obligatory high five, Phil was concerned that this might be all the training Mighty Mike planned to provide. And he was right. Mighty Mike was a hell of a salesman but he didn't know the first thing about leadership.

Phil's first day at work consisted of hanging around, shooting the breeze, and waiting for his turn with a customer. Traffic was slow on Mondays and after 10 hours, Phil headed home without so much as a nibble. But he wasn't discouraged. It had been new and exciting and his associates had told him amazing stories of untold riches ➜that had been made on this very car lot.

By the end of his first week, Phil had put in 60 hours. He had seen four customers—three just walked off and he'd TO'd (turned over) the fourth to Steve, their "number one closer," who couldn't close that one.

Late Saturday night Mighty Mike called Phil into his office. "Philly," a term of endearment Mighty Mike had made up for him, "Philly, in this business you have to sell, sell, sell and you haven't sold, sold, sold. But you're brand new and I'm going to give you another chance. Go ➜home tonight and thumb through your address book, call your friends and family with money, and get them to come in and buy a car from you." His frame shook as he chuckled at his own advice. "Philly, give me five."

Phil hung on for another week with no sales and no paycheck. Then Mighty Mike let him go declaring, "Philly, you're burning the customer base." And, according to Steve, that meant he wasn't closing the walk-ins and so he was taking opportunities away from the real closers like him.

The following week Phil applied to a foreign dealership across ➜the street, and this time things went far better. International Motors had a 3-day training program for new hires. Their program spelled out the rules and regulations of the dealership—how the various departments worked from service to finance. And, most important of all, it included 2 full days on the basics of selling cars. His new sales manager, Harry Upton, answered all his questions and made him feel at home.

Next Phil was told to shadow (that is, follow around) Sam Spiegel, a high-integrity salesman with 20 years experience. Sam was great. He explained the ins and outs of ➜the dealership and how to effectively sell their specific brand. He provided constant supervision and walked Phil through the paperwork until he was sure of it. Like a giant jigsaw puzzle Phil, with Sam's help, put together the pieces of his new job. His confidence was growing. He felt good about the dealership and the quality of the cars and service his customers would be receiving. And by the end of the second week, Phil had sold two cars and earned $400. It was a start in the right direction and Audrey was delighted.

Who Failed: Phil or Mighty Mike?

➔ What a difference a leader makes! Phil experienced quite a contrast between the leadership of Mighty Mike and Harry Upton. Mighty Mike expected Phil to "sell, sell, sell" but he didn't realize that he had to gear down to teach, teach, teach.

The quality of leadership is most important in 1st gear when we're first starting. Look what happened when Phil headed across the street to work with Harry Upton. Harry started Phil off slowly, teaching him the ins and outs of his company and its divisions as well as the basics of selling cars.

Phil's wife, Audrey, ➔ played a powerful leadership role in the development of his new career. It was masterful how she shifted gears with Phil. She geared down to face the problem head on: they needed income and he needed to find a job. Then she geared up to devise a creative solution: do something you love. And Audrey recognized that solution was selling cars. Next she overcame Phil's objections when his ego got in the way. Step by step, day by day, she guided her husband from feeling stuck and confused into sustained goal-directed action and income, even though it was uncomfortable for ➔ him and for her.

Next Sam Spiegel stepped in to provide Phil the additional knowledge and self-confidence he would need. Their gears matched perfectly—the 1st Gear of Success and the 1st Gear of Leadership. Phil was well-prepared to produce in 2nd gear, and he did. This is the kind of leadership that will be needed by millions of Americans who will be starting or restarting their lives and careers in the next few years.

As their coach we sometimes forget how important it is to have someone beside us when we're brand new at something. Like when you had ➔ your learner's permit and your dad, mom or driver's ed instructor sat in the passenger seat next to you answering your thousands of life-saving and car-saving questions: Will this car fit between those cars up ahead? Can I parallel park in that space? Why does that police car behind me have those lights blinking on top? Asking these questions sounds silly to us now, because as experienced drivers, those judgments are programmed in our brains. But when we were learning, they weren't there and we needed someone experienced to fill in our holes in terms of self-confidence, knowledge and experience, as ➔ well as, to take responsibility for our safety.

When we are leading people in 1st gear, it's important for us to gear down into our "starting something new" mindset—the mindset you're in when you're first learning how to use a computer, surf the Internet or scuba dive. As leaders, if we fail to do that, we mistakenly assume these tasks are as easy for new learners as they are for us. We underestimate timeframes and difficulties. Or we assume that others have the experience and decision-making abilities we have. We catch ourselves thinking, "Come on, that's easy" or "What's →wrong? Are you stupid"? No, they're not stupid. They're simply new and inexperienced.

When we're learning or relearning, we need our leaders to believe in us. If they can't imagine us succeeding at this job, task or skill, then it will be impossible for us to have confidence in them until we can build our self-confidence. In 1st gear we need to know that our leaders have the time, skill, ability and willingness to get us from not knowing to knowing, from failing to succeeding and ultimately to leading others.

Yes, leaders make a profound difference in the 1st gear of →selling cars or providing customer service. But they have an even more powerful effect when they lead us skillfully in the 1st gear of life. Or if they fail to. When leaders fail, their errors reverberate through the whole leadership chain, especially if those leaders are parents.

- OK, now count the number of arrows in the left-hand margin of the portion you read. Each arrow represents 100 words.
- Next count the number of words you read past the last arrow and add those totals together.
- Divide the final total by 3 to obtain words per minute.

Is your reading speed high enough?

Sad to say, most business people read at 250 words per minute not because their brain holds them back but because years ago their 2nd grade teacher told them, "Always read slowly and carefully, one word at a time." And they are still unconsciously following these old rules and limits.

Grass Roots Tip
Today you need to be able to read 1 000 words per minute to keep up with work and competition and enjoy a balanced life. There are many excellent speed reading courses available and we urge you to take one in person or online.

In the early grades, you were in the 1st gear of reading so those instructions were appropriate. But they are producing Information Overload now—and stacks of unread stuff piling up on bedside tables and office credenzas around the world.

You must be a variable-speed reader

For technical documents you will need to read more slowly. For pleasure you may want to give yourself lots of time to see, hear, feel, taste and smell what the author is creating for you. But, when it's reading you need to get done effectively and efficiently, here are some powerful updated techniques you will want to start practicing immediately.

Decide on your outcome and time frame before you begin

Knowing your desired outcome and time frame up front allows your brain to perform more effectively, efficiently and creatively whether you are reading a book, proposal or e-mail, attending a meeting or leading one, meeting people or listening to the news.

To immediately become outcome-oriented, simply ask yourself: "Why am I doing this? Why is this important to me?" Determining your outcome up front applies to everything you do, at work and at home and is especially important in your leadership. When you delegate an outcome, you need to make sure your team member knows precisely what you have in mind so they can follow through to completion and satisfaction.

Now reset your timer for 5 minutes and reread the article you just read with this outcome in mind: Which gears of success and leadership were the individuals in the story in? Stop working when the timer goes off and move ahead to the next new skill.

RapidScanning

Grass Roots Tip
Always know your outcome and available timeframe before you begin reading.

Remember how rapidly your brain comprehended those jumbled, misspelled words! Learn to trust your brain's ability to work far more quickly and efficiently. RapidScanning significantly reduces the time it takes for you to obtain maximum value from articles, manuals and books.

Most people sit down to read a book from the beginning. But, given today's pressures and overload, after a few pages they either find themselves dozing or thinking about something they had forgotten to do. When they return to the book, they start over at the beginning again. And again. And never get through it!

Here's a more proactive approach to getting the outcome you want from reading a book.

RapidScan the whole book first

1   When tackling a book, read the Table of Contents first. Authors provide the main branches for your Mind Map up front. In fact, whether authors draw a Mind Map or not, they have the central idea and main branches of their book in mind as they write.
2   RapidScan the book all the way through, the way you glance through a newspaper to decide what to read in the time you have. Get a sense of the whole and the outcome you want from reading it. Decide up front how much time you want to spend and set a timer so you stick with that time frame.
3   On your second RapidScan, return to the beginning of the book. This time rapidly read the first and last paragraph of each chapter, bold headings and summaries. Glance quickly at charts and graphs. Mark the pages you will Deep-Read with paper tabs or Post-It notes.

4   Now that you have pre-digested the book, Deep-Read the parts that matter to you and enjoy the outcome you had in mind when you purchased, borrowed or added that book to your pile. And take a moment to notice the pile is shrinking.

To increase your comprehension, use the 5-Finger Technique.

If you find yourself zoning out as you read, find 5 KEYWORDS or phrases on each page. Review them on your fingers—1, 2, 3, 4, 5—before turning the page. This technique retrains your brain to pay attention instead of giving over to distraction, fatigue or sleep—zzzzzzzzzzzzz.

Grass Roots Tip
Practice RapidScanning for key words until your eye/brain automatically searches them out and increases your comprehension.

The proof of the pudding

Susan and Richard did an introductory *Managing Information Overload* workshop and one of the participants just happened to be the new publisher of *The Miami Herald*, Jesus Diaz. Afterwards, he asked them to teach these skills to his executive committee at the paper. Unfortunately Jesus could not attend that session, but he heard all about it when he returned and called to tell them how frequently his executive team was using the skills they had taught them—in talks, in meetings and to communicate new ideas.

Several months later, Susan and Richard were invited back to *The Miami Herald*. This time to teach these updated information skills to the next layer of their organization, their top 200 managers. And then after that, there were 2000 additional Grass Roots employees. How could they teach Managing Information Overload to all of them most cost- and time-effectively? They spent the next six months creating an e-course to do just this. You can find it at our website www.technologyofsuccess.com. Here is a sample of the feedback comments they received:

> To say you guys were a hit would be an understatement. When I returned to town, I asked my executive team, "How did it go?" Twenty minutes later, I was feeling sorry for myself for missing it. So we invited you back to train me and our management team. I just saw the feedback. I could not agree more. It was a terrific course.
>
> Jesus Diaz, **Publisher**, *The Miami Herald*

> We all boosted our reading speed significantly, several of us almost doubling it. The strategy for digesting reports and manuals has proved a great time saver.
>
> Rick Hirsch, **Senior Editing Team**

Outcome-oriented e-mail—quickly and memorably send and receive messages

Are you also in Inbox Overload? Many business people receive 200 plus e-mails a day. How many do you usually receive and send? What is your e-mail reading speed? Do you have a strategy for RapidScanning them and Deep-Reading the most vital ones?

Times have changed. Today fewer messages are written by hand or pecked on a typewriter, licked, stamped and mailed at the post office to be delivered several days or weeks later. We now have instantaneous e-mail. So there's no reason not to send and receive as many messages as you want to anyone anywhere. Or is there?

E-mail is free, right?

Apparently so, but not really. How much time and money is e-mail actually costing you? To find out—divide your annual salary by 120 000 minutes (40 hours a week × 60 minutes an hour × 50 weeks a year) to get your salary per minute.

Next multiply your salary per minute × 3 minutes per e-mail. That's the cost per e-mail to you—and your organization! So if you make $60 000 a year that's 50 cents a minute or $1.50 an e-mail. 100 e-mails a day costs $150.00 a day and consumes 5 hours of your time! Not to mention what it's costing your employer!

Tell the truth: Are you addicted to e-mail, checking it constantly—when you get up, all through the day, before you go to bed?

Take control of your e-mail. Check it at specific times and let regular senders know what those times are—like 10:00 a.m., 2:00 p.m. and 5:00 p.m. Tell people that if they need you immediately, they should call or stop by. When you read e-mail, shut your door, turn off your phone and focus on your messages and outcomes.

"Corporate America sends more than 7 billion e-mails a day," according to International Data Corp. What would it mean to you and your organization—if most of the e-mails you sent and received were cut by 80 per cent? It's possible. Here's how…

Send more effective e-mail

Always use the subject line. Like the central image in a Mind Map, it immediately says what your message is about—the outcome—and why your recipient should open it.

Grass Roots Tip
Use the formula on this page to find out what each e-mail is costing you.

MANAGING
INFORMATION
OVERLOAD

Assume they are busily racing along in 2nd gear. So it's up to you to get them to slow down to read your message and requests in depth and follow through as requested.

Pre-digest your message before sending. What exactly do you want? Use fonts that allow your e-mails to easily slip into their brains. Bold keywords. Add color, clip art and pictures but always check file size before sending so you don't overload your recipient's inbox.

Receive e-mail more effectively

RapidScan all e-mail up front. Read subject lines and/or first paragraphs. Delete irrelevant ones. Prioritize which need immediate action and which to respond to later. File reference material.

Next study your most important e-mails. Address each point requested and ask for clarification if needed.

Send relevant e-mails to relevant people

- Make e-mails 1 page or less. When scheduling a call or conference, include topic, location and time in the subject line.
- Put most important things first. Most people don't read past the first screen.
- Spell out your outcome and the actions you want them to take in detail. Include time frames so they can meet your requirements.
- Put all requests to the same person in one e-mail if possible.
- If the list is extensive, pick up the phone and discuss. Back and forth e-mail queries take time.
- When you're tempted to cc or bcc, ask yourself: what do I really want the copied person to know? Individualize the subject line to include specifics on why you're forwarding the message to him or her.
- Edit forwards. Cut and paste instead of making recipients fight their way through a long string of messages to be opened and opened and …
- Use Send All and Reply All wisely! It can be a major source of Inbox Overload. One CEO Susan and Richard work with disabled Reply All in his company's system to save everyone time and money!
- Respect relationships. Think about others preferences and boundaries before forwarding their message.
- Don't send jokes routinely. Or you'll be routinely deleted and lose your e-credibility.
- Lead by example. Do unto others what you want them to do unto you.

Remember what makes Mind Maps user-friendly—color, keywords and phrases, variety of type, images, bolds and underlines. Include these elements in e-mail as well so they'll be easily digestible and memorable to the brain.

And pass these Managing Information Overload guidelines on to frequent e-mail partners—coworkers, vendors, clients and customers.

Now put these ideas to work. Read the following ...

From: Jim
Date: January 18, 2007
To: Harry
Subject:

Hi Harry,

Just wanted to catch you up on things here. Since the last meeting, Joan has been out sick. She broke her toe at our group outing. Richie left the group. He's now in India. So we're a bit confused and disoriented for now.

You remember that we'd talked about our next meeting being in February. Given all these changes we are going to have to put it off until March 3 when everyone will finally be able to attend. Hopefully they will be able to do their follow through by then. Joan is supposed to report back on the Milo project. Richie's replacement, Jean Baxter, will need to be briefed on what she has to present at the meeting on the Williams account. Do you know of anything else that will need to be handled?

See you then,
Jim

(144 words)

OR ...

From: Jim
Date: January 18, 2007
To: Harry
Subject: Meeting date change and follow up

Next meeting March 3
Follow through:
Milo project—Joan.
Williams account—Jean Baxter, Richie's replacement, needs briefing on presentation she'll make.
Anything else?

(29 words)

Grass Roots Tip
Review some of your recent e-mails and see how you could cut them by 80%.

What would it mean to you and your organization if the majority of e-mails sent and received were CUT by 80 per cent? You know now how that could happen.

OUTCOME-ORIENTED MEETINGS MAXIMIZE TIME, ENERGY AND FOLLOW THROUGH

"Meetings are 'the hidden landmines' of Information Overload. Most people have never been trained to organize their thoughts, to listen on purpose or keep meetings on track. So meetings wander on and on, start late and run over, and attendees walk away muttering—what a waste of time! And I've got so much to do!"

Make meetings worthwhile—set your outcomes in advance. Ask yourself up front—Why are we meeting? What do I/we want from this meeting? What needs to be done afterward and by whom?

Sitting through a boring, off-course meeting can drain you for the rest of the day. But participating in a purposeful one can move you and your project ahead dramatically.

Take a break after 50 minutes. Your brain can focus for up to 50-minutes. Pressing on after that—without taking a break—becomes less and less productive and more and more exhausting.

Meetings are like text. Only 10 per cent are key. Drawing a Mind Map during the meeting will force you to remain focused on your outcomes. If you're getting together for the first time on this subject, create a new Mind Map. If you've met before, review your previous Mind Map beforehand and add to that map as you meet. Insert a question mark (?) or follow up (FU) in areas that will need to be dealt with after the meeting. Be sure to bring your Mind Map to the next session.

Grass Roots Tip
Increase the effectiveness of your meetings. Take breaks after 50 minutes.

Distributing Mind Maps is an ideal way to circulate the results of your meetings. Mind Maps are a powerful way to organize a presentation. Hand out copies and work from it as you speak. Or speak first and then handout a Mind Map as you review. Mind Maps make your presentation memorable and impactful, include your contact information and date. Mind Mapping keeps meetings on course and insures follow up steps by all attendees are pursued to completion.

Make meetings worthwhile. Set outcomes in advance. Do you need to meet? Or could the outcomes be reached more effectively by e-mail or a call? Would another approach save time and energy? However, remember, a key benefit of meetings is rapport and team-building.

Start on time and if your outcomes have been achieved, end early. If they haven't, plan how and when to complete and end on time. Respect attendees' plans and commitments at work and at home.

Mind Map the meeting as it unfolds. Are you on track? What else is there? What decisions need to be made? Allow participants to voice opinions. Their input needs to be heard. Don't railroad. Create consensus and ownership. Re-direct hostile individuals and comments. Switch back to the agreed-on agenda.

Was it worthwhile—considering the time and salaries of participants?

PURPOSE-FULL LISTENING

Maximize your opportunity. Sit close to the speaker. Turn off cell phones. Bring paper and pen/pencils. Speaking happens in real time. If you miss what is said, it's gone. Tune up and tune in.

Stay focused. See, feel and pre-experience what you hear and look for missing details and information. Make sure the hologram you are creating is detailed and multisensory. Ask questions if it isn't. If you catch yourself chatting or daydreaming, retune and refocus or use the 5-Finger Technique.

You enhance relationships dramatically by letting others know you are listening by letting them know they are heard. "Uh hah, yes, I hear you saying ...."

Notice which gear you are in as you listen

"Are you in 1st gear, trying to learn new information, needing immediate input and direction, rights and wrongs, dependent, anxious but eager?

"Or in 2nd gear, working to get a project done, meet bonus standards, a deadline or budget?

"Or in 3rd gear—open to ideas and insights, willing to offer input and pre-experience potential futures—new products or services, new ways of generating results?" says Susan.

Be sure to listen to everyone around you. Consider their ideas and how they connect to your ideas and outcomes. The most powerful ideas come when you least expect them—driving, showering, talking to a stranger or child. From the people you may least expect to get them.

FYI: The idea for the outside elevator came from a janitor. The idea for the bar code came from a graduate student. The idea for your organization's new

Grass Roots Tip
As you listen, analyze which gear you are in and make sure you meet that gear's needs.

breakthrough product or system may be incubating in your mind right now—
and need only one more piece to become full blown.

Susan says, "To succeed in the future you will need to get comfortable operating
in 3rd gear.

"Creating—new links, connections, associations, new products, services,
industries, new ways of living and doing business together."

CONCLUSION: THESE SKILLS WILL ALLOW YOU TO USE NEW INFORMATION BETTER THAN THE COMPETITION

No, technology may not be making our lives easier. But it's not technology's
fault. It's ours—our use of outdated skills and approaches most of us learned in
elementary school and haven't updated since.

Three-gear, proactive leaders know that managing Information Overload
needs to be at the top of their current To-Do List. The future success of your
business will depend on your team's ability to digest information and convert
it to knowledge more and more effectively, efficiently and creatively. Proactive
leaders know that they must make time to shift people into 1st gear to begin
updating their reading, e-mail, listening and meeting presentation skills—their
information skills now. Proactive, three-gear leaders also know they must allow
team members to practice their new skills over and over to get them up to speed
and ready to use for 2nd gear productivity.

WHAT'S NEXT?

In the next chapter, Tony Dottino looks at how neuro-science research provides
new insights into our thinking and behavior. This information will give you
and your team the competitive edge you are seeking.

ACTIVITIES

1   Mind Map the next four meetings you lead or attend.
2   RapidScan one book a week during the next month.
3   Make sure the subject line of your e-mail tells the whole story.
4   Be sure to include the exact actions you want the recipient of your e-mail to complete and when.
5   In 1 month, redo the Reading Speed exercise and check on your progress.
6   Draw a Mind Map of the most important project in your work or personal life.

GRASS ROOTS
LEADERS—THE
BRAINSMART
REVOLUTION IN
BUSINESS

104

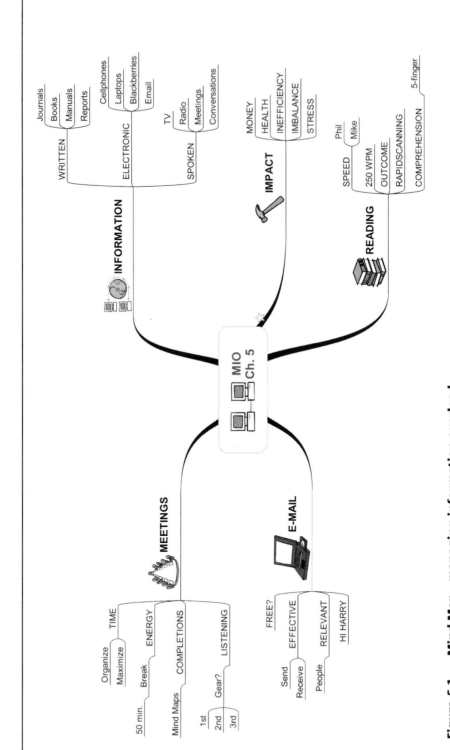

Figure 5.1   Mind Map—managing information overload

CHAPTER 6

The Seven Principles of Grass Roots Leadership

OVERVIEW

Businesses are at the forefront of the revolution in thinking. In an environment that is global, complex and competitive, we look at some of the advantages accruing to a company which recognizes that human resources are the key to long-term success. We describe the seven Brain Principles in practical terms and the benefits a company enjoys when it applies each principle in harmony, the utilization of cognitive science to enhance leadership, creativity, teamwork and communication skills of managers and Grass Roots workers.

ASSETS IN THE BILLIONS

Imagine your company owns a computer with the ability to receive and transmit information using a variety of input/output devices, such as visual, auditory and tactile. It has unlimited memory available, with built-in redundancies to ensure that vital data is never lost. How much would that computer be worth if it could use this combination of input devices and storage capacity to continually add to its database of knowledge? How much would that computer be worth if it could use the knowledge it gained from experience to reprogram itself, so that mistakes were less likely to be repeated? And how much would that computer be worth if it had the ability to program other computers so that they also learned from its experiences? How much would that computer be worth to your company? Millions? Billions?

As you are reading these sentences, you are using the most powerful tool ever known. Your brain is that computer—worth billions! Our research and experience have consistently demonstrated that the brain's capabilities are greatly under-exploited. We have also seen the dramatic improvements possible when the brain's capabilities are used more fully.

If your company had human assets worth billions and you learned that only a fraction of those asset's capacity was being used, would that worry you? If the efficiency of your human capital improved tenfold, how much would that add to the profitability of your company?

USE YOUR BRAIN

In the Grass Roots workshop Tony Dottino conducts there is a ground rule for the participants. "In any solution to a problem or an opportunity you cannot ask for more headcount or more than a very small amount of money, less than $1000. Arrive at a solution that doesn't require more of either!"

Eight weeks after a workshop he came upon Nakita, a nurse who was a participant in the workshop. She had immigrated 10 years prior from Russia to the United States. This day her facial expression was different from the tense, stern, angry look she had on the second day of the workshop. Now it was cheerful, more relaxed and a smile was trying to break out.

Nakita spoke with a noticeable level of emotion and respect,

> *Mr Dottino, I come from Russia and at the beginning of the workshop I thought I was there again. You told us we could not have money, nor more people, and you weren't going to fix our problem. You suggested that we had all the people and money we needed to solve many of our own problems. I thought you were crazy and you had no idea what life was like on the floor.*

The team's problem involved the delays between radiology and the emergency department in getting test results back to the doctors. The inability to get doctors to write clearly so radiology could do their job immediately was creating extra phone calls back to the emergency department. Finding a nurse who then knew where the doctor was so they could clarify the order was taking more time than needed. This created delays in getting patients tested, that eventually led to delays in getting them discharged or admitted.

The team thought they needed an extra secretary to track down the doctors so they wouldn't need to bother a nurse. That was a reactive solution not a proactive one. In the midst of the day-to-day crisis of an emergency room there was no time to talk to one another, just react to the next crisis. But talk to one another was exactly what the team needed to do. Tony wasn't going to have them ask the chief nursing officer for budget money to hire a new secretary.

As Nakita continued talking, she smiled and spoke with passion.

> *We met with the radiology department, emergency room doctors and nurses. The Grass Roots team showed them the analysis of how many times this problem is occurring and the wasted time between all three groups that could be saved. In addition the benefit of getting the patient admitted or discharged quicker was important to all of us.*
>
> *Everyone now understands the impact that we have on one another and the doctors have agreed to make a point of writing more clearly. The nurses promised the doctors less interruptions and faster test results. No one had ever stopped to*

realize how much wasted time we had. Over the last 6 weeks, patients are being discharged 1 hour sooner and we are not interrupting doctors as often.

The fact that we were able to sit together and communicate as a team was the most important lesson we have learned. By using our creativity we found a solution that will save the hospital overtime and get patients on their way quicker. The best part, you were right, we didn't need to spend anything, only better utilize our time. You taught us how to use our brains!

Jack Welch, the former CEO of GE, would certainly agree with her as revealed by a comment he made:

There is infinite potential for savings. The human mind is always able to find a better way to do things.

Many of today's successful companies realize that it is the ability of people to harness their natural intelligence to create and apply technology that is responsible for generating extraordinary financial results. They understand that technology is the result of the application of human intelligence.

The authors believe that successful businesses have always depended on brains, and that thinking, creativity, teamwork and communication will continue to drive the innovative corporation towards success, to survive, to prosper, to innovate and to succeed— to soar beyond all competition.

Astute companies know that future success depends on being able to fully utilize its human resources that exist within the organization. Successful corporations in the future will be intelligence-driven, realizing that intelligence is not just capacity—stored knowledge—but also the ability to make the most of it. The sum of these two will create the competitive advantage.

OUR MARVELLOUS BRAIN

Imagine how much more you could achieve, if you could learn to improve how it works. What if simply learning more about how your brain works could help your Grass Roots team grow in both their personal and professional life?

During the past 25 years, the number of people working in the field of brain research has grown from 500 to over 30000, according to Ronald Kotulak, author of *Inside the Brain*. The brain has been featured on magazine covers more often during the 2000s than at any other time, and cover stories in publications such as *Time*, *Newsweek*, *New Scientist*, *Discover*, *Scientific American* and *Science* have chronicled many of the breakthroughs and puzzles uncovered.

What if, as a result of all this research, new tools could be created to revolutionize the way each Grass Roots employee viewed their work? What if they were all born naturally creative? What if the more they learned, the easier it was to learn more? What if the people who have been telling them that they can't learn to do certain things are wrong?

Well, this book argues that all these statements are true. The fruits of this research are a technology that enables each individual to increase their intellectual capital. As with any new technology, at first it may be difficult for society to adapt to it and the changes it brings. A few pioneers will try it out, and as their discoveries prove worthwhile and more people learn of them, it will cause a snowball effect, until eventually, the majority of the population will adopt the technology.

During this pioneering stage of the study of human intelligence, there may be many struggles, hardships and setbacks to deal with. Yet the Grass Roots people who persist will reap great rewards, they will become the future leaders of their organizations.

The vast amount of neuroscience research now appearing on TV, radio, and the print media provides new insights into thinking and behavior. People who are finding pragmatic applications for applying these lessons are demonstrating outstanding results. The time has come where utilizing these lessons is now mandatory for organizations that want to compete in today's economy.

BRAIN PRINCIPLES

Despite your brain's amazing complexity, here are seven principles that Tony Buzan developed after years of research and study. When Tony Dottino first heard him present these at a workshop on creativity he attended, it caused him to think, "Every person in IBM should know what these are." Today he sees the value they provide to executives, managers and Grass Roots workers and speaks passionately, **"Every person in the world should know what these are!"** Each of these principles is a part of the operating system your bio-computer— for that is what the brain is—uses for its thinking and learning.

THE SEVEN BRAIN PRINCIPLES

1   The brain synergizes information, so that 1 plus 1 is 2 or more.
2   The brain is a success-driven mechanism.
3   The brain has the ability to mimic actions perfectly.
4   The brain craves completeness (it needs to fill in the blanks).
5   The brain constantly seeks new knowledge and information.
6   The brain is truth-seeking.
7   The brain is persistent.

Brain Principle 1: The brain synergizes information, so that 1 plus 1 is 2 or more

Research has shown that the brain has synergistic powers. This means that one thought triggers another, which in turn triggers another, and so on. Imagine receiving a message at work saying that an urgent letter has arrived at home. How many different thoughts will be triggered in your mind by this initial piece of information? This is divergent thinking: our ability to start from one central idea and to move onto many ideas. It means we are capable of creating our own internal universes of knowledge, networks of thought, memory banks, and uniquely innovative and inspirational ideas. Convergent thinking, on the other hand (which is what is measured by most IQ tests), is our ability to narrow from many ideas to one, such as selecting one vendor from a list of 20.

Stop!

Take this simple test. Stop thinking! Shut your brain off and do not think any thoughts for the next 10 seconds.

If you aren't able to complete this test because you were thinking, then you have passed the more important test. You are alive and your brain is working, 24/7.

When the brain is vigorously thinking and learning, each neuron develops more connections (axons and dendrites—see Chapter 8) to communicate with other neurons. This process creates a more sophisticated, intricate and complex bio-computer. What we think, the way we think and the way we think about thinking literally change the biological structure of our brain.

Creativity occurs when the brain's synergistic ability combines and links existing knowledge with new ideas to create new thought patterns. It happens naturally when members of an organization exchange ideas and direction. Synergy explains why new ideas and associations fed into the existing knowledge base lead to breakthroughs in creative thinking. Each Grass Roots team member becomes a vital ingredient.

The brain's ability to synthesize new and existing information explains the acceleration of technological innovation. Because each generation of people start with all the accumulated knowledge of their predecessors, we have a knowledge base upon which to build. Each new breakthrough or discovery of information adds to that knowledge base, so that the pace of technological advancement and creative thinking accelerates. An example of this is the advances made in computer hardware and software over the last 15 years. Communication vehicles such as the Internet which can transfer knowledge and experience between users from around the globe mean that the rate of change will accelerate exponentially.

Lack of familiarity with this principle sometimes causes frustration for those who attend a business or self-improvement seminar or read a book on this topic, who frequently complain: "Most of the material I already knew! I didn't learn much new!"—and they stop thinking. If they applied their knowledge of synergy it would mean that even if 99 per cent of the material was familiar, the 1 per cent which is new will trigger new associations and ideas. These associations will build upon existing knowledge to create new ideas, which will in turn create more new ideas. Even one new idea or thought from a seminar or book can eventually generate a breakthrough idea. That is why we stress that every person can trigger valuable ideas—listen to all of them.

Synergy follows the GIGG process

You may be familiar with the computer acronym GIGO—Garbage In, Garbage Out—and apply it to your thinking. However, we feel another acronym reflects the synergy principle more accurately: GIGG (negative).

Based upon what you now know about the brain's structure, what do you think happens when the brain has garbage entered into it? Because of the synergy of the brain:

Garbage In, Garbage Grows

Our brain builds a garbage dump which accumulates all the junk it receives. All new junk entered is added to the dump, and the dump grows exponentially because of synergy. Negative thinking, pessimism and cynicism breed more of the same. Imagine the implications of this if you and your employees expend most of your mental energy on negative and cynical thoughts about your company. That thinking will become more prevalent until it pervades the organization, turning your own creative energy against your company and yourself!

The opposite of "Garbage In, Garbage Grows" is GIGG (positive): "Good In, Good Grows" towards a positive outcome. Just as the brain's synergy can be destructive when fed negative thoughts, it becomes radiant when given positive inputs. A person whose brain is synergizing positive thoughts to generate more positive, creative thoughts is using what we call "Radiant Thinking." We use this term because a brain working in this fashion becomes like a sun, radiating light in all directions. This means that as well as being self-destructive, the brain can be self-enhancing. It is important to recognize that in most instances, we control the information entered into our brain. We control what the Gs in GIGG will represent.

It's time for 5 minutes of homework

At the end of the first day of the Grass Roots Innovation and BrainSmart Leader workshops Tony Dottino conducts, he usually assigns homework for each attendee. They are to go home that evening and have a 5 minute conversation with someone and begin it by asking, "What good things happened in your day today?" At the end of the 5 minutes they can talk about anything they wish, including the problem events of the day. He then requests that they do this at least once a week for the next 6 weeks.

At a Grass Roots Workshop follow up session, 6 weeks after the initial exercise, Shirley, who has been a nurse for more than 25 years, stands up and her facial expressions announces to everyone in the room, it is time to stop talking and pay attention, something is up.

She begins by advising the class that her initial thoughts on the GIGG homework were not favorable, "It was the dumbest thing she had ever heard." Life is loaded with problems, how can anybody dismiss the misery of it all and talk about the good things. But she was true to the assignment and advised the class that she did the homework.

Her daughter and grandchild are living with her and as she began the dinner conversation with the question, her daughter was wondering what was happening. Usually the evening conversations are short and not very joyous. However, this time the conversation took a different direction and lasted 90 minutes. Laughing, getting excited, being happy and enjoying the evening together was the result.

Shirley advised us that her daughter couldn't wait for mom to get home the next night do it again. At this point of the story her eyes began to well with tears as she advised the class that before the GIGG exercise, life at home was tough, conversations were either non existent or ended in arguments. However Shirley was now reporting that for the last 6 weeks things have been wonderful, she has rediscovered the relationship with her daughter and its fun. They laugh at dinner rather than argue.

But then Shirley goes on to finish the story, with that big smile and eyes popping from the sockets, her voice moving from mellow to strong and confident. An insight! She professes that after the first week of doing this with her daughter and seeing the results, it got her attention. It occurred to her that she might be able to bring this same energy and new found enthusiasm to her work associates and patients. Maybe she was coming to work a bit grumpy everyday and it was time for a change.

She began each day with a smile and a question, "What good things happened in your life last evening?" At the nurses change of shift there was an energy boost to start the day. This story has a happy ending for the hospital's patients, because as the whole staff started their day with this pleasant opening it set the synergy for the days actions in motion. Patient SAT scores went up by 15 per cent and the nurse manager received the month's recognition award for the largest increase in patient service scores.

Grass Roots Tips
Use these methods to maximize the benefits of synergy:
• Evaluate people's buy-in to the organization's goals to ensure focus.
• Learn to recognize and select appropriate GIGG for each person's brain.
• Develop education plans to build new pathways of thinking-/creativity.
• Start and end each day with identifying the positive situations of the day.

THE SEVEN PRINCIPLES OF GRASS ROOTS LEADERSHIP

An article published in July 26, 2006 on *Knowledge@Wharton*, "The Effect of Mood on Work Performance" references recent research that suggests a persons mood in their private life has more significance on their work performance than previously thought.

With the years of experience we have had in doing this homework exercise, we totally support the conclusion presented.

Brain Principle 2: The brain is a success-driven mechanism

When you set a goal, your brain will guide your thought processes, consciously and unconsciously, in a direction that helps you achieve success. The more precisely and consistently an organization's goal is defined, the easier it is for Grass Roots teams to take the actions to reach the target. That is why it is vital to describe desired outcomes in sufficient detail that it can be visualized and referred to later as progress is measured and tracked.

How many times have you heard someone stress the importance of writing down goals as a tool for success? Yet fewer than 10 per cent of those we have encountered have done so. Why is writing down goals important?

The act of writing down a goal and then reading it clarifies and reinforces the message. Combine this with a conscious action to review them from time to time creates a clear focus. Without this additional emphasis, the criteria of success can become distorted.

This Brain Principle also explains the importance of having clearly defined customer requirements. During our encounters with customer focus initiatives, we have found that companies with a clear definition of customer requirements consistently outperform those whose customer requirements are ambiguous or confusing.

In order for your brain to work at its optimal level, you must provide it with clearly defined end results and criteria to evaluate its progress. When allocating time priorities on a work project, make sure you allow time to write your goals down: because it will have a tremendous impact on your effectiveness. If possible, create images of what the finished product will look like. Encourage yourself to write down additional goals too, since they provide fuel for creative thinking.

Brain Principle 3: The brain has the ability to mimic actions perfectly

Copying the work of others is usually considered cheating during formal education, but this does not apply in the workplace. The brain learns best by copying others. The brain has the ability to learn new skills quickly by imitating others who are proficient at that skill and studying and imitating someone

GRASS ROOTS
LEADERS—THE
BRAINSMART
REVOLUTION IN
BUSINESS

112

else's work helps you improve your existing skills. Unless you are taking a test to measure your knowledge, copying is OK! Trying to learn without taking advantage of this Brain Principle is counterproductive. Imagine an infant trying to learn to speak, and being told by its parent, "Don't copy the words Mummy just said to you! That's cheating! Make up your own!" To see this Brain Principle in action, observe an infant learning a new skill. The infant studies the role model intently, trying to duplicate the behavior exactly as modelled. Using this ability, plus Brain Principle 7—persistence (see p. 117)—the infant learns the new skill quickly through closely observing and mimicking practice.

Our brain works both consciously and unconsciously to duplicate behavior and skill performance to perfection by searching for a model to imitate. After identifying an acceptable model, it consciously studies the behavior and mimics it.

The brain also copies behaviors on an unconscious level. When we listen to someone speak, the brain unconsciously detects the speaker's favourite phrases and mannerisms. Without even realizing it, we start mimicking them, often using the same phrases.

During a meeting with an executive team, several managers made a presentation of an operating plan to the chief executive officer. The CEO of this company frequently uses the word "remarkable" to describe data or behavior which is either unusual or impressive. In the presentation of the operating plan, each presenter used the word "remarkable"—an average of six times during each 10-minute presentation. Remarkable!

We need to be more aware of our brain's natural ability to mimic activities, otherwise we may begin mimicking inappropriate or poorly performed behaviors. We may not even realize that we are mimicking the behavior until we have "perfected" it. If this occurs, we will have to consciously search for a new, more appropriate model to follow, to replace the old. The longer this old, unacceptable behavior has been established, the longer it will usually take for the new, acceptable behavior to replace it (see Chapter 7, TEFCAS).

The mimic principle means that the thinking patterns of our brains will reflect the environment in which we exist. Many experts on psychology and self-improvement advise that to become more successful, we should associate with successful people. To apply this knowledge, we should examine our associates and note the behaviors we are duplicating. Do they provide us with a model for success, or are they modelling inappropriate behaviors?

By combining the mimic and synergy principles, you can create a formula your brain will follow to achieve success, but you must do this consciously. For example, do you deliberately select your role models and associates, or do you just "go with the flow?" Are you careful when selecting reading material

Grass Roots Tips
Use these methods to maximize the effectiveness of the Grass Roots success-driven mechanism:
• Develop a clear, documented picture of goals. This provides several benefits:
  – It forces everyone to clarify thinking by eliminating any ambiguity about what needs to be achieved.
  – It stimulates creativity by making a brain think imaginatively about goal definition and goal fulfilment.
  – It reinforces commitment to achieving the goal by strengthening its imprint.
• Check and note progress regularly.
• Establish interim milestones, and celebrate small successes along the way.

Grass Roots Tip
Use these
methods to
maximize the
benefits of
mimicking:
• Associate
  as often as
  possible with
  people you
  respect.
• When a
  conversation
  in a group
  of people
  becomes
  negative,
  attempt
  to keep it
  realistically
  positive.
• Ask people
  who their
  mentors or
  models are
  they use for
  learning.
• Select suitable
  role models
  for the skills
  and attitudes
  you wish to
  develop.
Read *Scientific
American*,
November 2006,
"Mirror Neurons
and the Mind"

or television programs to view? Do you search for people who are already successful at a goal you desire, and examine their behavior?

Now that you understand the mimic principle, consider the impact of lunchtime conversations spent with co-workers bombarding you with negative thoughts about the workplace. The mimic principle means that your brain will begin to copy these attitudes until they are firmly entrenched. When you combine this with the synergy principle, the GIGG outcome is disastrous. If you associate with cynical, pessimistic people, you will program your brain to think about all your experiences in a similar fashion. If you surround yourself with negative people, you will program yourself for failure.

Now consider the opposite. If your brain is exposed to people who are successful, innovative and happy, it will mimic and learn those positive thought patterns. By associating with positive people, you program yourself for success.

Brain Principle 4: The brain craves completeness—it needs to fill in the blanks

How many times have you heard someone begin a story and then pause, saying, "I really shouldn't be telling you this." Don't you feel like screaming, "Get on with it! I want to know how it ends!" This happens because our brain craves completeness. When the brain is given incomplete information, it tries to fill in the blanks anyway. The Greek philosopher Socrates often stimulated discussion and debate among his students by asking them challenging questions, and then responding with another question. He consistently made them aware of the gaps in their knowledge, which his students eagerly worked to fill. Hence the practice of using a series of questions to uncover the truth is often referred to as "the Socratic method."

The best leaders are those who know how to ask the right questions, providing incomplete stories, thus having people creating their own answers. Therefore when used in this fashion, it's an excellent tool to stimulate creativity in people.

Grass Roots Tip
Use these
methods to
maximize the
benefits of the
completeness
principle:
• To
  communicate
  effectively
  with someone,
  they need
  to have the
  same picture

However, if you receive a message from your boss which says, "Please see me at the end of the day," what does your brain do? It will not stop working until it generates an answer to the question, "What does the boss want to see me about?"

This anxiety about what is going on explains the hours employees spend swapping rumors and searching for information on the corporate grapevine. When employees hear rumors about an organizational change, their brains crave an understanding of what is likely to happen. Another instance of no news is *not* good news! When left unintentionally open it can create lots of extra work, tracking down the source of false beliefs.

The implications of this principle in day-to-day life are limitless. Think of all the people you communicate with on a daily basis and the words you use, the actions you take and the pictures you create in their minds. Imagine all the opportunities for misunderstandings that may have resulted.

A participant in a workshop got a note from the secretary and you could see the person's face drop as he glanced to read it. Noting the immediate change in facial expression the instructor stopped his teaching to ask, "Is everything okay?" The students response, "I don't know." So it was suggested that the student leave the class and respond to the message, "Please call home as soon as possible before coming home after class, Your honey."

After 5 minutes the student returned, saying, "I will kill her when I get home. When I first read the note I got so frightened that something had happened, my mother has been ill. All she wanted was to make sure I stopped and picked up a loaf of bread and some milk before coming home."

So much for the brain craving completeness, managers should always make sure that their Grass Roots employees are not left at the wrong time to make things up. It is the fertilizer for grape vines and rumor mills at great expense and loss to productivity. When not having complete information, employees should ask managers to clarify.

Brain Principle 5: The brain constantly seeks new knowledge and information

Much like the rest of our body, our brain needs exercise to keep healthy and fit. It becomes stronger and more rigorous through the reinforcement of existing knowledge and the addition of new information. Like a well conditioned athlete, the more you exercise your brain, the easier it is to perform difficult mental tasks. Furthermore, the more knowledge and information your brain possesses, the easier it becomes to learn new information.

When your brain is fed new relevant information, it remains fit and at the peak of its mental powers. If your brain is left to stagnate, it becomes flabby and sluggish. You lose some of your mental edge. By adding new information dendrites grow to enrich the brain (see Chapter 8). Contrary to a popularly held belief, researchers have not found that learning new things becomes impossible with age. In fact, continuous learning throughout your lifetime may be one of the best ways to ensure that your brain remains healthy. A brain which is active and growing, even during later years, is much less likely to be susceptible to brain diseases which sap its vitality.

So it really is true: use it or lose it! As Warren Bennis insists in his book *Becoming a Leader*: "You can learn anything you want to learn." One example which emphasizes the importance of continuing education in a profession is the licensing requirements for public accountants in the United States. Most states

or image of what you've said as you have in your mind. Confirm this by asking them to describe the picture they have in their mind. This will provide you with feedback about how well you are communicating.

- After someone has requested you do something, check your understanding by repeating the request back to them.
- When brainstorming in a group, use as little detail as possible when trying to generate new ideas. By leaving many blanks, you will stimulate each person's mind to create solutions.
- Encourage completeness by beginning a sentence and letting others finish it for you.

require that after reaching certification, the accountant completes an average of 40 hours study each year on topics related to the profession. This requirement encourages chartered accountants to maintain their professional expertise, and keeps their minds physically fit.

To provide a benefit, the new information you learn does not have to concern something which is familiar to you. In fact, learning about something totally different from your existing knowledge base can be a powerful way of spurring creativity. For example, if you are a finance specialist, learning about the marketing side of your organization will improve your financial skills. It will broaden your perspective and provide more data for your brain to analyze when studying financially related marketing issues. We call this "making new connections"—taking different pieces of information and creating new associations between them. Regardless of your profession, you need to realize that once your primary, secondary and higher education is over, your true learning has just begun.

Brain Principle 6: The brain is truth-seeking

In their book *Brain Sell*, Tony Buzan and Richard Israel introduce the idea of the brain as a truth-seeking instrument. For the brain, truth means survival, which is why it strives to learn or discover.

We can see instances of the importance of this every day in the behavior of children. Why do they constantly demand fairness in their games? Why do they frequently ask the question "Why?" Because the truth is accurate information, and the brain is hungry for that information. Imagine that a man is crossing the street and sees a big car heading directly towards him at high speed. If his brain does not know the truth—that the impact of a car travelling at 100 miles per hour will have certain unpleasant effects on the human body— what will it do? It will make no effort to avoid the car.

The brain needs to know the truth to survive. The more accurate the information in its mental data bank, the greater the possibility of survival. This is why most people are uneasy when they lie. At a deep level, your brain knows that by lying, it may be threatening its own survival and that of others.

Dr Paul Brown, a noted psychologist in the United States, has studied the characteristics of successful leaders, coaches and managers for more than 20 years. His analysis has revealed that the primary characteristic people look for in their leaders is trustworthiness: "Can I trust/believe what this person is telling me?"

When people believe that the commitments made during a meeting will be honored, they are much more likely to take action. But violation of trust always has serious consequences in a relationship. Who wants to be lied to? "Give it to

Grass Roots Tip
Use the following methods to keep your brain fit:
• Read trade publications relevant to your profession at least several times per week.
• Meet with people in departments outside your functional area of expertise, and exchange ideas and knowledge.
• Take a course at a college or university on a topic which is of interest to you.
• Learn something new every day.
• Remember: you can learn at any age. Make the decision to keep learning.

me straight" is how many people phrase it. Integrity is an extremely important characteristic for becoming successful.

As our brain edits its inputs, it constantly evaluates the new data using this criterion: "Can I believe this, or is it garbage?" Once the brain decides to accept the new data as valid, synergy combines this with existing knowledge to trigger new thoughts and ideas.

One of the problems we frequently encounter is that people do not judge data accurately, or they have beliefs and ideas with little basis in fact, or they fail to update themselves. Many times, the question "When did you first acquire that belief?" evokes the response, "Well, 20 years ago ..." or "When I was in school ...." The appropriateness of the information has never been re-evaluated, to see if it still applies.

Brain Principle 7: The brain is persistent

One of the brain's most important attributes is its ability to persist, to continue striving for success no matter what the odds. The brain, using its synergistic, creative skills, will continue generating ideas and plans, in order to reach the goal. However, it is vital to focus on the defined goal, not the obstacles.

Any time our brain learns a new skill or creates a new thought, substantial effort is required in the initial attempt. Imagine an explorer hacking a pathway through a dense tropical jungle. The journey is the most difficult the first time. Each subsequent trip down the pathway becomes easier until, after many journeys, little effort is required.

Our brain works in a similar fashion. Having a thought for the first time is the most difficult. Each subsequent time we have the same thought, we make it easier to have the same thought again. The more often we have a thought, the more likely we are to have the identical thought in the future. The implication of this pattern is that the brain naturally persists towards a goal that is in focus. When it stops persisting, we should question our commitment to reaching the goal.

When striving to accomplish a difficult goal, there is normally a moment of truth. Our first attempts may result in failure, leading us to question our ability to succeed. In his book *Learned Optimism*, Dr Martin Seligman explores the importance of persistence.

When people feel helpless and believe that a problem is both pervasive and permanent, they tend to give up trying to resolve it. However, unlike many adults, infants do not dwell on the concept of "failure." They are preoccupied with the desired goal, the finished product. They do not bombard themselves with negative self-talk, such as "I can't do this!" or "I'm so clumsy/stupid/

Grass Roots Tip
Use the following methods to maximize the benefits of your truth-seeking brain:
• When someone shares new information with you, note the process your brain goes through to evaluate its accuracy.
• Have you ever said, "That's not fair!" This feeling is triggered by your truth-seeking brain. Listen to the number of times your work associates describe business situations with this phrase. What are your thoughts when you hear this phrase?
• Check the current validity of your fundamental beliefs.
• Gather and validate information in a new situation, or an old one that feels uncomfortable.

Grass Roots Tip
Use these methods to maximize the benefits of persistence:
• Read the biographies of famous people you admire. You may be amazed to learn about the setbacks/failures/discouragements they overcame on the way to success.
• Find a few people you trust to support you in your progress towards an important goal. Ask for their assistance in keeping you focused on achieving the goal. Look to them for encouragement when you doubt your chances of success.
• The next time you are learning a new skill, monitor your self-talk. Distinguish between positive, neutral and negative statements. Does your self-talk need adjustment?

awful!" Their brains' natural persistence allows them to keep working until they achieve what they want.

Keep this in mind the next time you are trying to do something difficult. If your first reaction when you hit a snag is to flood your mind with negative self-talk, modify it to be more confident and persistent: work in a brain-friendly fashion. With your amazing brain at the helm, knowing how to steer, you can only succeed.

PROFILE: WHAT HAPPENED TO CHARLEY?

Charley was a Grass Roots employee for a utility company when he attended a GRI workshop. After the first days session was finished he asked if he could borrow a few of the articles that were referenced. He took them home with the promise to read and return them in the morning. You could see his truth seeking brain searching for the facts, were the brain principles for real or just more management propaganda.

As we mentioned earlier as part of each Grass Roots workshop we assign homework. Each participant is to go home and initiate a conversation with someone to practice their GIGG.

It was Charley's wife who advised Tony Dottino 6 months after the workshop:

> Upon coming home from the first day of the GRI workshop as we were sitting at dinner, he had his usual grumpy and stressed look. At first his demeanor spoke, kids watch what you say because daddy has had another bad day at work. He began to start his normal evening chatter about how lousy everything was, when he stopped in mid sentence. Charley seemed to be in deep thought and was staring with a look we had not seen before. We were all ready to hide, what happened?

The family was trying to fill in the blanks with the worst of possibilities and could never have imagined what was going to happen next.

Charley remembered his GIGG homework, an instant 180 degree turn. He began asking his family members (wife and sons aged 9 and 12) to share their good experiences of the day. His wife couldn't believe who was sitting at dinner, what happened to him, as she continued filling in the blanks. It must have been a company brain washing session. But they have tried before and it only lasted a few days before things reverted to normal. To put more bewilderment into the night, Charley asked his son if he could help him with the night's homework. He was excited about this new information and knowledge he received during the day's session. It was called Mind Mapping and Charley was going to see if it would help his son with his homework. Since his son was "labeled" as learning disabled this was a real chance to take something new and see if it really worked.

Tony Dottino heard this part of the story 4 weeks after the workshop when Charley was explaining the benefits of the Grass Roots workshop to a group of company executives. But who was this person talking, Charley didn't look like Charley. First, he cut his hair, shaved his beard, changed his wardrobe and talked with such confidence and energy. The first part of his presentation was a big thank you to the company. His son had just gotten an A on his science test and the teacher was puzzled, how did he do this?

The company executives were wondering if this was the chronic complainer, who never had anything nice to say about anything or anybody. Where did this new employee come from and what was the magic pill? Let's order a few million before the supply runs out was there call.

What happened to Charley has happened countless times to the Grass Roots people that have learned to navigate the waters utilizing the seven Brain Principles. Dad set some new goals, an adjusted criteria of success for his career, a more positive educational focus for his sons, and a rekindled romance for his role as husband. He did his reading and locked in on the "brain facts" as he called them. The night he took the reading materials home he couldn't sleep, he had read them after his son went to bed and his brain began synergizing on a whole new world of possibilities.

"Charley Jr is going to ace his next series of exams." So after their dinner conversations, father and son would sit down to do a few Mind Maps of the days school studies. Dad had realized, he was the model for the kids to mimic, it was going to change. If this brain principle material was going to work for home then Charley thought, why wouldn't it work at the office. By being persistent with the proper GIGG he decided it was time to put all of his energy into making a difference at work.

This GIGG thing was working, the dinner table was becoming a fun happening. There was a continuous flow of excitement each night and both boys were doing much better at school. At his job, he got a new boss who saw a light shining and decided to ignore some of the talk he had heard about Charley. Charley became the Grass Roots leader on a number of improvement projects and was delivering tangible results to the companies bottom line. He was rewarded with a promotion to manager. Who would have ever thought after 17 years in the company someone that no one thought had a chance to make it, finally did. Charley always seeks out his Grass Roots team members for the best solutions to the challenges he faces everyday.

But to close this story with the best ending possible, lets go back to Charley the husband. His wife called to speak with Tony Dottino as we mentioned above, with the following words, "I do not know who you are and may never meet you, but I can only say, THANK YOU FOR GIVING ME MY Charley BACK, I ALWAYS KNEW HE HAD SUCH GOOD IN HIM AND WHATEVER THIS GIGG THING IS YOU TAUGHT HIM, IT WORKS!"

CONCLUSION OF THE BRAIN PRINCIPLES: THE BRAIN IS NATURALLY CREATIVE

The brain links and associates new ideas and sensory inputs with its existing knowledge and experience base. Every new input is connected to your core knowledge, and builds upon it. This synergistic linking of new ideas to existing knowledge is the engine's fuel for persistence. All these factors contribute to success when a clearly defined goal is established.

Creative people take advantage of this linking and associating power by encouraging dialogue with others. They learn everything possible about issues that matter, and create an environment which encourages and nurtures ideas during the formative and developmental stages. Mimicking and benchmarking are used in a positive way to feed knowledge into the biocomputer.

You have a capacity for creativity that is beyond anything you could imagine. Challenge your truth-seeking brain by trying different experiences. Remember these seven Brain Principles, and check your actions and results against each of them.

WHAT'S NEXT?

We have learned seven principles that impact the way people, create, relate and communicate with one another. Have you ever done a crossword puzzle and just by changing the sequence of how you responded to the clues, filled in the missing letters? In the next chapter we will give you a practical order in how to use the seven Brain Principles. It will increase your ability to be successful as a Grass Roots Leader.

ACTIVITIES

1   Make a list of four of your favorite role models and ask yourself the following questions with regard to each:
    Role model's name
    What attracts me to this person?
    What can I learn from this person?
2   Starting tomorrow, have lunch-time conversations with people that are focused on helping you achieve your goals.
3   Write down three business goals that you want to achieve in the next month, and then three action steps you will take towards achieving each of these goals.
    Goal 1
    Action step 1
    Action step 2

Action step 3
Goal 2
Action step 1
Action step 2
Action step 3
Goal 3
Action step 1
Action step 2
Action step 3

4   At the close of your next three conversations, once completed, check the other person's mental pictures by asking them to describe the conversation to you so it can be verified for accuracy.

5   At the next meeting you attend, note which Brain Principles are being used:
    Meeting Date
    Brain Principles

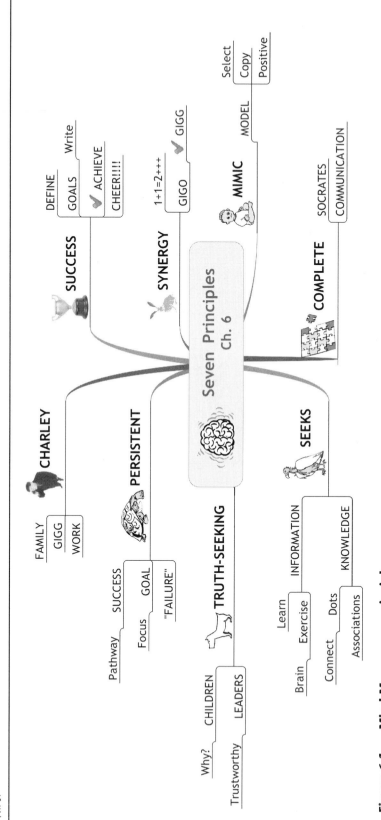

Figure 6.1   Mind Map—seven principles

GRASS ROOTS
LEADERS—THE
BRAINSMART
REVOLUTION IN
BUSINESS

122

The Lifeline to "S"

OVERVIEW

In this chapter, you will be introduced to a new way of thinking, known as TEFCAS. TEFCAS is a process for organizing your brain's thinking towards achieving goals. It lays the foundation for building an organization that knows how to communicate with purpose and focus.

THE POWER OF TEFCAS

The powerful business tool we are about to introduce to you is not a new computer or any other form of hardware. It is not an innovative piece of software. It won't require that you make radical changes in your office or production line. It won't take months of training.

What it will require of you is the willingness to change the way you think, the way you approach problems, the way you work towards your goals and how you give feedback to people.

It was at the same workshop mentioned in Chapter 6 that Tony Dottino heard Tony Buzan speak about TEFCAS. As he spoke about the importance of accurate feedback that is necessary for the brain to make the right adjustments, his inner voice was screaming. "We (IBM), are doing it all wrong and if we don't correct it, we will self destruct."

When working to explain problems to senior executives, managers would take unpleasant messages and spin them so well, that the problems only existed in the minds of the Grass Roots workers. The result were poor management decisions. Resources and time were wasted on an endless search for the truth and reality. What Tony Buzan told his brain: "By giving humans inaccurate feedback you short circuit their ability to be successful." What he worried: "If the whole management culture operated in this way and kept filtering the front-line messages to the senior executives, could IBM go out of business?" Unfortunately that question got too close to being answered.

TEFCAS is an acronym for the steps involved in this new approach to achieving success:

- Trials
- Events
- Feedback
- Check
- Adjust
- Success

In this chapter, each step will be described and you will be shown how it can be used to help Grass Roots workers, managers and executives have accurate feedback and direct communications with each other, that helps everyone reach goals—both personal goals and the company's.

Your brain is capable of creating limitless thoughts and ideas. Imagine what would happen if you could direct all that creative power towards achieving the company goals as well as your personal goals. That is exactly what happens with TEFCAS.

THE END IS THE BEGINNING

Paradoxically, we are going to start at the end—with the "S" in TEFCAS. The "S" stands for *Success*—the successful outcome, the target or goal. It is what all your efforts are for, what they are designed to accomplish. We use the term BIG S to designate the organizations top priorities that every employee must support. It is the major outcome an organization has defined for which it marks itself as unique. You may think of it as the vision. The key is that each Grass Roots employee must find some part of it which helps them to achieve their personal S. So as you will find there are different layers of Success and we use the BIG S to distinguish the ultimate.

When a baseball team begins their season, the BIG S may be to win the world series, while during the course of the season the pitchers may want to win 20 games, the batters may want to hit .300 and some may want to hit 40 home runs and have 100 runs batted in as their personal S. The first S for everyone is to win their division, which is then followed by their next S being the conference, which is followed by the ultimate World Series Event, winning it all.

Your success, your goal or target, may be a 10 per cent increase in sales for your company, the development of a new widget or a decrease in cost for the department budget. A personal success or goal might be a promotion, or more time to spend with your family. The company's BIG S may be to increase profit and the stock price by 10 per cent. Each quarter may have its own S and as the year moves along each quarter will have its own outcomes. In this chapter the terms S, goals, and outcomes will be used interchangeably.

GRASS ROOTS
LEADERS—THE
BRAINSMART
REVOLUTION IN
BUSINESS

124

The other letters in TEFCAS will be dealt with in order, but the discussion starts with the last element because a clear picture of what constitutes success is what makes this powerful tool work.

As seen in previous chapters, if you have only a vague idea of your destination when you start out on a journey, you will waste a great deal of time en route. You will take wrong turns, and may end up going in the wrong direction. If you finally arrive, you may not even be aware of it! Something similar happens when you don't provide your brain with a clear picture of what a successful outcome is, for yourself, your team or your company. The more specific you make the definition, the more effectively your brain will work to achieve that success.

From the Brain Principles (Chapter 6) you know that the brain links and associates new information to existing knowledge. The brain also likes to "fill in the blanks" when it receives information that it believes is incomplete. If a goal is vague, each person hearing that goal will generate their own associations about what that goal means. For example, "being a world class organization" could mean being number one in market share to a sales and marketing person, being first in profitability to a finance person or having the highest employee morale to a person in human resources.

With such a variety of definitions, each person will take actions to move them towards their own understanding of the definition. When the different definitions pull staff in conflicting directions (as could be the case with "first in market share" versus "first in profitability"), the results can be disastrous—the brains' rival definitions will lead them to compete against each other, the success mechanism will work against itself, and the organization will suffer.

The commonest single reason for failure in achieving a goal is lack of buy-in to a goal that starts with a poor description of the goal. Therefore, the first step in applying TEFCAS is to define "success" as clearly as possible.

In Chapter 6, it was said that the brain is a success-driven mechanism (Brain Principle 2) and will work towards whatever has been defined as "success." It will work endlessly to bring a successful outcome—*as long as it knows what a successful outcome is*. Before assigning work to their employees, the first thing a leader does is take the time to articulate carefully and in detail what a successful outcome would be.

An organization's BIG S is an attractive future for Grass Roots people which inspires your creative brain to help you achieve it. It gives you direction, helps keep you focused, stimulates your creativity and challenges limiting beliefs.

In the 1960s, President John F. Kennedy inspired NASA workers with his BIG S of putting a man on the moon, and returning safely, resulting in one of the largest management and organizational challenges ever undertaken. Many skeptics at the time scoffed at the idea, but the BIG S energized NASA employees to meet the challenge.

Whenever the authors sat down with an executive, a management team, or a team of employees working on a team project, the very first thing they would ask them to do is to describe what a successful outcome would be like: "What are you trying to achieve?" "What is this thing going to look like when it's finished?" "What is the end result that we're trying to get to?"

They would find many times that people didn't know what it was they were actually trying to achieve. There would be five people on a team, and they would have five different ideas of what their outcome was supposed to be. This indicated the organization's misalignment with the goal and a division within the team members. And that meant that much extra work was being created. People were working on things that didn't directly relate to the goals they were trying to achieve. And that was because no one ever took the time to clearly define or verify alignment to the goals.

Your brain never stops working. All day, it generates thousands of thoughts. It works even when you are asleep, integrating information and creating ideas. If you give it a goal, a target to shoot at, your brain will bend those thoughts, focus them and organize them to find the best way to achieve that goal. As the authors now understand from what they have learned about how the creative brain works, it needs to be given a precise destination for it to create the road to get there.

In addition, remember that the brain is not only success-driven, but also truth-seeking (Brain Principle 6). Therefore, the target must be reasonable, one that it is possible to achieve. If you were to select the goal of learning to fly by flapping your arms, for example, your brain would recognize that as impossible, and it would expend little if any effort trying to find a way for you to do it.

The goal should not only be reasonable, it should be something you are passionate about, something you truly want to achieve. If your enthusiasm for the S is lukewarm, your brain will make only half-hearted efforts to reach it. If you hit an obstacle it will make excuses for why the goal is unrealistic and stop trying to reach it. Therefore, you must examine your commitment towards the goals you want to achieve. Why are they important to you? Will you stop at the first point of resistance, or will you be passionate enough about the goals to devise solutions to any problems that may arise? The answers to these questions will help you understand the level of commitment you have towards your goals.

At this point, you may choose to stop and refine your desired outcome, based on the level of dedication you feel towards it. You are trying to link your goals with your emotional brain, so that your cortical skills blend with your emotional thinking.

GRASS ROOTS
LEADERS—THE
BRAINSMART
REVOLUTION IN
BUSINESS

126

Convincing your brain that you truly mean to achieve a goal you set entails using your imagination—envisioning, feeling and even tasting the fruits of your efforts. Picture yourself achieving your goal. Feel the handshakes from peers and managers. Hear the words of congratulations. Count the pay rise or rewards that you will receive. Taste the meal celebrating your success.

Blending your cortical skills, your senses and your passion creates the devotion to the outcome that will allow you to consistently overcome obstacles.

Opening a Grass Roots Workshop, a senior executive of the organization defined the company goals. He explained where he needed their help and why it was critical for them to be in the workshop. When he was finished Tony Dottino then asked the attendees, "What was said and how does it make you feel?" As a few people got up enough courage to speak it became clear that they didn't clearly understand what was meant by "being Baldrige compliant" (Baldrige is a USA quality award with a set of seven standards), nor were they up to questioning, "Reaching the company excellence goals." What were they and how are they measured were the questions not asked.

As further clarification was then made by the senior executive the question came back to "How do you feel about them?" This session continued with a level of concern, stress and questioning of whether the goals were realistic.

Eventually the organization had some additional working sessions on clarifying the goals, why they were important and the urgency of why they needed to be met. The work projects started coming together and before long the executive team was celebrating success.

When people closest to the work have the understanding and commitment to the company goals the creativity of the workforce flourishes. Therefore it is imperative that a management team invest the right amount of time and demonstrates a level of patience to ensure everyone is focused on the same definition of "S." A myth in today's fast-paced world, people think they don't have enough of time to clearly define goals. Unfortunately by not taking the time to do so increases the number of wasted hours spent in trying to hit the moving target.

TRIALS AND TRY-ALLS

Once you have provided your brain with a clear goal, one that is achievable and that you are passionately committed to, your brain will automatically go on to the next step of TEFCAS: it will begin trying to achieve that goal through a series of *Trials*.

Grass Roots Tip
Use these methods to maximize success:
• Write down your goals and display them, so that everyone involved can generate thoughts on how to achieve success. Make certain you have the full participation of your team.
• Since the brain generates ideas continuously, 24 hours a day, it is important to have a means to record your thoughts. You could keep a tape recorder or a notepad on your bedside table to capture your ideas.
• Don't pass judgment or set limits to ideas before trying them.
• Abandon the "We've tried it before and it didn't work" attitude. Try again.
• Try the same idea differently. This time, you may be more successful.

THE LIFELINE TO "S"

However, rather than trials, perhaps it would be even more useful to think of the "T" in TEFCAS as standing for *Try-alls*—for the brain will try everything in order to reach your goal.

You are now unleashing the formidable power of the brain's natural creativity. It knows where you want to go, and it begins generating ideas for how to get there until it finds the path that works. Your thought processes become aligned with your goals. You now have the strongest thinking machine ever created, your brain, working for you to design the path on which you must travel to achieve success.

Since the brain's thought processes are continuous, you are able to generate patterns and design strategies on a 24-hour-a-day basis. Thoughts and ideas may be formed while you are taking a bath, exercising, driving to work or at 3 a.m. while you are sleeping.

When your brain is on "automatic pilot," it is uninhibited, free of opinions and judgements. It is at its creative best. And it will continue its generating, creative behavior as long as you are enthusiastic about achieving the outcome. It has an infinite capacity, and it will persist for as long as you tell it to.

While your brain will continue to work on the best method of reaching your goal automatically, you can help by actively feeding it new information. In the business environment, one way to help facilitate our Try-alls is to find out whether someone else has already achieved our desired outcome. Our brains can then mimic the necessary behaviors or processes (Brain Principle 3). The business term for using the mimic principle is *benchmarking*.

The diversity of knowledge and experiences gives a Grass Roots team an excellent chance of trying things not previously thought of. Its important for the management team to support them and encourage them to keep on going when hitting obstacles.

A series of events

The Try-all process can be exhilarating. Your brain is generating dozens, perhaps hundreds of ideas intended to help you find your way to your goal. But ideas aren't much use until they are put into action.

The Trials or Try-alls step is the planning stage. The *Events* step is the action stage. We've planned, now it is time to take action. This causes an event.

We use the term "event" to avoid investing too much importance in a particular occurrence. An event is just one step on the way to success, not the *only* step.

Grass Roots Tip
Use these techniques in your Try-alls:
• Remember that your brain has an infinite ability to generate ideas. Stay focused on your goal, and give your brain time to generate the Try-alls necessary for success.
• Share your Try-alls with other people who share your definition of success. This will generate new try-alls that you had not previously considered.
• Find suitable models to mimic.
• Assess your commitment level.

If you start with the idea that the first action you take, the first thing you do to try to achieve your goal is *the* answer, you will be discouraged if it fails, and first steps will often fail to provide you with your defined success. If you accept that an Event is just one step on the journey towards ultimate success, then the fact that it didn't work out (or did) is relatively unimportant.

Too many people see any Event that doesn't result in progress towards a goal as a failure. They develop that into the idea that they themselves are failures—an attitude that can discourage further efforts. On the other hand, the person who recognizes that all Events are part of a process leading to success will accept that unexpected negative results are just as important as—maybe more than—positive ones.

Always remember that the Event is not the goal. Some people remain stuck in the Try-alls stage because they make that mistake. They act as if they have only one chance to succeed, that if one Event fails, then it's all over. With very few exceptions, you will have many more than one opportunity to achieve your success.

Even if the Event does not achieve the desired outcome, you have learned new information that can be used to assist you in reaching your objectives. Events should never be labelled as "failures," whatever their outcome.

The care and feeding of feedback

To evaluate Events, we need to have some way of providing our brain with information on how well we've done—*Feedback*.

In some ways, Feedback is the most difficult step in TEFCAS, because some of it will be perceived as negative. We all have a natural desire to avoid what we think is negative feedback. The impulse to "kill the messenger" when they bring bad news is very common, especially in many executive offices of large organizations.

But in the larger sense, as long as it has integrity and pinpoints events that moved us away from the agreed definition of success, there is no such thing as negative Feedback. All Feedback is positive, because it provides us with valuable information. We define "good" Feedback as any Feedback that helps the person receiving it move closer to achieving their goals.

Good Feedback must be actively sought and encouraged. Far too often, managers and team leaders surround themselves with sycophants who tell them exactly what they want to hear, rather than what they need to hear to be successful. No one wants to tell them that something didn't work as well as was expected, or didn't work at all, so they fudge, equivocate or gloss over any problems.

Grass Roots Tip
Use these techniques for handling Events:
• Events are part of a process, and outcomes should be studied so that you may learn from them.
• As people carry out actions and errors are detected, remember that they are only one Event in the course of the total plan.
• Failure is part of success. Accountability should be assigned to the lessons learned.
• Share what is learned from "failures" with others.
• Success is also an Event!

Reward the messenger

There is a scene that recurs day after day in many companies. An executive will ask a worker how a project is going. "Fine," the employee may say, "Everything's going OK." When the executive leaves, the employee walks down the hall and tells some co-workers, "This is an utter disaster." When the employee is asked why they didn't tell the executive the truth, a frequent response is, "He just doesn't like to hear bad news. And any delay or deviation from plan is perceived as bad news."

This occurs when executives who request Feedback appear insincere. Perhaps they have been known to heap unfair criticism on others who have told them that a project was going badly. Blaming the messenger for the bad news will only ensure that bad news never reaches the boss until it is *really* bad news—and too late. Rather the manager should **REWARD** the messenger, he has just provided the **LIFELINE TO SUCCESS.**

Pinpoint

In addition to making it clear that you want honest Feedback, you must make it equally clear that you want the feedback to be as specific and detailed as possible. Feedback should also be directly related to the goal.

Take the example of a manager we encountered who wanted his staff to work more closely as a team. If he asks for Feedback on how well the team concept is working, he needs detailed examples of exactly what is happening, and how it relates to the goal.

Good Feedback he received began with a restatement of the goal. You say your goal is to have your employees sit down as a team to develop recommendations for this new project. But some of your workers won't even talk to each other. Others are making individual decisions without getting everyone's ideas that are costing time and money. And some members are arguing and blaming each other publicly for project delays.

That would be excellent Feedback, because it is specific enough for the manager to see where they are going to have to make some changes. The Feedback is pinpointed, and directly relates to the goal of bonding into a team.

Feedback is not a one-way process. You must be prepared to give it as well as receive it. The same rules apply whether giving or receiving Feedback: it must be honest, specific and related to the goal.

Know the S

When offering Feedback to someone else, you must know what their goal is. If you wish to provide Feedback to anyone, you must know what is their goal and what they consider a successful outcome. If it's someone who has told you he wants to be the best employee in the city, your Feedback should take that into account. For example, you might say something like the following:

> *Harry, your procrastination in getting your paperwork done on time hurts both the company and yourself. Erratic delivery of supplies means we sometimes have to shut jobs down. And that certainly doesn't contribute to your goal of being the best team player in the city.*

When you give Feedback that is tied to the goals of the person receiving it, you also avoid personal and emotional confrontation. The issue becomes the actions that need to be taken or adjustments that need to be made, rather than issues of personality or character. You aren't telling anyone that they are a bad person, only that they need to do certain things differently (adjust their Try-alls) to achieve their goal.

Without Feedback, we can only assume that the path we are following will lead to our goals. In this case, we are filling in the blanks generated in our brain with nothing more than suppositions and hypotheses. Truthseeking Feedback is the lifeline to Success. Useful Feedback provides a measurement of the effectiveness of the actions we've chosen to take in order to achieve our goals. It also provides us with the data to plan towards future Adjustments and Try-alls that will be necessary in order for us to reach Success.

Check the Feedback

After you have received Feedback, you need to *Check* whether it is valid and accurate.

If the Feedback given is inaccurate or incomplete, then if you act on it, your journey to success may be jeopardized. Therefore, any Feedback you receive should be assessed to determine if it has merit. The best way to check Feedback is to compare it to Feedback from known reliable sources.

If a foreman who was told that filing his paperwork late was a problem wanted to check that Feedback, he could ask several other people (peers, subordinates, other executives within the organization) if they agreed with that assessment. However, if you do decide to ask another worker, if the Feedback is to have integrity, they must not feel threatened and thus obligated to give you the answer they think you want.

In addition, once you have Checked the Feedback you have received, you must accept it. If you perceive it to be inaccurate, then it may have a negative impact on your thought processes. Remember that the brain is truth-seeking (Brain Principle 6), and if it doubts the integrity of the input, it will discard it accordingly. The blind acceptance of Feedback without Checking to confirm that it is factual, relevant and effective, could introduce negative inputs which could redirect your action plan away from your goals.

Accurate Feedback is invaluable, and can lead us to reach our goals, as we exercise our prerogative to act on shared information and knowledge. All Feedback received should be assessed to establish whether it is warranted and justified. Once Feedback has been Checked, it can then be used to change and Adjust action plans we've devised, to bring us one more step closer to achieving Success.

Making adjustments

The "A" in TEFCAS stands for *Adjust*. It is the final step on the way to "S," the Successful outcome of your goal.

Adjusting is the moment of truth. After defining your goals, considering Try-alls, performing Events, receiving Feedback and Checking, you must decide whether to Adjust your actions—and if so, how? In this stage, once you have accepted the Feedback as accurate, you will begin to Adjust your actions so that you achieve your goal.

When you reach this point, you may be reluctant to Adjust your Try-alls. You may resist the idea of doing things differently. Instead of modifying your actions, you may instead rationalize, "Well, I didn't want to be director of my department by next April. Being manager is just fine with me."

When this happens, you are not Adjusting your Try-alls, but instead are adjusting your definition of Success—you are Adjusting your goal, rather than your action. Sometimes this may be appropriate, but if you retain your goal and keep it in mind, your brain will create new Try-alls to generate different Events until it achieves Success. You will begin to Adjust the actions that must be taken to achieve your goal.

TEFCAS SUMMARY

The steps of TEFCAS are:

1 **Define success**, as the brain is success-driven and needs a clear goal towards which it can work.
2 **Try-all** the suggestions your brain creates in its attempt to map out the course of action you must take to succeed.
3 **An Event** will occur as a result of the Try-all you implemented.
4 **Receive Feedback**, it is the lifeline to success.

Grass Roots Tip
Use these techniques in Checking:
• Occasionally Check the company S, to ensure that it is still relevant.
• Check Feedback to verify that it is specific and measurable.
• Check whether an Event took you closer to or further from your goal.
• Check the action you need to take next.

5   **Check** before you accept the information, as the brain is truth-seeking, and needs accurate data to adjust properly.
6   **Adjust** according to the Feedback you gathered.
7   Repeat the TEFCAS process as necessary.
8   **Attain Success**, as you defined it.
9   Celebrate!

Test this model by applying it to a situation where you are currently not as successful as you would like to be, and you will begin to see how you can use TEFCAS to reach your goals. Figure 7.1 summarizes the model in graphic form.

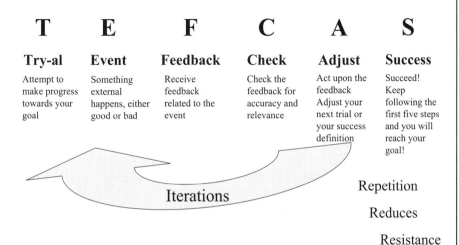

The brain's success mechanism follows a consistent model

T	E	F	C	A	S
Try-al	**Event**	**Feedback**	**Check**	**Adjust**	**Success**
Attempt to make progress towards your goal	Something external happens, either good or bad	Receive feedback related to the event	Check the feedback for accuracy and relevance	Act upon the feedback Adjust your next trial or your success definition	Succeed! Keep following the first five steps and you will reach your goal!

Iterations

Repetition

Reduces

Resistance

Figure 7.1   The TEFCAS model

EVERYONE HERE IS A VIP: CANDACE JONES

The Holiday Inn Arena in Binghamton, New York, wasn't the worst Holiday Inn in the region, but had a number of challenges. Guest are more stressed, their demands are relentless, they want the comforts of home, and the industry has problems finding staff.

At the helm was general manager Candace Jones, a perfectionist with a sincere desire to make the hotel a winner—a desire that seemed to be constantly thwarted by intangible factors she couldn't quite identify. All she knew for sure was that poor morale, lack of initiative and a pervasive attitude that anything that went wrong was somebody else's problem was translating into unhappy guests. She needed to motivate her employees.

• Your brain will Adjust for the next Try-all. You determine what will be Adjusted.
• As long as you are committed to achieving your goal, don't give up at the "moment of truth" stage.
• Allow your brain to find alternative solutions.
• Sometimes just a minor Adjustment will lead you to success. Don't assume that an Adjustment to your Try-alls must involve radical change.
• Consider looking for different perspectives from different people when creating new action plans. You may use benchmarking or other sources of ideas.

One of those unhappy guests was Tony Dottino, who stayed at the Holiday Inn Arena. There had been serious problems with the hotel's air conditioning system and, after three room changes, Tony's temper was as hot as the rest of him.

Candace directed that a letter be written to Tony, offering free accommodation on his next visit. "Tell him if he tries us again and we still can't get it right, then we don't deserve his business," Candace said. When Tony received the letter, he was impressed, and noted the fact that Candace seemed committed to making her customers happy. So the next time he was in Binghamton, Tony stayed at the Arena, this time meeting Candace.

When Candace learned about Tony's line of work, she was intrigued. Maybe he could shed some light on her problems. As the two strolled around the hotel golf course, Tony asked Candace, "What is your definition of success?" She told him that she wanted to take the hotel "further." He pressed her to elaborate, and realized that part of her frustration was the result of her failure to communicate a clear picture of success to her staff, because she didn't have a clear enough idea in her own head of what she wanted.

The big S

Tony finally wrested from her what she wanted to do: *treat every guest like a VIP, and create an atmosphere as much like home as possible for them.* However, Tony noticed that there was some negativity on her part. It was agreed to start a Grass Roots training program.

In their first session, Tony asked the hotel staff to Mind Map their frustrations. What they revealed was astonishing. "Many times in meetings I had asked, 'How am I doing?,'" but they were never comfortable giving me the unpleasant truth," said Candace. "At the session with Tony, however, they did speak their minds. It wasn't easy listening, but it was a positive step, because it forced me to come to grips with some things I needed to improve upon."

Candace learned that she treated her staff like incompetent children. For example, one day she had led all the department leads around the hotel looking for problem areas. There were cobwebs on the ceiling. The brass in the bar wasn't polished. A storage closet was a mess. "I'm totally disappointed in you," she lectured them. "You are supposed to be professionals. Why do I have to baby-sit you?"

Humiliated, embarrassed and demoralized, no one was brave enough, until the session with Tony, to answer her question. Without realizing it, Candace had sapped everyone's desire to take initiative, because whenever anyone did something on their own, she'd take it over, criticize the way they had done it, or instruct them to do it some other way.

GRASS ROOTS
LEADERS—THE
BRAINSMART
REVOLUTION IN
BUSINESS

134

"I was frustrated, and thought they weren't supporting me by taking the ball and running with it, but how could they run with it when any time they tried, I'd intercept it?" she said. "My approach made them feel, 'Why bother if she's going to do it herself anyway?'"

Testing the S

The first step in tackling this problem of control—and it was a big step for Candace—was to let go, delegate and accept the fact that there was more than one right way to handle a situation. When Tony asked employees to Mind Map what they thought Candace's goals were, none of them matched the Mind Map Candace drew. It was quickly obvious why she hadn't been getting the results she had sought—everyone had a different idea of what she wanted.

"I'd tell people I wanted to take the hotel further, and they'd nod, but no one ever asked me, 'What are you talking about?'" Candace remembered. "I just assumed they knew, and their misunderstanding made it even more frustrating. When they did something other than what I wanted, I assumed they weren't in my boat, rowing with me."

Once that problem was acknowledged, they worked together to create a group Mind Map, to come to a consensus about what specific steps needed to be taken for success. It was agreed that customer satisfaction was the most important result, so their central image was a big smile.

"To me, friendliness and a positive attitude were *major* points," Candace related, "and I knew they were contagious—a smile from me would transfer to my staff, and down to the customer. I realized that any time I passed on a bad mood to my team, they were likely to pass that on to staff, and then on to guests. I realized that my behavior was duplicated all the way through the organization. Looking back at the smile on the Mind Map, I was forced to acknowledge that the buck truly stopped with me."

Making adjustments

The exercise also helped Candace discover who would never be "in her boat." "This was the first time I had ever seen my teams clearly," she said. "Two people ended up leaving our employ, and it was much easier to deal with their decision to leave after seeing their Mind Maps." Finding replacements for those two people was not easy. But when they did, the map helped find the right fit. Candace learned that every time you have disruptive team members it makes the goal of providing customer service more difficult to achieve. So having the right team teams members was worth the wait.

With all these changes, the hotel is running smoothly, and morale is considerably improved. "My goal is to continue development of staff and the management team by allowing them to feel a part of the decision-making process," Candace said.

The Grass Roots Revolution

Each employee from housekeeping to managers are encouraged to be a "constant, caring, friend" to a guest. Every month she conducts two Grass Roots sessions to hear the staff stories of how they made a guest happy. They capture these stories on mind maps and at times can easily see how a customer response could have been done better. By acknowledging their stories in a positive synergy, it motivates every employee to feel a part of the decision-making process in making a guest feel special.

Candace has seen that these sessions build skills in the staff that empowers them to be spontaneous to guest situations. On a rainy day a housekeeper noticed a guest standing at the front door without an umbrella. The housekeeper got an umbrella and before she finished had escorted four guest to their cars. Another quick thinking maintenance worker noticed that their ATM machine was out of order and a female guest was concerned about walking about the area to the local bank. His offer to walk with her was graciously accepted.

Just in time

While Candace was busy improving her management style and employee morale, she had to deal with challenges of a city in decline. Binghamton had its problems and the Holiday Inn Arena was right in the middle of that city. People were shopping in the suburbs, and businesses were flocking to areas near main traffic arteries.

The situation was bleak, the looming future even bleaker. There was doubt whether the hotel would survive. Two large companies had recently moved out, taking 3 000 people with them. Occupancy was at an all-time low.

Candace identified a team of key employees and had them work to identify the main problems. They had to do some analysis of them and come up with ways to overcome them. Try-alls from the TEFCAS model would ultimately save the hotel. Instead of sitting around wringing their hands and reacting, they came up with the following action plan.

They identified the following negative factors:

*   The hotel's mainstay in the past, convention bookings were going to larger venues.
*   Five small non-full service hotels opened in the area.
*   The hotel was older.

GRASS ROOTS
LEADERS—THE
BRAINSMART
REVOLUTION IN
BUSINESS

136

Candace received from the team ways to turn these negatives into positives. Since convention bookings were down, they needed to attract different customers. They decided to market the hotel as an affordable destination for golfers. Deals were forged with local golf courses, employees went to travel trade shows and developed brochures. By the second year, 27 per cent of the increased occupancy was due to golfers.

The profile of the travelor had changed. Female, retirees and extended stay people were becoming a more significant part of the travel business and they all want to feel special. With "constant, caring, friends" it had to lead to a higher rate of returning guest. During those dismal weeks from January through March when occupancy had usually been so low employees had to be laid off, the hotel offered skiing and horseback riding packages at nearby resorts, and courted tour bus operators. "We began attracting nine or ten busloads every weekend, with 400–500 people. This resulted in a very significant increase in revenue," Candace says.

Instead of being apologetic about the size of the rooms, they marketed them as "cosy," and made sure that everyone was friendly, welcoming and helpful at all times. 'We know we aren't the Ritz Carlton, so we made it our goal for every customer to leave saying it was the best stay they'd ever had. We wanted them to leave with a smile on their face—to feel like they had found a little piece of home here.'

Since Candace joined the Holiday Inn Arena team, she has had ups and downs but has consistently grown revenue and profits. People return again and again because the team lives by their word and if they make mistakes they will make it right. This creates a loyal base of returning customers.

Candace's "Lifeline to Success?" The Holiday Inn Arena team getting instant feedback from every guest and knowing how to create the right outcome for each event.

It wasn't easy, but working with the Grass Roots employees, they have taken her vision and made it into reality. She has transformed the hotel's fortunes, and those of many others, and made the Holiday Inn Arena a special place to work and stay which is why they call it "Always the Place to Be!"

CONCLUSION

TEFCAS's applications are limitless, and it can be used to define your next course of action. TEFCAS is a powerful tool that allows you to be in control of the problems you face every day in order to ensure your success. The authors use it constantly, and are convinced of its power and influence. It is one of the most powerful lessons managers and Grass Roots people can utilize to enhance their ability to influence change in an organization.

WHAT'S NEXT?

This chapter provided a pragmatic sequence in taking desired outcomes and providing the details in the steps that need to be followed to reach your "S." But if you have taken up the sport of golf or watched the professionals on TV your realized there are bad days and there are good days. In the next chapter, we share with you the most important ingredient of your own success. It's your formula for learning how to learn and bring about change in an organization that is sustainable.

ACTIVITIES

1   Write definitions of both your business and personal desired outcomes.
2   Create a Mind Map of all the ideas you generate to make progress towards your goal.
3   Develop a support group of three people with whom you can share and develop your goals.
4   Practise giving Feedback to a business associate where you can provide information about specific behaviors you have observed which cause them to miss their goal. Provide suggestions on how you think they could do better. (Note: always ask the person first if he or she would like Feedback.)
5   Next time someone gives you Feedback, verify the Feedback with at least two other sources. List both the consistencies and the inconsistencies.

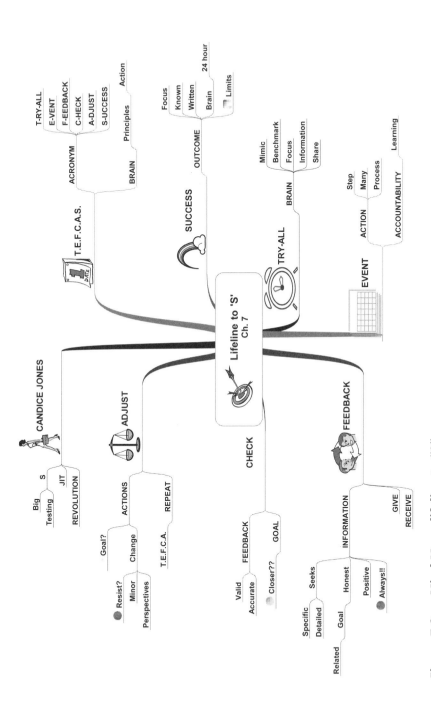

Figure 7.2   Mind Map—lifeline to "S"

CHAPTER 8

Grass Roots Power

OVERVIEW

Enthusiastic and excited people consistently generate ideas and new ways of doing things, but their ability to do so can be reduced by their self-imposed limits or how you communicate thoughts and messages to them.

We've all seen teams of athletes draw on the diverse skills of each member to achieve success. To communicate effectively, you must first understand the thinking skills you possess, and the way you process information.

MANAGING CHANGE

Skills inventory

How you behave and react today is determined by your prior knowledge and beliefs. As new events in your life occur, your brain associates, connects and files the new information into your existing database. Memories and experiences are interlinked like the roads and highways on a map. If you travel the same path more than once, you learn most of the bumps and turns on the road.

Think of a childhood experience when you first began to build a new skill, such as speaking, writing or playing a sport. Do you remember gaining confidence in your new skill? How did that affect your eagerness to practice and continue learning? Now contrast this feeling with the first time you believed you were unable to learn a new skill like drawing, writing or memorizing multiplication tables. From childhood, many of us have been taught that we just weren't born with the aptitude for certain skills, and because we were not born with them, there was no possibility we could ever master them through hard work and practice. We may have been encouraged to identify and believe in our limitations. This belief becomes a self-fulfilling prophecy because it causes us to short-circuit our brain's success mechanism and closes a road in our mental network. This means we fail to develop our full range of cortical skills, which in turn reduces our ability to be creative.

Trusting her Grass Roots team

Jayne, a Chief Nursing Officer at a 400-bed hospital, had just come out of a meeting in which the finance manager had issued a fourth quarter decree: no overtime, no discretionary spending, no travel, no off site or nursing meetings, no consultants and no temporary staff. And he immediately followed that up by reminding them they must meet their patient service targets and their stretch goal.

Once out of the meeting, Jayne slipped into reactive mode and Blackberried her assistant to schedule an emergency directors' meeting. This decree had been a real blow to Jayne. She had worked proactively all year to optimize her resources but several recent crisis situations forced her to use up her reserves. And now this.

In that emergency directors' meeting, Jayne read the list of restrictions and saw her team shaking their heads, "Here we go again. Short term decisions we'll pay for next year." The energy in the room plummeted and the sense of imminent defeat was palpable, for them and for her.

The next day Jayne remembered questions she had heard in a Grass Roots session: had anyone communicated with their leaders? Had anyone shared their overall targets with them? Had they made sure their leaders understood the challenges they faced? Had they brainstormed with them for ideas? No, no, no, no, no.

So Jayne conducted sessions with each of her director's teams, gave them details of key goals and metrics, where targets were and weren't being met. Jayne and her directors answered questions and provided additional information and asked team members to take a few days and get back to them with ideas. And they did. Here are two that proved very valuable:

Grass Roots identified problem 1:

The physical therapy department had a high rate of appointments missed or cancelled on the morning of the scheduled visit. As a result, the 12 therapists had a productivity rate less than 75 per cent.

Solution 1: When the therapist finishes with a new patient, they walk the patient to the scheduler's workstation and tells them how many return sessions the patient needs and how often. The scheduler dialogues with the patient to find the best day of the week, preferred hours, work schedule and driving restrictions and so on. Together they create a calendar for sessions that best match the patient's needs.

Cost Savings: This project resulted in $115 000 increase in revenue. Productivity increased more than 90 per cent and morning cancellation dropped by more than 50 per cent.

Grass Roots identified problem 2:

A Grass Roots team of isolation nurses knew that gowns and supplies were being wasted unnecessarily. Here's why: to avoid leaving the room with the infected patient to obtain additional supplies, having to degown, regown, wash and start over, isolation room nurses tried to anticipate all the supplies they could possibly need and bring them in all at once. But this was expensive because once the patient was moved from the room, unused supplies were considered contaminated and had to be discarded.

Solution 2: The nursing team suggested creating an isolation room supplies cart that was positioned outside the isolation rooms. When something else was needed, a nurse could simply reach out and get it, without having to degown and regown. The supplies would be taken as needed.

Cost Savings: This idea resulted in $100 saved per patient times 12 patients a day.

Jayne's Grass Roots teams were able to identify problem areas the managers didn't know and put together pragmatic solutions that delivered on-going results. Using their knowledge and creativity, Jayne's teams were able to make their revenue and expense targets—without ever having to impose most of the decreed restrictions. And her teams' spirits soared because their ideas were heard, implemented and highly effective.

What was most surprising to the directors was that Grass Roots teams could come up with solutions that had real cost-savings attached to them—solutions they would never had thought of given their distance from the problem.

YOU CAN DO IT!

The truth is that our brain has the ability to learn *any* skill, and open *any* path, if we are interested, find the right model to follow, have access to good coaching, and practise.

To fully develop your brain, you must continue to add to your stock of skills, and to develop those skills you need to improve. For example, if your profession relies on skills that are predominantly left-cortex, such as accounting, work on developing several of your right-cortex skills, like music or drawing. If your profession requires skills that are predominantly right-cortex, such as art, work on developing left-brain skills, like logic or foreign languages.

Why should you try to improve seemingly "irrelevant" skills? Because when the brain is working well, there is constant communication between the left and right sides of the brain's cortex. The two sides of the brain working together in harmony generate ideas and natural creativity.

Einstein and Disney did it

It is not surprising to learn that innovators like Einstein or Disney developed each of the cortical skills to a high degree. Albert Einstein is considered by many to be the greatest scientist of the twentieth century. We are all familiar with his scientific ability from his development of the theory of relativity, but it was Einstein's vivid imagination that allowed him to understand the relationship between mass and energy, and the interdependence of space and time. Einstein claimed that his first insight into the theory of relativity came from a daydream in which he imagined he was riding a light beam towards the end of the universe. To his astonishment, at the end of his imaginary journey he had returned to his starting point!

On a somewhat different level of achievement, Walt Disney is well known for his colourful imagination, his storytelling ability and his creation of the cartoon characters Mickey Mouse and Donald Duck. He could also pay intense attention to detail. During construction of Disneyland, he guided Disney 'Imagineers' in applying scientific precision and meticulous attention to the smallest details to create attractions which were designed to stimulate both the left and right cortices of the brains of park visitors.

As cortical skill development takes place, your brain possesses an infinite ability to link and associate new ideas with existing knowledge. Any limitations on generating new ideas stem from self-imposed belief systems. Regardless of whether these limits were developed on our own or with the assistance of a parent, teacher or coach, we have the power to decide to remove them.

How big is the memory bank?

A common misconception is that our brain has a finite amount of storage for new ideas and knowledge: if we use valuable brain space to learn skills which do not immediately apply to our profession, we run the risk of "running out of room" for more important information. The reality is that the more we learn, the easier it becomes for us to associate and link new knowledge—in effect, our brain has a unique ability of creating new pathways. As we remove roadblocks that have been placed in the highways of our brains, we discover new roads that have yet to be traveled. Your level of skill mastery determines how fast you can navigate these roads, but they can be traveled by anyone.

Do the math

The human brain has more than 100 billion cells called *neurons*, each one made up of a sending branch called an *axon* and receiving branches called *dendrites*. When an axon sends a message, it can connect with up to 100 000 adjoining cells. Each cell that is connected with the first neuron can connect with another 100 000 neurons. This linking and connecting of cells creates memory traces and thought patterns. With so many possible combinations available, how many unique thoughts and traces do you think the brain can create?

When you combine the unlimited biological potential of the brain with the seven Brain Principles outlined in Chapter 6, you discover that the information you input into your brain dictates the direction of your own thoughts. This will either provide the resources to overcome obstacles that block our journey to success, or else the reasons why we really can't do something. To take advantage of this, you must first understand the GIGG, Brain Principle 1, more clearly.

Start by thinking about how you have defined success, and whether or not you have placed limits on your definition because of some incorrect beliefs. Remember that the brain is truth-seeking, and will act on what it believes to be true. At times you may want to question how and why you accept some of your beliefs to be true. Write down reasons why you believe them to be so; revalidate or question those reasons and perhaps discard them, and realize that they may not be appropriate in the present (for example, perhaps your brother told you years ago that you would never be an accountant or be able to add up numbers).

WHAT IS IN YOUR FIRST POSITION GIGG?

So how do you begin to direct your brain to overcome barriers and limitations? The first step is to examine closely the type of information you are putting into your brain. As explained in Chapter 6, your brain takes all new information, and links and associates it with existing knowledge. This information becomes the starting point for creating new ideas, and acts as an investment in the development of your Intellectual Capital and people power. To maximize the return on this investment, you must ensure that the type and quality of your input are consistent with your individual goals. Some typical sources of new information are TV, newspapers, professional journals and the people with whom you interact on a daily basis. Although you will not always have direct control over everything you store in your long-term memory, you need to be aware that the quality of the information you take in determines how well your skills inventory grows. Even your own thoughts can act as inputs, influencing whether your brain is willing to accept the value of developing new skills.

Your brain follows the model of GIGG, and you ultimately control whether the first "G" will represent "Garbage" ("Garbage In, Garbage Grows") or "Good"

("Good In, Good Grows"). If your inputs currently fall into the "Garbage" category, you can make the necessary changes to convert them into "Good." Your brain unconsciously uses the mimic principle to model and duplicate the behavior and mannerisms of your associates. If these behaviors include cynicism and a lack of positive thinking, your brain may accept this input as true, and thus program itself to fail. If you combine negative thinking with additional "Garbage" inputs, your brain will program itself to fail very quickly and effectively.

It is natural to want to vent problems and frustrations. Co-workers experiencing the same frustrations will relate to each other easily, and will strengthen these feelings further. The combination of "Garbage" inputs and the mimic principle could cause you to fall in with the consensus before you realize your thinking has changed. Without even being aware, you may have built a roadblock, which obstructs your creativity. Whether you are a manager or junior member of staff, you must be sensitive to the input you receive and that you provide to others. The quality of your thoughts will determine whether a team of creative, excited thinkers or a group of negative, apathetic whiners surrounds you. You choose the direction of the thoughts you generate each day.

EXERCISING YOUR BRAIN

New information combined with existing knowledge keeps your brain alive and generating new ideas. This provides the fuel to keep you moving in the direction of your goals. Some of the resources you need to develop improved input are probably within reach right now. With a little persistence (Brain Principle 7), you can usually find a model representing your goals for your brain to mimic (Brain Principle 3). An excellent source of information is to read a book on a subject which interests you. Feeding your brain positive, useful information helps strengthen your mental powers.In fact if you believe what DaVinci taught us that everything connects to everything else, then you can even read something that doesn't interest you and see what new thoughts it triggers.

BRINGING THESE LESSONS TO ACTION

This was done with a client in a workshop Tony Dottino was doing on Information Overload. During a segment of the workshop he was taking the above lesson and putting it to work. Out came a stack 20 magazines, he put them on table and asked each participant to take one that they would find most dull and boring.

At first, on hearing the exercise you could just see the disbelief on their faces, why would anyone want to read something of disinterest? But, each person took one and was asked to scan it and read an article that was least likely to be fun. Many of them didn't believe this would lead to anything of value. Most felt that the lesson they were taught about their brain's ability to link and connect would not work. However they were encouraged to limit their disbeliefs and go through the exercise so they could be their own laboratory of discovery. They were going to learn for themselves if they could associate new information to their existing work experiences and find out if they could create new thought patterns.

After each person read their articles, Tony grouped them into teams of four and each person had to share three things they learned from the reading which associated to their business plan. As each employee shared their new thoughts you could hear each voice speak a bit louder. Sparks began to fly and there was a new wave of energy beginning to create a new belief. This could actually work, we may find some new ideas.

As each team got up to make their presentation, it was amazing. The first team spoke for everyone, "When we started this exercise we had no idea that this would actually work. It gave us new pathways of thinking. that led to several new ideas for meeting our business plans. This is unbelievable" or should they have said this is believable? As each of the teams made their presentation the whole room lifted into a whole new level of belief and excitement. They formulated action plans that have led to creating several new marketing plans. One they got came from an article about a teenage computer genius that caused them to question their whole internet marketing strategy. A number of new insights were gotten and the results they have gotten has led them to visiting the local library on a quarterly basis. Team members are being alternated every quarter and the fun and excitement they now have is creating strategies and marketing plans that are leading to real results.

Some of this story is a bit vague because they are in a very fierce competitive battle in their industry. It is their request not to divulge what they believe is their new secret weapon, GRASS ROOTS POWER with an ability to create new pathways of thinking.

Find the right model

Another way of gaining information is to ask questions of someone who has already mastered a skill you wish to improve or acquire. Our experiences have continually demonstrated that the most successful people in a company are least likely to be asked by their peers to share the secrets of their success. Sometimes our ego keeps us from asking our closest allies for help. People are usually eager to talk about their triumphs, and enjoy the experience of sharing with others how they achieved it.

Here are some techniques to improve the quality of your own input and of the input of those around you:

- Remember the concept of "Good In, Good Grows."
- Avoid negative reinforcement of ideas. They cause brains to cultivate skepticism and hinder their ability to generate solutions for existing problems.
- Ask questions of people who excel at skills you wish to mimic.
- Be aware of the quality of sources of information that provide input into your brain.
- Visit the book store monthly and scan the front covers of magazines. See if you notice a trend of hot topics.
- Consider new sources of information, such as books, the Internet, college classes or professional training.

Tony Dottino saw an example of this tendency when meeting an artist at the Metropolitan Museum of Art. His curiosity was interested in learning more about art, and asked the artist what he was working on. During the next hour, the artist passionately described how he drew his paintings using various tools. He explained how he studied and visualized his subjects with far more attention to detail than untrained eyes. The one-hour art lesson enabled Dottino to view all paintings from a new perspective, because his brain had developed new relationships and connections to an existing interest.

The importance of listening

Listening is an integral part of communication. In surveys we have conducted with thousands of Grass Roots workers it comes up as their number one request of Grass Roots employees to their managers, "Can they just learn to listen to what we have to say, it just may give them an answer to a problem they want to solve?" It also shows that management cares about its workers. As we listen to other people speak, we often start forming opinions about what they say before they are finished ("It's not going to work, it's a terrible idea and they don't know what they're talking about!") By doing so, we've deprived our brain of the motivation to listen, to explore these possibilities and create new ideas. When we are able to suspend our judgments and preconceived beliefs, it opens the possibilities of creating an infinite number of new ideas.

Likewise, if a person's opinion is in the minority in a group meeting, we tend to ignore it, treating them as out of the box, as "not part of the team," whereas they may be presenting missing information that could lead to creative solutions. It might be time to move the box to surround this new thinking. When listening to others express their ideas, listen to gain understanding, build compassion and communicate your own point of view without antagonizing others.

LEARNING TO MANAGE CHANGE

How do you take all of this information and knowledge and apply it to effect change in your business life? Learning to manage change has become the greatest challenge in many companies. Because of the acceleration in technology and the increasing sophistication of customers, even the largest companies have had to try to become nimble and flexible. Despite the latest technology available, many companies still find it a struggle to implement change rather than just react to it. Why is this the case? To answer that question, you must first understand how we think when we learn, and how we develop new habits.

Learning to learn

You are probably familiar with the term "learning curve," which is used to describe the process of improving a skill through practice and experience. We sometimes refer to it as the "change curve," because people learn as they are changing. If you had to draw a typical learning/change curve, what would it look like? Most people draw a curve that resembles the one in Figure 8.1.

In fact, every learning curve that people have drawn at our request looks similar to the one shown in Figure 8.1, the only variation being the gradient of the curve. Yet this diagram is inaccurate.

What would the consequences be if you found that the learning curve of the human brain looks nothing like the curve in this example? What if you discovered that learning new skills does not occur evenly over time, but instead has many peaks and troughs?

What do you think the learning curve of the human brain looks like?

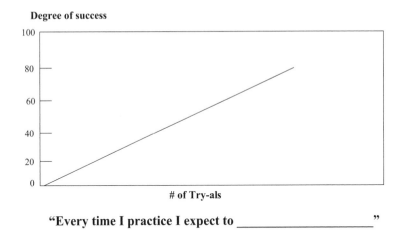

"Every time I practice I expect to _____"

Figure 8.1   The common idea of the learning curve

The learning/change curve is not smooth

Although your brain is constantly learning, the integration of new knowledge into your existing knowledge base does not occur evenly. In your own experience, have you felt that despite practising a new skill, your mastery of that skill undergoes occasional performance dips? Have you ever felt that a skill you have already mastered is deteriorating? Well, the good news is that both of these occurrences are perfectly normal!

Figure 8.2 gives a much more accurate representation of what the learning process of your brain looks like.

You may have already noticed some important differences:

- **The learning process is not smooth**—Your improvement in a skill will involve many peaks and troughs. There will be times when your improvement in a skill will occur rapidly. There will be other times where your mastery regresses, and you will struggle just to maintain the status quo. Both of these experiences are normal, and both occur regularly during the learning process.
- **The learning process contains many troughs**—You may have noticed that the curve contains many downturns, and at least one instance where the skill mastery is not much greater than at the very beginning of the learning process. We have illustrated those points on Figure 8.2 with a drawing of a "big black hole."

What normally happens at the big black hole?

Try to remember the last time you were practising to strengthen a new skill. Do you recall a time when you felt you had hit rock bottom? What type of self-talk did you give yourself when that happened? What things do you think most people say to themselves at this time? Our surveys have revealed that the worst (and most common) self-talk at this point is: "I can't do this! I give up!"

Now imagine that you understand that the learning process contains many periods where progress in skill acquisition is flat or reverses itself. Ask someone who plays golf if they have ever experienced this. Would your self-talk be different if you believed those downturns were both normal and temporary?

At this point, your most helpful self-talk would be, "How interesting! How fascinating! What can I learn from this?"

When you believe that learning is constant and smooth, any failure to progress must be perceived negatively. This encourages negative thinking and self-recrimination, because *any* slippage, however minor, is seen as an indication of failure. Regression is viewed as failure, which in turn associates itself with other thoughts of failure. Your thinking will become more pessimistic, because each of those negative associations will trigger other associations. You will unleash a self-doubting, self-defeating cascade of thoughts that will reinforce the belief "I can't do that," and give up (an example of Garbage In, Garbage Grows).

If you accept that learning naturally occurs in uneven bursts, temporary deterioration is not catastrophic. You will no longer view it as an indictment of your own ability, a failure, but as a normal, expected event. This separates the emotional reaction and fear of failure from the event, and allows your brain to deal with the issue without any negative thoughts.

GRASS ROOTS
LEADERS—THE
BRAINSMART
REVOLUTION IN
BUSINESS

150

Picture the contrast between these two outlooks on learning and events. Consider the impact that will have on you, your organization and its view of "failure." Is failure seen as a bump on the road to success? Or is failure viewed as a dead end, or a mistake that deserves to be punished? How your company regards failure will greatly influence whether or not you have a dynamic, innovative organization. (For a detailed treatment of this theme, see Tony Buzan's video *If at first ...*, produced by Charthouse.)

What are some of the typical responses to failure?

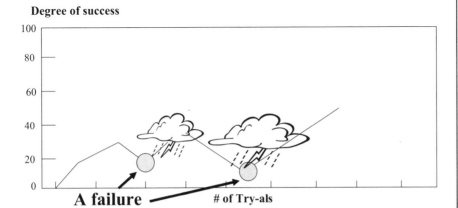

Figure 8.2   The true learning/change curve

LEARNING TO CHANGE BEHAVIOR

You are now ready to combine the information and knowledge you have learned in this chapter and use it to effect a change in your life by altering a behavior or habit.

Let's assume that you have a behavior or habit that you would like to change (such as arriving to work late each morning). If you wanted to develop self-talk that would maximize your chance of changing this behavior, what would it be?

Your brain will take any self-talk that is entered into it, and associate it with existing thoughts. If you reprimand yourself each morning after you are already late, saying to yourself, "I won't arrive late tomorrow," your brain will emphasize the phrase "arrive late tomorrow." This self-talk will actually increase your probability of being late tomorrow, and other days in the future! Your goal must always be positive, and must include the outcome you hope to achieve. In this instance, it should include something like "arrive at work on time" or "become more punctual."

However, if you develop positive self-talk that is factually incorrect, such as "I am someone who arrives to work on time' when you are often late, your brain will reject this input. You will recall from Chapter 6 that the brain is truth-seeking (Brain Principle 6). If it is fed information that it knows is inaccurate, it will discard that information.

On the other hand, if you develop positive self-talk that is factually correct but is not related to time/action, your brain will accept the information, but not act upon it. For example, if your self-talk is "I will arrive at work on time," that statement may be true, but it is based in the future. Since this statement is not based in the present, your brain will not act to make it true. The behavior change will be left to occur "later," and later will always be redefined so that the behavior never changes.

If none of these approaches will work, what self-talk *should* you use to be effective? Your input must be:

- **positive**—stating the goal as a positive outcome
- **factually correct**—not an expression of what you would like the truth to be
- **in the present tense**—so that your brain is moved *immediately* into action and continues.

We recommend telling yourself, "I am becoming punctual." That statement meets all the requirements above, and more importantly, it takes into account your learning curve. What if you begin repeating this phrase to yourself today, and tomorrow you are late for work? Would the above self-talk still be correct? Yes, because you are in the *process* of becoming punctual. Since the learning process is uneven, it allows for events such as arriving at work after your specified time. You still allow yourself opportunities to learn from the occasions where you do not meet your goal on a given day, but you avoid the frustration and negative thinking that accompany viewing the event as a "failure." Persisting with this self-talk will move you along the road to success, until your brain has reprogrammed itself to be punctual.

Consider your organization's views about change. Is it nurturing, saying, "You can do it!" or is there cynicism and resignation when newly defined goals are not met immediately? Are goals phrased so that they are consistent with how the brain learns to modify its behavior? Are the goals phrased positively? For example, if you have a 10 per cent error rate in a process, will your goal be to lower the error rate to, say, 5 per cent? It would be more effective to state the goal in terms of the desired success rate—95 per cent.

GRASS ROOTS
LEADERS—THE
BRAINSMART
REVOLUTION IN
BUSINESS

152

Are your goals in line with current reality? Does the executive team tell itself, "We are a world-class provider of information services," when the reality is that you are struggling to hold onto your existing customer base? Your goals must be positive, but they must also be honest.

Finally, are your goals based in the present, therefore requiring immediate action, or are they phrased so that action may be delayed until the future? Do you have goals which say, "We will become the industry leader in XYZ," or are they defined as, "We are in the process of becoming the industry leader in XYZ." Even that small distinction will affect the chances of your organization achieving its goal.

PROFILE—TESTING THE LIMITS OF THE GRASS ROOTS MANAGERS

The American Society of Composers, Authors and Publishers (ASCAP), founded in 1914 by Victor Herbert, Irving Berlin, John Philip Sousa and many others of the great composers and songwriters of the time, is the world's leading organization in the protection of the intellectual property rights of creative artists. With over 300 000 members, ASCAP's revenues ($750 million in 2005) are distributed directly to its writer and publisher members, based on the performance of their works, after a small operating expense is deducted.

At the start of the new millennium, ASCAP's visionary CEO, John LoFrumento, saw himself facing major challenges. With music at the vanguard of a myriad of rapidly changing technologies, and a storm of legal and legislative action on copyright, how could ASCAP sustain its preeminent role as the champion of music creators, effectively protecting them and ensuring they could continue to earn a living at their craft?

Two things were critical to him. The first, was to create a stronger more cohesive creative community to speak with a louder and clearer voice on copyright issues; a force that would be uniquely ASCAP, leading to greater membership and greater market share.

Second, to invest in his front-line managers in a new way, tapping into their rich pool of intellectual and creative capital and allowing them to lead. He wanted a new program specifically directed at this leadership opportunity. He named it MOVE; not an acronym, but a message—he wanted people who were ready to move into action and take on true leadership assignments.

To bring his MOVE program into reality, he tapped Marshall Tarley. Marshall had taken on some of the most critical and complex challenges in both line and staff areas, and had consistently delivered results. Importantly, he had been mentored by Tony Dottino and Tony Buzan for years. He had absorbed and utilized the tools of the BrainSmart Leader and GRI, and had these disciplines as a basis for a leadership program. The program he rolled out was a rigorous 8 months of readings, workshops and applied learning. It included Mind Mapping, TEFCAS, Brain Principles, management theory, leadership and the brain, work assignments and much more.

When it was done, LoFrumento wanted more. He wanted to take these new leaders and stretch them further, challenge them like never before.

He culled four teams from the graduates (three graduates per team), each from different business disciplines, ensuring diverse thinking. He assigned each team to an executive sponsor. Utilizing the brain principles, he phrased each strategic project as a single question.

This stimulated an explosion of thinking, which quickly led to a dilemma for each team—should they interpret their projects narrowly, limiting their risk and playing it safe; or should they use the question as a springboard to brainstorm broadly, take prudent risk and reach into new areas of thinking and opportunity for the business? Each team decided to take the risk, to enter territory where no one had gone before.

They started with intense research, internally and externally. They interviewed ASCAP's most important customers, board members and senior managers. Next, came brainstorming, using Mind Maps to stimulate and capture the divergent thinking of the team. Then, they converged on the ideas they believed would make a critical difference in the business. They had to navigate the organizational dynamics and senior management, and find the strategies to get their ideas accepted and championed by those in authority. After months of work, they presented their ideas to the senior management group. They were vetted, sent them back for redrafts, and eventually asked to present to the Board of Directors.

Many of these ideas shifted paradigms of thinking within the organization. The board asked piercing questions. Finally, with the influence of the CEO, the board approved these new initiatives. One of those ideas, was the *I Create Music ASCAP EXPO*—a new way to reach out to ASCAP members and beyond, and create a greater value, a creative community of diverse yet like minds in a learning and mentoring environment.

"Ideas are great," LoFrumento said. "But, ideas are worthless without execution." These teams, however, were on fire with enthusiasm. They carefully reached across the boundaries of the organization from one department to the next and began to assemble the liaisons and collaborations that were needed. Accomplished songwriters and legends were asked to share their time and genius at EXPO to teach, to mentor and to perform.

The excitement built and began to engulf everyone in a collegial spirit of, "What can we do to make this great? Whatever it takes, we'll do it." Internally, from the entry level administrative person to top management, everyone was pulling in the same direction. Accomplished songwriters started calling ASCAP asking how they could be a part of EXPO; asking how they could contribute.

And, on 3 days in April of 2006 in Hollywood California, 1 200 paid attendees and hundreds of mentors, panelists and performers converged in this new phenomenon called *ASCAP EXPO*. This first-ever conference of its kind rose to a unique level of shared experience of mind and soul.

"You couldn't believe the excitement everywhere you went," one of ASCAP's own board members said. "I've been attending music conferences for 40 years, and this was the best I've ever experienced."

How can you measure the success of these projects? From the end of ASCAP EXPO in April 2006 through the end of the year, ASCAP Membership grew by 29 000, 11 per cent. And, this first year event finished in the black, providing a small amount of revenue to reduce operating costs, thereby returning more royalties to members. ASCAP EXPO has become a new jewel in the crown of the organization. It has raised the level of the ASCAP experience into a rich community of shared artistic endeavor. It has raised and somewhat altered the perception of ASCAP to so many who look at the organization from various segments of the industry and beyond. It is continuing to do so, and it has opened a new business arena for the organization.

The other three projects made considerable contributions as well. One licensing area embarked on entirely new strategic approaches, yielding increases in revenues and implementing a cutting edge web-based customer-relationship/ sales-relationship system. Another put ASCAP Radio on the air over the internet, launching the organization into new pathways that they are just beginning to explore. Still others saved costs while creating new ways to solidify relations with some of ASCAP's most influential members.

It was a great deal of work that was on top of an already crowded work agenda. There were difficulties, obstacles and discomfort. In good spirit, they persevered, and they delivered important, creative and insightful initiatives to senior managers and the Board of Directors, and made important long lasting impacts to the organization and its business.

By reaching down to his front-line managers, LoFrumento opened the door of opportunity for the organization as a whole, and galvanized the organization to execute and reach a peak experience of success.

CONCLUSION

We live in a world that perceives technology as the driving force for change. We should remember that it is *people* who create, improve and apply technology to bring about this change. It is vital that each employee take a periodic look at his limiting beliefs and realize this. No technology would exist without the applied creativity of people. Today, people exchange much more information at higher speeds than ever before, thanks to such tools as the Internet, fax machines and cellular telephones. However, we need to be constantly alert to the need for the human brain to be in control, supported by the marvels of modern technology. The human spirt to learn and create is endless!

WHAT'S NEXT?

Realizing that your brain has infinite capacity to create and the importance of the right feedback, self-talk and synergy we will look at a critical element that brings it all together in the workplace. Studies have shown that the support managers provide to employees is vital to the results that employees produce.

Chapter 9 will look at the manager's role in building an environment of trust and clear communication so there is no confusion about the support a Grass Roots Team can depend on receiving.

ACTIVITIES

1   Start a reading group and have each person visit the library monthly with objective to read something not familiar to themselves. Relate the reading to the company goals.
2   Write a letter to someone complimenting them on their success. Tell them in what way this has altered a belief you previously had.
3   Introduce yourself to one new person each month, and list five interesting things you learned about each person. Review the journal quarterly.
4   Join a volunteer group and take a leadership role, work to uncover their limiting beliefs.
5   When returning home at the end of the day, let your first 5 minutes of conversation be about "good things" that have happened to each family member during the day.

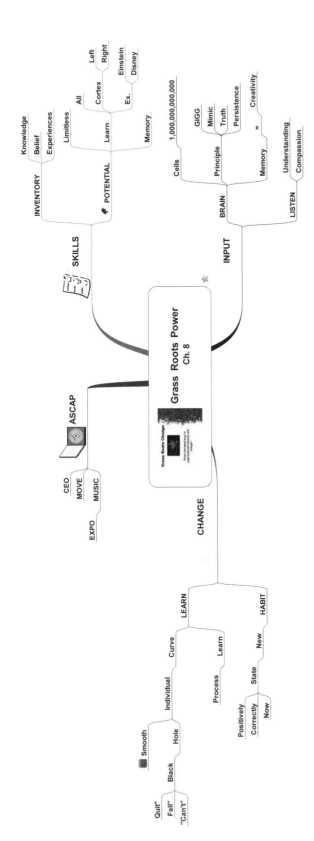

Figure 8.3   Mind Map—Grass Roots power

The BrainSmart Leader

OVERVIEW

There is no shortage of management books today that describe the secrets of unleashing employee creativity, improving morale, maximizing the benefits of diversity and creating powerful teams. You may have read many of these books yourself.

Managers have a key responsibility in keeping a Grass Roots Revolution alive and focused on the Big S. This chapter illustrates by means of a case study how a concept of BrainSmart Leaders can apply the Brain Principles covered in Chapter 6 to build trust and confidence within their Grass Roots teams. Communication is vital for a Leader, so we explore this in detail. It focuses on bringing together two concepts into a powerful force to gain competitive advantage for an organization.

BRAINSMART LEADERSHIP

In *The BrainSmart Leader,* published by Gower in 1999, Tony Buzan, Tony Dottino and Richard Israel introduced the concept that leaders need to learn how to inspire and build enthusiasm within their workforce to ignite the endless flow of creativity which exist within each employee.

Few would dispute that the most significant asset of any company is its people. Since this belief has become so widespread, why do so many companies still continue to squander the intelligence of their employees? How many annual reports have you read where the company refers to its employees as its most valuable asset, only to announce a downsizing resulting in thousands of redundancies soon after?

How can you realize the potential of your staff? By harnessing their power and tapping into their natural creativity and Intellectual Capital, as described in this book.

Like any valuable asset, the intelligence of your workforce must be maintained and nurtured by providing an atmosphere that is both challenging and stimulating. As we mentioned in Chapter 6, the brain needs to continually learn new information in order to remain vibrant and creative (Brain Principle 5). One way to accomplish this is to encourage your employees to continue their education, whether internally through company-sponsored training programs or externally through university courses. Since the main objective of education is to exercise their brains, studying topics with which they are unfamiliar will be most beneficial.

To secure the greatest return from your human assets, you must realize that *everyone* is creative. Your ability to tap into the excitement, enthusiasm and energy of your staff will ultimately determine the long-term performance of your company. Managed properly, the combined intelligence of your employees will lead to success; managed poorly, it will lead to disaster.

Consider the results a group of people can generate when they are committed to a leader with a clearly defined goal. To make the best use of this power, the leader must encourage everyone in the group to ask, "What is the best way to relate to people?" and "How does my thinking mechanism work?"

GREAT LEADERS ARE GREAT COACHES

The next time you watch a sporting event featuring a team that consistently wins, observe the coach. Effective coaches play several roles that are essential to their teams' performance. They need to be visionaries, with a clear picture of what their programs and teams must accomplish. They must be excellent communicators, defining this vision clearly for their players so that they also believe in it. They must motivate and inspire their players. They must be teachers, providing their players with the technical instruction necessary to make the most of their ability, and they must evaluate talent, offering feedback on performance so that their players know how well or poorly they are performing. Although coaches don't throw, kick or hit the ball during matches, their ability to fulfil these roles determines whether their teams will win or lose.

BrainSmart Leaders are coaches. They have to encourage their Grass Roots members to stretch their limits to perform in ways they never thought possible. They must have a clear definition of the team's SUCCESS and have the ability to evaluate the buy-in from each team member to it. Longer term they are building a team which can work cohesively to translate the "S" into reality.

Leaders do this by understanding the workings of the brain, applying the seven Brain Principles and TEFCAS to the structure of their work and their teams to achieve maximum impact.

GRASS ROOTS
LEADERS—THE
BRAINSMART
REVOLUTION IN
BUSINESS

160

CASE STUDY

The new boss arrives

Joe Friday is a successful accountant with XYZ Corporation. Joe's department is responsible for reporting the business results of the domestic operations for his company's manufacturing and service organizations. One day, Joe was in a meeting that was directed by the Organizational Development Department advising him that due to organizational changes being made he would have a new manager, Jane Doe. The present manager Mike Merryfield was being moved to the Export Accounting division. Although Jane had managed other groups within the business results reporting function, she had no firsthand experience with Joe's department.

To make her transition to the new department as smooth as possible, Mike spent a few days showing her the ropes. He introduced her to the staff who handled the main activities of the department, and explained the key work processes that existed within it. Because of Mike Merryfield's hiring pattern and emphasis on training, the staff combined many areas of expertise, with a balance of technical and practical knowledge.

Once Jane began to play a more active role, the staff quickly noticed the differences between her management style and that of Mike's. Before the first month had passed under her management, Jane held a departmental meeting where she laid down many new rules without explaining why they were necessary. Although all her staff worked on a fixed salary basis, Jane demanded that they notify her whenever they took a break for lunch or any other reason. The new rules and oppressive supervision started to create mistrust.

Jane expressed concern that her staff was unable to analyze the output of their work properly. Her solution was to require them to provide her with finalized data earlier than the normal set schedule. This request alarmed the staff, because they had already reduced their cycle time considerably, and further reduction would require a large-scale redirection of their efforts. Furthermore, it didn't match the department's goals for the year.

Staff trust and confidence continued to decline over time, and tension continued to build within the department. In later departmental meetings, Jane publicly reprimanded staff members for making mistakes, even when they resulted from trying to formulate new solutions to improve the service for important customers. She demanded to be notified of all new projects, regardless of scope, for pre-approval. During one of the meetings, Jane declared without any explanation, that all staff members were required to work the following weekend. It didn't seem to matter that several team members had already made travel plans with their families.

The group's frustration continued to increase as morale began to fall and the department's focus became clouded. Lack of trust and confidence in management grew as the department began work on a special project.

Jane seemed to welcome ideas and input at project meetings, but she never followed through with actions. If a minor change was proposed from the original plan for the project, Jane resisted it. This inconsistency led to a lack of a clear direction toward any goals. Jane behaved as if she felt she could not rely on anyone in her department, and must carry its workload alone.

The staff soon found that Jane became easily frustrated by any deviation from her commands. Her motto became, "I want everything to work perfectly, all the time, the first time." Because of the changes rippling throughout the organization, this goal seemed impossible to the staff. They felt she wasn't willing to listen to their concerns and work as a team. Under Mike the team had worked to provide lower and lower error rates by creating timely solutions as issues arose. As it became evident that any mistakes would be punished, less innovative and creative ideas were generated by the department. Now creative ideas represented such a high risk, and everyone became preoccupied with minimizing the chance of being blamed. The unfortunate consequence of this mindset was that it united the Intellectual Capital of the department—against its manager. The survival instincts of the employees meant that each member developed a defensive attitude regarding any issue linked to Jane.

A silent civil war ensued, with both sides interested only in winning small battles. The frustrated, demotivated subjects withdrew from their despotic, intolerant ruler. Communications between staff and Jane became selective, and problems were hidden.

Department meetings became silent, and creativity evaporated. There was no leadership to provide the guidance necessary to align the department team. All of this led to an unexcited, unenthusiastic workforce that led to customer dissatisfaction. With the erosion of the trust and confidence in their manager, the team was unable to begin a communication process to address its concerns.

Trust and confidence: the brain is truth-seeking (Brain Principle 6)

Surveys have shown that people consider trust and confidence the most important factor determining how they communicate and interact with each other. When building relationships, trust is bestowed upon others cautiously, like a precious gift. It takes time to develop, and once betrayed, never fully returns. When it is present, it opens doors, breaks down walls and unleashes creativity. Trust increases our willingness to listen to new ideas and to take risks. Lack of trust causes us to retreat to safe territory, and inhibits our ability

GRASS ROOTS
LEADERS—THE
BRAINSMART
REVOLUTION IN
BUSINESS

162

to think freely and creatively. Trust must be earned, and once won, should be nurtured carefully.

Since Brain Principle 6 tells us that the brain is a truth-seeking device that acts on what it believes to be true, the results of these surveys should be no surprise. A leader should recognize the power of this principle to ensure that their Grass Roots team focuses and takes action towards reaching a common goal. How much easier it would have been for Jane if she had shared her goals with her department, and created a group consensus. She would not have felt she had to do everything on her own and, more importantly, she would have tapped into the natural thinking processes of her experienced staff.

With the advent of change programs, the job security of many employees has been threatened. As changes are introduced into the organization, sharing information plays an even more critical role. The brain seeks knowledge and information so that it can make connections and associations about a topic (Brain Principle 5). When it is given inaccurate or incomplete information, or no information at all, it will work to fill in the blanks (Brain Principle 4). The synergy principle (Brain Principle 1) comes into play, and the brain generates possible scenarios, fuelling the rumor mill.

If a management team wants to restrict the influence of the rumor mill, it needs to communicate information to its staff that fills in the blanks in a way that is credible. The Grass Roots people who hear this information will then be able to use the synergy principle to take appropriate action. This leads to a natural process which generates ideas that can provide innovative solutions to customer needs and business problems, and build enthusiasm among the group.

Since the success of any organizational change effort is largely determined by the creativity of team members and their willingness to take risks, it is vital to earn and maintain their trust. An effective way to do this is to share information with them so they can generate solutions that are focused on the correct goals. Senior management must always try to create an environment where trust and confidence can be built and nourished, and recognize that the words they use and actions they take will be mimicked by their staff (Brain Principle 3). A management system where there are daily crises has a difficult time in sustaining the trust of the Grass Roots employees. They begin to question direction and their own survival. They lose confidence and begin to question their desire to follow a leader who takes them into crisis day after day.

Companies where trust is low or non-existent tend to have high staff turnover. Although employees are generally encouraged to continue their education in order to keep their skill sets current, a company with high stress and a low trust environment that pays for its staff's education will not benefit from its investment, since employees will take the benefit of this training to another company with whom they are more comfortable. Thus, low trust companies find themselves in a double bind: if they invest in training their employees, they will not reap the full benefit because the additional skills make it easier for unhappy employees to find better jobs with a competitor, whereas if they restrict the marketability of their employees by limiting training, their workforce's skills will become outdated, and eventually obsolete. In either case, their Intellectual Capital will be drained until it cannot sustain performance.

FEAR OF RETRIBUTION?

Tony Dottino was working with a manager who was working extremely hard at getting her employees to identify problem areas and share their ideas in bringing solutions to them. There was a critical point where the Grass Roots teams were going to test this with a problem they thought might embarrass the manager. They were deeply concerned that though the manger was speaking the words, this situation was so embarrassing that all this talk about open communications was only talk and there would be retribution. The major issue concerned the loss of employee productivity due to their not having some of the basic tools necessary to do their jobs. What made this day particularly interesting was the company Chief Operating Officer was going to be in the room to hear about the employee problems along with the manager.

When it came time for the Grass Roots team to share their concerns there was much trepidation, a long pause, some hard swallows but finally the words and emotions of frustration. After listening quietly, the manager told the employees that she had no idea this issue was causing so much pain, loss to their department metrics, and impact to their customer. She promised to support their efforts in working with the fiancé team to get them the tools they needed to perform their jobs.

After the session was over, the COO commended the manager and team for being able to have an open and honest conversation that would lead to improving customer service. Rather than criticize the manager for not knowing about this sooner, he commended the manager for building the trust and confidence of her employees to speak openly and honestly, so the business could move onto solving its problems.

There is nothing more powerful in building trust and confidence within an organization than matching words with actions and the employees were recognized for being leaders in "straight talking to management."

WHAT IS "SUCCESS"?

The importance of communicating any changes in your company's missions and goals to your employees must not be underestimated, as they are more

GRASS ROOTS
LEADERS—THE
BRAINSMART
REVOLUTION IN
BUSINESS

164

likely to trust you. Employees with diverse and up-to-date skills can recover from adversity and transform themselves much more easily and quickly. Contemplate the same situation in a company with outdated skill sets where no trust exists. The workforce will become defensive, risk-averse and skeptical, with everyone watching their backs. Some disgruntled employees may even secretly delight in the failure of the company, as just deserts for past sins. An unhappy employee may even regard the collapse of the company as success!

Successful managers do not just build trust within their own organization. To remain successful, a company must have strong relationships with its customers, built upon trust and reliability. For example, if you promise a customer 100 per cent of their requirements, you will disappoint them if you deliver only 80 per cent. On the other hand, you could notify your customer that the best you can deliver is 80 per cent of what is requested, but ensure you do so. In the former case, there will be anger, mistrust and you may lose future business. In the latter, there are no broken promises, the relationship with your customer is not jeopardized, and the customer's trust in you will be maintained or strengthened. The customer received what was promised, even though it was less than what they wanted, so they could make contingency plans.

Jane Doe from XYZ imposed new rules on her staff without taking the time to explain the reasons for them. This created mental blanks in the minds of her staff that were filled with scenarios of mistrust and hostility. An ineffective manager who tries to implement new rules unilaterally will meet resistance and cynicism. New rules that are not explained to staff are likely to be bent or broken. In the case of Jane Doe, departmental meetings were negative experiences for everyone, adding to the mistrust. The brains of the departmental staff used the negative inputs from these meetings to create new links and associations, which were also negative. Their brains also invoked the mimic principle (Brain Principle 3) to model the excessive criticism and lack of trust demonstrated by Jane. The combination of all these factors eventually turned the department against its leader.

BrainSmart Leaders can introduce new rules easily because they develop trusting relationships with their employees. They first gain their trust by confiding the reason behind the new rules and justifying their actions. They reinforce this trust by inviting feedback from their employees. They do not become defensive when faced with criticism, and are willing to change or eliminate rules that prove to be unsound after hearing their employees' views. They may request the assistance of their more experienced staff to make the transition easier.

When Jane was setting new goals, she achieved neither consensus nor alignment, and she failed to give credit to the group for work they had already done. When establishing new goals, it is always important to explain to your staff the need for them, especially if they need to stretch themselves to achieve it. If your staff feel the new goal is impossible and feel no ownership in setting it, they will not draw on the persistence principle (Brain Principle 7). Their brains will not generate ways to achieve the goal, but reasons why it cannot be achieved.

The public humiliation and reprimands for failure further compounded the resistance Jane's staff displayed towards the new goals. These attacks triggered her employees' defense mechanisms. Had Jane approached failures by saying, "How interesting, what can we learn from this?," she would have unleashed creative, positive thinking.

Leonardo da Vinci believed that everything connects to everything else, and a manager must realize that a person's brain does not shut off work issues while at home, nor ignore home issues while at work. Several of her employees had already made travel plans with their families that could be cancelled only with great difficulty. Forcing an employee to choose between work and family divides the attention of the brain, rather than letting its thoughts flow naturally. As a result, the employees who gave up time with their families to work mandatory weekends spent much more time at work thinking about their families than they would have otherwise, "I really miss my family. I am angry that Jane's worries about our schedule have taken priority over my personal time. Jane is more concerned about her own success then with keeping my morale high." This further increased the tension between Jane and her staff, and fostered an "us against them" mentality.

Trust and confidence provide the climate that allows open, two-way communication to take place. This communication of information and knowledge allows our brain to make appropriate corrections towards the achievement of its goals, and provides the basis for building long-lasting relationships.

Trust and confidence are key factors in determining a company's ability to implement change and make full use of its existing Intellectual Capital. The synergy of creative thought processes is more effective when it operates in a comfortable and trusting environment. To be successful, each manager must produce a stable environment that allows any potentially risky situation to be evaluated with mutual respect. If the uncharted pathways of our brains are thought to be littered with mines, no one will take the risk of attempting to travel on them by coming up with new ideas.

COMMUNICATION

The brain learns best through association, by linking new information to existing information in a synergistic fashion. Your life experiences define the connections your brain makes between two pieces of information in a fashion that is unique to you.

GRASS ROOTS
LEADERS—THE
BRAINSMART
REVOLUTION IN
BUSINESS

166

To maximize the effectiveness of your communication, learn to communicate using skills from both sides of your brain. In addition to communicating numbers, facts and statistics (left cortex), you must also use images, colours and rhythm (right cortex), but remember that because no two brains are identical, the mental picture you have of what you are communicating may differ from that formed by your listener. We are only familiar with our own associations, so we cannot assume that the same reactions and responses will exist in others. Consider, for example, what temperature would be considered a "warm day" by a resident of New York compared to someone from Florida. Contemplate the confusion among the different functions of an organization when the executive team promises "dramatic" work and performance improvements because of a new re-engineering program. Imagine the variety of responses when company leaders are asked to quantify what they mean by "dramatic" or 'significant," and the problems that could result.

Very often when people are introduced to others, they are labelled by the person introducing them. If we know the person making the introduction, these labels are often accepted as "truth" by our brain before it makes its own determination of the validity of the label. You have probably seen examples of this when listening to two different people describe the same object or person. Have you ever wondered how two people can view the same object and have totally different perspectives?

Filling in the blanks

When Joe explained the processes, it is likely that he left blanks in Jane's mind. A manager often lacks sufficient details to explain problems or issues to someone else properly, so detailed explanations of unfamiliar processes are best left to the person who does the work. A BrainSmart Leader who joins a new organization can use this knowledge to help understand the organization by determining whether the person doing the explaining is filling in blanks or creating them—an excellent way to evaluate how well a person knows their job.

Unfamiliarity with every detail of a new department can exacerbate the normal feeling of being overwhelmed that a new manager experiences when taking on a new position. The manager's thoughts in this instance can be best described as, "I hope someone here knows what's going on until I figure out how to survive."

While it is relatively easy to transfer information by speaking, it is very difficult to truly *communicate* while speaking, since the same word can trigger different associations in different people. Communicating effectively with someone requires that you communicate "brain to brain." A combination of trust and your knowledge of the skills inventory of your listener is helpful here: you can use these to communicate in a fashion that links your thoughts to their cortical skills through their five senses. With this is mind, you should begin a topic of

Grass Roots Tip
Building trust and confidence:
• Use as many of your five senses and the cortical skills as possible to convey the exact meaning of your thoughts.
• Remember that the brain is truth-seeking, and acts on what it believes to be true.
• Respect the trust employees have in you.
• Remember the importance of feedback.
• Be caringly honest with others.
• Remember that it takes time to earn trust.

From the brain's point of view, trust and confidence translate into truth and belief, so BrainSmart Leaders should concentrate on building trust and confidence with their Grass Roots employees.

conversation by asking some key questions to establish a base of information and knowledge.

Because of Mike's training, the staff had areas of expertise, including a balance of technical and practical knowledge. Jane could have assessed the skills of her department in terms of the ten cortical skills of the brain to assess the strengths and weaknesses of the group as a whole. For example, sitting with each person to learn about their job, she could map their dominant cortical skills. By doing so, Jane could draw up an inventory of the skills of the department and see if there were any cortical skills missing, such as "big picture" thinking, imagination, logic, or lack of details and technical knowledge.

Associations—do we match?

Words are powerful communication tools, and they evoke a multiplicity of associations that cause us to interpret them individually, as uniquely as our experiences. To show the power of the associations of words, draw a circle with the word "money" at the centre, and draw ten lines radiating from the circle. Think of ten words that you associate with money, and write one word on each line. Keep your responses to yourself. Then ask four other people you know to perform the same exercise on their own. When you have all completed the exercise, compare your ten words with the others, looking for complete matches. With a group of four people, it is quite common to find no matches at all. At best, you may find one or two word matches between two people.

Jane alienated her entire department after the first meeting by communicating requirements that implied that the department was not trustworthy. The associations to this message—whether conscious or unconscious—evoked resentment and defensiveness among her staff. Had Jane communicated her concerns to the department, recognizing the associations that her team would make, they could have worked together to develop a solution which addressed her concerns, but in a much friendlier atmosphere. For example, Jane could have asked to be kept updated on new projects, not simply for pre-approval (which implied that she was the only person who could be trusted to decide whether or not a project should be undertaken), but because she needed the knowledge to manage the workload of her department more effectively (which would have implied concern about keeping the workload manageable and equitable). Both requests would have asked for the same information, but the latter would have resulted in a much less hostile environment.

All these opportunities could have provided the staff with an excellent role model and coach to mimic. Imagine the influence she could generate by being the model for building trust and confidence, leading to open communication. Through this model, the staff would have a basis to share their concerns with her. This opening could provide them with the possibility to persist and not feel so helpless when generating ideas to reach their organizational goals. Finally, in trying to gain the knowledge and information necessary to make her

GRASS ROOTS
LEADERS—THE
BRAINSMART
REVOLUTION IN
BUSINESS

168

comfortable as quickly as possible, the group could have drawn up Mind Maps to assist the communication process.

What's the picture?

When communicating with someone, whenever possible, create a picture or image in the mind of the listener, using vivid words that describe the scene. If the image is clear and trust exists between speaker and listener, the concept is quickly understood and immediately accepted. A trust-filled environment with open communication channels plus effective communication leads to infinite creativity. Imagine a workplace where innovation and breakthroughs happen regularly. Think of a company where people are excited and motivated about their jobs, where they actually look forward to coming to work each day. At this company, productivity is world-class because open and honest communication channels across all functions and levels of management allowing problems to be quickly identified, communicated and resolved. Risk-taking is considered an important part of the creative process, and failures are viewed as providing a unique opportunity to learn. Customers rave about the quality of service provided, and feel their input is valued and respected.

Now consider the alternative. Picture a workplace where innovation is scarce, and risk-taking is openly discouraged. "If it was a good idea, somebody would have already thought of it" is the company motto. Information is viewed as a jealously guarded asset, and is shared on a "need-to-know" basis only. Communication serves merely to transfer limited information back and forth, but the information is fragmented, and frequently taken out of context. The workforce is cynical about attempts to improve working conditions or customer service, and staff turnover is high. Productivity is low, and continues to deteriorate as each person protects themself, and avoiding blame for mistakes wastes energy. Competition among departments is fierce, and the failure of other departments is viewed as an opportunity for your own department to look better in the eyes of senior management.

Which company would you rather work for? Which company do you think will outperform the other? Which company do you think will eventually be struggling just to survive?

The assets of a company reside in the skills of each individual. It is the ability of a BrainSmart Leader to nurture these skills which leads a company to long-term success. In your interaction with others, you have the opportunity to establish a model for others to follow. So what will it be? Will your communication be honest and helpful, or disingenuous and misleading? Will your work environment be exciting and encourage innovation, or boring and encourage finger-pointing? Will your communication be interesting and informative, or dull and useless? You decide.

JEAN TURCOTTE, THE JOURNEY TO MAGNET STATUS

When Jean Turcotte became a Nurse Manager responsible for 100 nurses in the Cardio Vascular Intensive Care Unit (CVICU) at Florida Hospital in Orlando, he had the opportunity to embrace the journey toward "Magnet Status." Magnet Status is being sought by many hospitals across the United States as recognition that empowerment and teamwork of the bedside nurses exist. Its primary purpose is to ensure nurses feel that they are part of the decision-making process as it relates to their patient care responsibilities.

Grass Roots Tip
Here are some other suggestions for improving communication:
• In building trust and confidence and setting the course of communication in Grass Roots relationships, you may begin by asking a person what they view as the important values and standards they use to measure their progress over time.
• Ask Grass Roots people for their ideas on solving a problem you have.
• Share knowledge and conduct coaching sessions where you teach them something related to their job performance.

Jean reported the results of his unit's efforts to the Senior VP's of Florida Hospital at the monthly strategy meeting and the Assistant VP of Leadership Development commented afterwards, "Jean you resonated with the team this morning. You gave them a slice of the real world along with a sense of the genius residing in the hearts and minds of our everyday employees!"

Jean describes one of the projects his unit team tackled—"managing equipment and work orders" or getting equipment fixed more efficiently.

> The unit needed a consistent method for repairing broken equipment and ensuring it was returned to circulation as soon as possible. This was accomplished by:
> * Inviting a unit secretary to participate in the project. She became highly motivated when management began setting clear expectations and establishing individual accountability. Doing this allowed the team to realize this person had more potential than she had been allowed to demonstrate. The truth was they had never expected more from her.
> * Understanding processes and setting clear expectations for all departments involved meeting with other departments (biomedical repair, engineering) and appreciating each department's contribution to the process. It helped us to identify short-comings. Little had they realized how many short-comings were owned by CVICU!
> * Building interdepartmental relationships. Once the unit had improved the processes and had a better understanding of their responsibilities, there was a tremendous improvement in relationships. There was less need to blame others as things were now getting done. The focus for everyone became, "What more can I do to assist you?"

The concept of Magnet matched Jean's philosophy of leadership. "Leaders should realize that those performing the job should be aware of rules, regulations and guidelines that govern their practice and should be responsible for their own practice."

Remember Jean's quote from the first chapter, " I believe that, as a Leader, one day removed from the front line I am outdated." Therefore building communications, teamwork and trust among his unit members is critical for the efficient practice of patient care.

An active Nursing Practice Council (NPC) was already in place and had a good level of motivation but lacked organization, business skills and, to some degree, purpose. A NPC is the formal structure to bring nursing teams together for shared decision making, from the bottom layer of nursing up through the Chief Nursing Office.

Though Jean was an advocate of Grass Roots teams, he had some degree of insecurity at the idea of a team of motivated employees who would be able to identify opportunities, develop strategies and implement change in the unit.

"Wasn't this unit of Florida Hospital now my responsibility and running it my job?" he thought initially. "What would my director and vice president think if I couldn't keep up with my own staff? Why did they even need me?"

The answer was, of course, he was needed to lead, support his teams, coach them in building their own skills and help clear obstacles that were in their way while the group became the leaders of change.

He shares a second NPC team project that has several lessons for managers.

- **Auto-resetting of bedside monitors**
  Monitors that should have been configured to reset automatically, were not. (The "auto-reset" monitor button would alarm more than was necessary). This cost bedside nurses time since they would have to respond to reset the monitor. "When I started in my role as Nurse Manager I met with Biomedical Engineering to try and fix the problem with no success. The former Nurse Manager had done the same. We were told that it was a 'software issue' and could not be changed."

  When the NPC decided to look into this, Jean was going to inform them that this was futile as two managers had already addressed this. "I didn't want to see the team waste their time or take on something that was not going to be successful. I then decided to let them go through the motions since sometimes we are not successful and it would still be good practice."

  The council actually took a different avenue than the administrative route, using their own connections from the relationships they built, and found someone who indeed knew how to modify the software. In the end they were successful in getting the monitors to auto reset. They celebrated their success, the staff were very happy to save time, the hospital saved resources, and Jean had learned a lesson.

His team of NPC members appreciate they have a leader who trusts in their ability to make a difference and has a fluid process of communications. Jean believes if you align employee goals to company goals, you create a solid foundation to build strong relationships. In addition, he isn't afraid to admit weaknesses and ask for help from his team. By sharing challenges and allowing his nurses to assume leadership roles, it leads to two benefits: if they are

- Focus more on communication skills that appeal to all five senses and to all cortical skills. Try new ones each month.
- Check your communication—ask for feedback on the meanings and associations you created while communicating.

successful then the team celebrates, and when they aren't, then everyone has a healthy dose of learning for growth.

Jean always has an open door when he is on the floor and makes a point at the beginning and ending of his shift to walk the floor so the staff can share thoughts, ask questions, and seek clarification of assignments. When he is not available, he ensures he communicates where he has been and what value any meetings he attends have to the unit.

At a leadership workshop that Tony Dottino taught, Jean saw the realization of his role as a force to remove barriers, provide support and resources, coach, celebrate success and revisit struggles. But he also recognized that his biggest role was to build a strong team of nurses and develop the skills of each nurse.

A number of his NPC members have attended the Grass Roots Innovation workshop (GRI) that we describe in Chapter 11 and you will read their stories that have been acclaimed by the National Teaching Institute. His unit has been able to reduce overtime costs by 10 per cent, improve their Gallup scores (employee engagement/morale survey) from 3.66 to 4.05 and build stronger relationships with other departments in the hospital.

What he sees from the "Front-line Transformation" is:

1   Leaders emerging.
2   Results that relate to his key performance measures.
3   Inter-departmental relationships that have built teamwork.
4   Engagement and satisfaction of providing a more efficient environment for patient care.

And of course the exposure that his staff have received in presenting and discussing with some of Florida Hospital's Senior Leaders. This is more of a gain for Senior Leaders than the staff themselves. I hope they see it that way!

CONCLUSION

Every leader who wants to exert a positive influence on their Grass Roots team needs to integrate the seven Brain Principles into their daily actions. Building trust and confidence to the point where people will communicate openly without fear of retribution or retaliation is essential to success.

WHAT'S NEXT?

To sustain a Grass Roots Revolution it is critical to have built an environment of trust and confidence. But with this environment must come a business vocabulary that everyone must speak so that all levels of the organization chart are on the same page.

The next chapter provides a clear definition of terms to ensure everyone has the same meaning to these terms. It empowers Grass Roots workers to speak with louder voices so executives find their message compelling. The fundamentals of process analysis are described in a sequence that facilitates the natural creativity everyone.

ACTIVITIES

1a Select an outstanding Grass Roots member of your team and develop a mini public relations program to inform others about your star performers.

1b Ask your star Grass Roots employees to do the same thing for someone they view as an outstanding member of their team.

2 List all the people who report to you. Each week write one positive sentence about each person. Review the list with each person every few weeks.

3 Schedule up to a 90-minute meeting with each of your employees to discuss their career goals and how you can be of help.

4 Carry out a time log of where you are spending your time. Analyze your list of activities and see if there are opportunities to teach some of these activities to your staff.

5 Based on the company vision, develop your organizational goals with your team so that they have the same focus as you do.

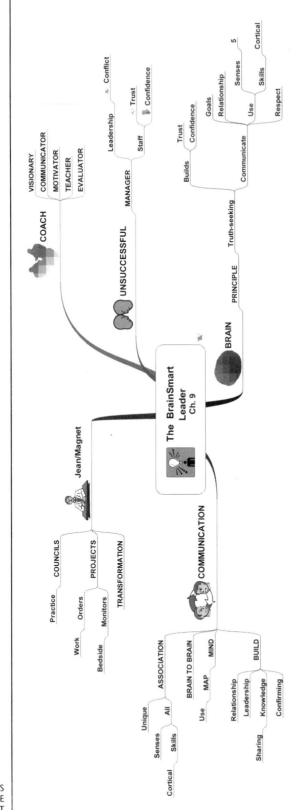

Figure 9.1   Mind Map—the BrainSmart Leader

GRASS ROOTS
LEADERS—THE
BRAINSMART
REVOLUTION IN
BUSINESS

174

CHAPTER 10

Building the Story

OVERVIEW

An in-depth knowledge of process analysis leads to permanent innovation in the workplace. It facilitates communication among managers, team members and customers. It improves teamwork and sparks the creative process. Through effective process analysis, the voice of the Grass Roots employee is heard, and they become change leaders. It provides the skills that are crucial to help managers transform from reactive to proactive. In this chapter the fundamental process analysis skills that each Grass Roots worker should master are defined.

When Anne Kelly was first introduced to Grass Roots Innovation (Chapter 11), she believed that no process analysis methodology worked perfectly. Each was effective some of the time, but none of them worked in all situations. No matter what program she implemented, all came up short in becoming part of the organization's culture.

Anne believed that in her current situation, she needed to find something that would result in a permanent change in the way people worked. This chapter provided the final piece that would help her make permanent changes to Station 11's operation.

THE REACTIVE MANAGEMENT APPROACH TO IMPROVEMENT

One of the major selling points of the reactive management approach for improving financial performance is that it looks easy to do.

A typical reactive management system has the following attributes:

- Budget reductions are made by executives, consultants and the finance team without input from the Grass Roots workers.
- Training is for technical skills and not critical thinking or interpersonal skills.
- Major communication gaps exist between executives, middle managers and Grass Roots workers.

- Measurements are not linked to customer requirements and are not conducive to taking immediate corrective action.

BUDGET REDUCTIONS

When an organization is having difficulty in meeting its financial targets, it is usually the combined efforts of executives, consultants and finance that drive action plans. Cutting headcount and reducing costs are their responsibilities. The underlying premise of this approach is that by increasing pressure on employees (and sometimes threatening their survival), the employees will be motivated to aggressively challenge how work gets done (thus reducing spending).

In the short term this approach can appear to deliver results, but as we stated in Chapter 1, there are times when the cost of decisions made today is not known until far into the future. When a previously unknown cost of a decision suddenly materializes, its unpleasant consequences can potentially jeopardize the organization's relationships with key customers and stakeholders. This frequently results in an increase in cost.

A comprehensive, bottom-up analysis is not done because it is deemed unnecessary. Why require so much organizational effort when comparable results can be achieved with much less effort? However, this approach falters when it comes to uncovering ongoing inefficiencies that inhibit the ability to deliver sustainable results. It also kills morale and the motivation for people to take initiative in leading change efforts.

Fortune Magazine of March 21, 2005 had an article that addressed this perfectly. The headline suggested that BRAIN SCIENCE is changing the way we think about retirement savings. A point made in the article is when you take decision making out of someone's hands and control it externally, then the person is apt to cut back on his own efforts.

We encountered a team of people who were excited about the contribution they were making in helping their department meet the financial challenges they were given. However, when company executives decided it was time to give edicts on spending and direct where cuts would be made, the enthusiasm of this team was quickly extinguished. They fell back into hiding and waiting to see how they could survive the next cycle of cuts, mostly by playing it safe.

EDUCATION PRIORITIES

In a reactive management system, training is focused on executives and middle management. Programs available for front-line workers are usually job specific,

GRASS ROOTS
LEADERS—THE
BRAINSMART
REVOLUTION IN
BUSINESS

176

technical skills are the priority and critical thinking, process analysis and interpersonal skills are for managers.

While it is current practice that only leadership understands the elements of process analysis, the true source of much process innovation are the front-line workers. By not training all employees with the skills and tools needed to sustain process innovation, the organization loses the benefit of their knowledge and experience. This is the skepticism referenced in Anne Kelly's story, Chapter 1; can an educational approach really capture the thinking of the Grass Roots workers and be productive on a sustained basis?

Reactive management leads to an organization having limited ability to:

1   spontaneously identify process problems;
2   conduct root cause analysis;
3   create proactive solutions;
4   develop new ways of conducting business.

The existing mindset that workers should focus on getting the work done without questions is never challenged.

For many years, Tony Buzan has been a pioneer in recommending to corporations that the best investment they can make is in teaching their employees the principles of *"Learning to Learn."* From his vast amount of research, he knows that there is no limit on the ability of people to learn new skills and add them to their tool box. This is true regardless of a person's age, gender or ethnic background. Current research even suggests that it is in our later years of life, age 50 to 60, that we have the potential to be our most creative.

We see a parallel from our business experiences exist in school systems. If we look at the financial pressures of many city public schools today, we see evidence that school boards have a bias towards funding technical skills and not creative skills. As school boards prioritize budgets, we are frequently asked by parents to speak to a school administrator or board member. Why? Because art programs, music, athletic and liberal arts classes are being eliminated due to budget constraints. When this happens, students learn to develop only one half of their brain.

This pattern can be found in corporations that debate the value of teaching their employees soft skills, such as interpersonal intelligence, communication, leadership, change management and creativity.

COMMUNICATION GAPS EXIST

In a reactive management system, process analysis work is taken only to the activity (groups of related tasks) level by the management team. It is felt that any attempt to dive deeper will not result in changes large enough to justify the effort. The focus is on eliminating and modifying major activities, and any work below that is considered too far down in the weeds to offer potential for real benefits and innovative ways of doing work.

However, almost every activity has a combination of beneficial and wasteful effort and the people doing the work have the experience to sort this out. Eliminating an entire activity is the business equivalent of throwing the baby out with the bathwater. Fat is cut, but so is muscle. Grass Roots workers may be unable to articulate the impact of changing activities on their workflow or the management system prevents them from giving their feedback, so executives are unaware of the repercussions of their actions until the consequences are significant. No one wants to communicate the bad news to their executives, that their decisions created more problems than solutions.

As part of a reactive change initiative, usually front-line workers are asked by a consultant to complete an activity dictionary, listing all major work activities and the percentage of the worker's time spent on each one. The project champion consolidates all of the activity dictionaries, sums all of the percentages associated with each activity, and usually concludes, "Wow, if activity ABC is eliminated we could save 1.25 Full Time Equivalent people!" If only it were that easy to eliminate 1.25 people while changing a culture to sustain results.

Unfortunately, the rough estimates of the time spent on each activity may open the dialogue, but without consensus there is no buy-in and commitment to live with the results. Therefore, nothing happens to change the organizational mindset. The communication process breaks down because no one believes they will be heard.

In addition, even an inefficient activity may be necessary until the root cause of errors has been identified and corrected. The audit function may not add value, but eliminating it could destroy value when the underlying process is faulty. When audits are eliminated before addressing the root cause of problems and empowering the workers, the customer becomes the catcher for the process errors. The reductions leave the remaining process vulnerable to an increase in error rates and cost.

As organizations attempt to reduce audit functions, so does the opportunity to catch small problems before they became big problems. Failures grow from problematic to spectacular as the communication gaps widen and panic begins to arise. Finally if an organization wants to empower people to identify cost

GRASS ROOTS
LEADERS—THE
BRAINSMART
REVOLUTION IN
BUSINESS

178

cutting opportunities, identify and solve problems then employees need some level of process analysis skills.

In Chapter 7 TEFCAS addresses to the importance of communications that have integrity so the organization can make timely adjustments. The profile of Jim in Chapter 1 describes this best—a million dollars lost since people were afraid to speak up.

MEASUREMENTS

Organizational measurements show what the problems are (for example, error rates), but they provide no insight into how they got that way (for example, faulty materials, unclear requirements). To successfully improve a process, in many instances existing measurements must be discarded. New measurements are created that are more effective in identifying the source of errors. The person doing the work must have spontaneous feedback so they can adjust immediately.

In one example, a client had placed an order for generators supplied by a company famous for its six sigma program. A key element of six sigma is its focus on using metrics to identify problems and measure performance. In this instance, the metrics were internal to the company supplying the generators, and were not tied to the customer. Unknown to the customer, a new engineer had taken over a key manufacturing role and decided to make an alteration to the manufacturing process for the equipment. The existing metrics did not identify the impact of this change on the quality of the generators. It was months later that the generators started failing at the customer's location causing equipment outages. It was months after the failures began that the source of the errors was finally identified, at a cost of millions.

Operating in a reactive management system was tolerable as long as the competition played by the same rules. After many years focused on improving operating results through productivity and cost reductions, the competitive edge delivered by such efforts dwindled. Companies discovered that they could not grow earnings forever solely by cutting costs. This demonstrated the need for a change in the organizational mindset.

EFFICIENT PROCESSES REQUIRE A CLEAR PICTURE OF SUCCESS

The output of a company is like a giant jigsaw puzzle that is being assembled for the benefit of a customer (we use "customer" here to refer to not only the external final customer, but also the internal user of the output of any process at any stage). Each employee contributes a number of pieces and eventually the puzzle is completed.

Quite often, employees work with their individual pieces without ever knowing what the completed puzzle will look like. This is a common cause of inefficient processes. What are the results? Workers and managers become preoccupied with overcoming crises created by having an unclear understanding of the final picture. In such an environment, there is usually absence of communication and a lack of skill in focusing on the root causes of problems and creating solutions.

The whole process works best when every employee knows exactly how their pieces of work link to the adjacent pieces, and to the puzzle as a whole. Once workers and managers improve their communication, everyone understands the whole process. This teamwork develops extraordinary power, creating solutions that improve the efficiency and effectiveness of the entire organization.

Team members should be taught how to define the output requirements of their activities, and how they relate to the process as a whole. Mind Maps can be powerfully employed in process analysis both to clearly define requirements and to show the integration of individual work effort into the bigger process. Clarifying customer requirements leads to an automatic improvement in work because of the brain's success-driven mechanism. The relationship between activities and tasks is revealed, sparking insight into opportunities for innovation. Grass Roots people learn "If you take any process and break it down into its component pieces, you will have a tool kit that you can use to solve any business process problem you will ever encounter."

An in-depth knowledge of process analysis leads to permanent innovation in the workplace because:

- It facilitates communication among managers, team members and customers.
- It improves teamwork and sparks the creative process.
- The voice of the Grass Roots employee is heard, through effective process analysis.
- Grass Roots employees become change leaders.
- It provides the skills that are crucial to help managers transform from reactive to proactive.

GRASS ROOTS
LEADERS—THE
BRAINSMART
REVOLUTION IN
BUSINESS

180

EFFECTIVE PROACTIVE LEADERSHIP AND PROCESS ANALYSIS BEGINS WITH A CLEAR DEFINITION OF TERMS

In analyzing, and communicating about, work processes, people tend to become confused because they do not distinguish the differences between a *process*, a *subprocess*, an *activity* and a *task*. People often use these terms as though they were interchangeable. They are not.

Tasks

Tasks are the detailed steps that a person performs in transforming input into output. A task is the lowest level of a person's work action or behavior that can be studied, quantified or analyzed. For example, the tasks for a clerk who sets up appointments for the sales staff might include phoning a prospect, making an appointment, and entering the appointment date and time on a master schedule.

Activities

Related tasks are grouped into an activity (see Figure 10.1). An activity will normally include 15–20 tasks.

Each employee typically performs several activities as part of their day-to-day job.

Each activity involves transforming something that they receive from another employee or department (input) into something different that is sent on to someone else (output)—this could be anything from adding parts on an assembly line to entering information into a database. For example, a white-collar worker receives information from other functions (suppliers) and performs a series of tasks to convert the data into a meaningful analysis. The analysis (output) is then sent to an internal customer, who uses it to prepare a monthly financial report. Examples of activities for a salesperson include identifying and meeting with new clients, informing existing customers of a new product offering, or creating a monthly report reviewed by the vice president of sales summarizing client contacts.

Subprocesses

A subprocess is a grouping of several related activities that are part of a bigger process.

What is an activity?

Activity defined:

"A series of tasks which transform an input into an output."

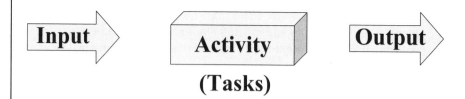

Figure 10.1　Definition of an activity

Link work activities into a process Flow to achieve maximum results

A process is defined as the organization of people, procedures, machines and materials into work activities sequenced to produce specified end results.

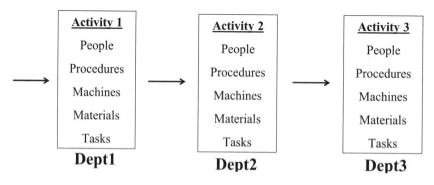

Figure 10.2　Process definition chart

GRASS ROOTS
LEADERS—THE
BRAINSMART
REVOLUTION IN
BUSINESS

182

Processes

Activities and subprocesses are linked together to form a process. A process involves linking or sequencing activities in an orderly fashion with the aim of creating some specified output for a defined set of customers (see Figure 10.2). Linking and sequencing are among the cortical skills of the human brain (see Chapter 4). There may be 30 or 40 processes going on at the same time in any company, performed by many different departments and people (see Figure 10.3).

Work processes and organizational structure typically have three levels

The organizational structure of nearly all companies involves three levels:

1   **Workers doing their daily jobs**—This is where tasks and activities are accomplished, at the Grass Roots level. There is often little understanding here of the processes that exist within the company, or how individuals' activities fit into each organizational process. Comments frequently heard here are, "I don't know where my work ultimately ends up; I just do what I'm told," or "It's not my job."

2   **Middle management**—Middle managers typically view work from the perspective of activities and subprocesses. Since middle managers are responsible for coordinating higher-level (process) views of work with lower-level (task) knowledge, to be successful they must understand tasks, activities and processes. They must also distinguish the difference between, "What is really happening" and "What is supposed to be happening." Comments frequently heard here are, "Do the top guys understand the impact of the change/project/effort they just asked me to make?", and "Do the front-line guys understand how much pressure we are under from the top guys to hit our target?"

3   **Senior management**—Top executives understand work at the process level, frequently having little or no knowledge of either activities or tasks. They create the ideal of what needs to happen. They must create a sense of direction and be grounded in reality to help them make critical resource decisions. A comment heard here is often, "Why is it so hard for our organization to be nimble and innovative? Do our managers and front-line employees understand that if we don't learn how to innovate, we will stop growing and our shareholders will demand a shakeup of the organization?"

In a crisis-driven system, the three levels are not aligned, leading to customer dissatisfaction and inefficient work activities.

In a proactive management system all three levels work together towards goals.

Much like the gears of a smooth-running machine, a process has a series of tight-fitting, interconnected parts

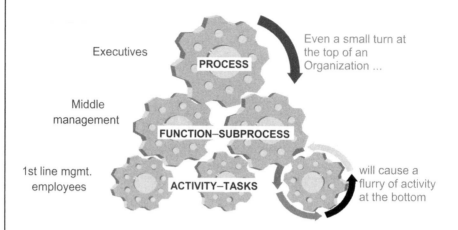

Executives

PROCESS

Even a small turn at the top of an Organization ...

Middle management

FUNCTION–SUBPROCESS

1st line mgmt. employees

ACTIVITY–TASKS

will cause a flurry of activity at the bottom

Figure 10.3   Gear chart

In a proactive organization, all three levels communicate using the same terms and make the same links and connections to the defined goals. When this occurs, company-wide agreement exists on how to prioritize resources to achieve these goals.

Executive (process) level

At the top level of the company, executives have a responsibility to set goals, direction and strategies—how to improve sales, invest capital, maintain happy customers—and then deciding what processes must be performed and what resources must be allocated to achieve them. They must see the big picture, the complete puzzle. A critical component of their effectiveness is resource allocation; the focus of the organization must be on driving improvement related to key strategic goals. However, executives frequently don't know the details of work that is performed at the Grass Roots level, and how executive decisions affect those workers. They must ensure that relevant information and knowledge is shared between appropriate people at all levels of the organization, so that informed decisions are made, taking into account the impact of those decisions.

Middle manager (activity/subprocess) level

Between the executives and staff are the middle managers, who frequently have the most difficult job in the organization. They must interpret decisions of the executives, translate them into activities and tasks, communicate them to the workers, and then confirm they are carried out properly. Interpretation can lead to pitfalls. In one company, the president and a director were talking in the cafeteria. The president expressed curiosity about maintenance figures in some of their service contracts. The director returned to his office and ordered his team to conduct a complete analysis of maintenance costs for the company's product line. When the report was sent to the president, the president called the director and asked what prompted the report. When the director said he ordered it as a result of their cafeteria conversation, the surprised president said that he had only been making idle conversation. He was not expecting a report that required two weeks' work.

Grass Roots (task/activity) level

At the Grass Roots level, employees often don't know how their work fits into the process. They don't know how it relates to the next person in the link. They don't know exactly what the consequences will be if their work contains errors, fails to be completed on time, or isn't it completed at all.

They don't know the overall goals and strategies of the company—they don't know what the completed puzzle, the big picture, should look like. It's not that they don't care; usually they are too focused on performing tasks to ask questions about matters that are not immediately relevant to their work. Unless an education program is initiated to transfer this knowledge, it can sometimes only be gained through years of experience and great costs to the company.

Companies that downsize often lose the experience of older workers. New employees spend a lot of time trying to learn about their pieces of the puzzle, so that they can understand how they contribute to the process. This often results in painful lessons, a greater unit cost per output, and a lower level of service.

One company suffered public embarrassment because a new employee didn't realize the importance of a particular piece of paper he handled. The employee took a printout from a computer and threw it on top of a pile of papers, then left for the day. The printout was the quarterly financial forecast that the president of the company was expecting to be on his desk the next morning. When it didn't arrive, the embarrassed president was unable to tell a number of Wall Street analysts the latest quarterly earnings. As this illustrates, a failure of communication can mean anything from a minor annoyance (in the case of the unwanted maintenance report) to the loss of public trust in a company's financial reporting (failure to send financial results to the company president). Employees' ability to paint word-pictures of their job activities paves the way for a review process that can help a company understand and measure the performance of that activity. This allows new links and associations to develop, leading to creative solutions to process problems. How do we take this thinking and use it to address the organizational issues, and how do we synthesize and bring together the diversity of opinion on a team?

"We are all connected to the bigger picture."

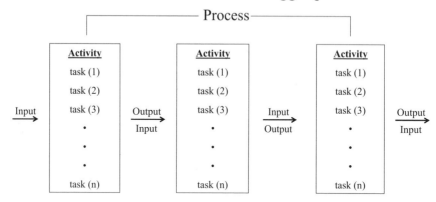

Figure 10.4   The bigger picture

BUILDING THE STORY—PERFORMING PROCESS ANALYSIS

Step 1: What are we doing?—create an activity list

The first step of bringing clear communications between the Grass Roots worker and the management team is to create an activity list. It represents a list of all the work that is currently being performed. The activity description should be as detailed as possible, and include both a noun and an action verb. A well-described activity allows an unfamiliar listener to form a clear mental picture of the work being performed. If the picture isn't crystal clear, the description isn't well-written.

After creating the activity list, add evaluative elements to each activity:

1   Estimate the potential for improvement, especially by improving activities that lead to errors or rework.
2   Gauge the effort needed to achieve the improvement: high, medium or low. For example, "high" could mean 6 people working full-time for 6 months; "medium" might mean 3 people working part-time for 3 months, "low" might mean 2 people working 2 hours a week for 2 months.
3   Identify whose approval you will need to make changes to the activity or tasks.
4   Estimate the time that will elapse before the actions produce benefits.

Step 2: How is this work really done—task analysis

The next step in the activity analysis process is to select an activity for task analysis. An ideal activity is one which has high potential for improvement, requires a small amount of time to achieve improvement, has a favorable approval authority and takes a short time to realize the benefits.

Performing a disciplined task analysis of current work allows the brain to see work as it is actually performed. From this picture, the brain questions why these steps are being performed in this sequence and manner, and may generate blanks which in turn lead to new sequencing. A detailed task analysis helps break workers out of "robot mode," where they are doing things by rote simply because that is the way they have always done them.

It becomes a critical step in the story line so managers totally understand how many steps are involved in doing a particular activity.

Step 2.1: How much time are we wasting—categorizing and prioritizing tasks

After listing all the tasks performed in the activity, the next step is to prioritize them based upon their importance, effort and nature. In evaluating the nature of tasks (why they are performed), we define them as falling into one of four categories:

- Required
- Failure
- Appraisal
- Preventive

Required tasks are those that are essential and/or mandatory. Even if we lived in a perfect world in which nobody ever made any mistakes, these tasks are necessary to transform an input into an output. An example would be filing paperwork with a government agency to demonstrate compliance with regulations.

Failure tasks are undertaken when something has gone wrong or a mistake has been made, resulting in the need for remedial action. With so much pressure on companies to reduce costs, this provides an excellent opportunity to eliminate expense and improve efficiency. Experience with the GRI program has shown that 25–30 per cent of staff time at the task level is spent doing something connected with adjusting, correcting, reworking or discarding work already done.

The most common reason for a failure task is an unclear or incorrect definition of a customer requirement. If the supplier of your information does not know the best format for you to receive input, you may receive input that requires

for improvement can be clearly articulated for each activity. Have the Grass Roots team relate each activity to customer requirements.

Grass Roots Tip
Proactive tips for task description:
- The detailed list should be drawn up in sequence to match the way the work is actually being performed.
- Ensure that all rework and corrective steps which are current tasks are included.
- Proactive tips for categorizing tasks:
  Normally, in the sequence of how tasks are performed a failure task will follow an appraisal.
- Prevention tasks maximize leverage to reduce failures.

Grass Roots Tip
More than a quarter of work done by employees involves correcting or adjusting for errors. Clearly,

BUILDING THE STORY

substantial rework on your part. If you do not have a clear definition of what *your* customer needs, you may be inadvertently supplying them with output that they need to be rework or discard. One example would be a new procedure that is put in place without clearly understanding the requirements of all the people who will have to implement it.

Grass Roots people become experts in knowing where time is wasted. It becomes a critical step in proactive management. What are the tasks that result in effort being wasted?

Appraisal tasks occur whenever there is a suspicion that mistakes are being made, or that output is not reliable enough to be sent without checking it first. An appraisal task involves inspecting or checking an output to sort good from bad. For example, if we prepare a letter, somebody might proofread it before we send it, or when somebody produces a financial report, before it is circulated somebody checks all the numbers against the accounting ledger. On average, 5–10 per cent of a company's costs are connected to appraisal tasks.

Preventive tasks are pre-emptive actions taken before an output has been created with the conscious aim of trying to avoid or prevent an error from being made.

Devoting resources to preventive tasks is more efficient and cost-effective than correcting mistakes after they have been made (see Figure 10.5). To implement a proactive management system, it is not enough to find and correct errors. It is equally important to identify the root source of errors, and make adjustments in tasks and activities to prevent similar errors from happening in the future.

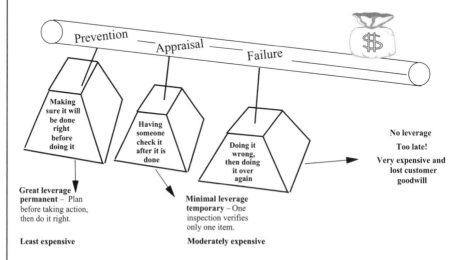

Figure 10.5   Moving from reactive to proactive—comparison of leverage for three types of task

Unfortunately, our experience indicates that very often *no* time is spent on preventive tasks—the organization is too busy fixing yesterday's problems. This is usually the first place where effort is reduced whenever resources become constrained.

As we learned in Chapter 6, the brain has an infinite capacity for generating new ideas. Learn to focus that ability to find ways to prevent problems, rather than spend effort finding ways to correct problems after they have occurred. This is not to imply that investing time in preventive tasks will be easy; if it was you would have already done so. In fact, you will temporarily *increase* your workload, since you will be correcting immediate errors at the same time you are adding steps to ensure that the errors won't happen again. Because of the increased workload required to do root cause analysis, the natural tendency is to concentrate on the fixes and neglect the preventive measures. If preventive actions don't lead to immediate improvements, they are frequently halted before the root causes of the failures are eliminated.

How people prioritize their activity list is critical to their long-term success. The goal of task analysis is to identify the tasks that offer the least added value to the activity. The best method for improving the efficiency of an activity is to eliminate failure tasks, and then minimize appraisal tasks. The use of Mind Maps is an excellent way to generate ideas at this stage.

Step 3: Why is this work important?—meeting with customers and suppliers

The next step in Activity Analysis is to obtain feedback on your activity and task list (the 'F' in TEFCAS—see Chapter 7). This may come from a manager or supervisor, the next person in the sequence, the previous person in the sequence (the supplier), or the person who receives the output from the worker (the customer). Feedback can also be obtained at a meeting in which several workers exchange ideas. You must decide what you will measure through this feedback, so that you can take appropriate action (see Figure 10.6).

The feedback will consider a number of factors involved in the process, including the cost to the company of implementing any solution, how long it would take to improve matters, and who in the company needs to approve any changes.

Meeting with your customers and suppliers to draw up a clear definition of requirements is the best way to eliminate failure tasks.

Measurements must be both thoughtful and identify immediate opportunities for improvement.

What will you measure and how will you use it?

Measurement means comparing outputs to user requirements

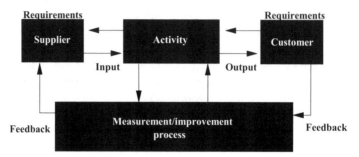

Taking action requires that your delivery system get feedback from your measurement system

Figure 10.6   Input/output feedback chart

Activity list

PART OF WHICH PROCESS: Nursing				✓ Noun ✓ Action Verb ✓ Specific ✓ Observable
GENERAL DESCRIPTION OF WORK YOU PERFORM WITHIN YOUR DEPARTMENT OR PROCESS (LISTING MAJOR OR ALL ACTIVITIES):	Y N	H M L	☺ ☺ ☺	1 mo. 3 mo. 1 yr.
Assess and review patient chart	Y	L	☺	1M
Implement doctor's medication orders	Y	L	☺	1M
Identify proper medication on discharge	Y	L	☺	1M
Complete patient charting paper and computer	Y	L	☺	1M
Gather equipment and supplies	Y	L	☺	2M

Y/N – Is there an opportunity for improvement in patient care?
H/M/L – What is the size of the effort needed to implement improvement
☺ ☺ ☹ - Is approval authority a happy, neutral or hostile person relative to this activity
1 mo (etc.) – Time before successful results realized

Figure 10.7   Example of an activity list

GRASS ROOTS
LEADERS—THE
BRAINSMART
REVOLUTION IN
BUSINESS

190

ENGAGING THE GRASS ROOTS TEAM

Activity Analysis begins when the team of participants creates a list of their daily work activities or those that are sequenced and are part of a process. Team members then select one from the list and perform a detailed task analysis with RPAF (required, failure, appraisal, preventive) times measured to pinpoint areas of improvement.

Participants are encouraged to start small—find an activity that can be immediately improved without a large time investment. As team members increase in confidence because of an initial success, they look for additional avenues for improvement. Figure 10.7 shows an example of an activity list from a nursing unit at a hospital.

Problems at the task-specific level are all too frequently compounded because of the failure to translate them into broader-based process management issues. This ultimately creates communications gaps, poor employee morale, inefficiency and additional process costs due to unnecessary spending. To help teams bridge this communication gap, Grass Roots Innovation (GRI) Workshops demonstrate how to use Mind Maps to organize thinking, structure the problem-solving process and improve communication in the brain blooming process.

Each team must agree on a key problem they are going to solve. The nursing team's tasks analysis of taking vital signs revealed that each time they performed this activity it takes 60 minutes, of which 30 minutes are spent in doing failure related tasks. Something isn't going right and they have to spend time adjusting. Because this failure task is done three times per shift, it is a constant source of stress and frustrations. Multiply the wasted effort of three failures per shift at 30 minutes per occurrence times the number of nurses in the unit and you get a large amount of unproductive time. This was identified as a key problem the team decided to tackle as their first Grass Roots project.

This picture of the problem is represented by the central image of a Mind Map. In the brain blooming process, each team member creates their own central image of the problem that needs to be solved; then the team combines the individual images into a central image for a team Mind Map. When a team cannot agree on a central image, this provides an early warning that they are not ready to produce meaningful results. It is revealing to compare the different perspectives that surface when team members compare their drawings. The communication that takes place while creating the central image for the Mind Map is powerful, and this common focal point is essential to generate creative solutions, and to build the team consensus necessary for implementation.

The main branches radiating from the central image are created for each of the elements of the definition of a process—people, procedures, machinery and materials. The branches are not added sequentially, but are completed randomly by team members as their search for the cause of the problem triggers ideas. Mind Mapping gives a team a clear vision of their goals. It requires the team to consider the entire problem by providing an overall picture. Once the team has agreed on a central image, the branches help them organize thoughts in a logical manner, and allow them to see the interdependence of the elements.

The process of creating the central image shows the team how individual members look at a problem in a unique way, and each unique perspective is integrated into the whole. The insights gained from the Mind Map help team members bridge communication gaps that exist between staff and executives. The pictures and branches make it easy for anyone unfamiliar with the day-to-day details to understand the whole problem and provide assistance.

In one phase of the workshop, the Mind Map created by the team showed team members that they could achieve a saving of 30 minutes per day simply by changing the sequence of tasks involved in performing the activity.

CREATIVE PROCESS IDEAS COME IN SMALL STEPS

It is wise to remember that important advances do not usually occur through large, unexpected jumps, but result from the clarity of the goal and the amount of time spent generating creative ideas. For this reason, to maximize team creativity, don't cut short the Mind Mapping brain-blooming session, either individually or in a group. The most common reason for failure to develop breakthrough ideas is that the group switches too quickly from generating ideas to evaluating them. Although this seems obvious, it happens all the time.

The additional time and effort spent by an individual or a group after they first believe they are out of ideas greatly increases the probability that an unrelated outside stimulus will trigger an insight—an "A-ha!"

Creative thinking is a repetitive process. The best way to increase creativity is to increase the number of small refinements that are made in each idea generated. This leads to increasingly innovative ideas.

At the beginning of a group attempt at finding solutions, the team must *decide* to be creative. Some people may have trouble with this concept—they don't understand how one can "decide" to be creative. Too many people think that you are either creative, or you're not. But creativity is an act of will. If you decide to be creative, you will discover, perhaps to your surprise, that you become creative. Why is that true?

GRASS ROOTS
LEADERS—THE
BRAINSMART
REVOLUTION IN
BUSINESS

192

Many people become less creative as they become more successful because there is greater personal risk in challenging the status quo by deviating from strategies that succeeded in the past. Their energy becomes focused on playing not to lose, instead of creating new ideas. Rather than working to generate new links and associations, their time is spent criticizing other ideas, explaining why "that just won't work."

It is an ironic twist, because experience and memory play a critical role in the creative process. They are the starting points to which new ideas are linked, associated and connected. The same experience that makes it easy to shoot down new ideas also enables a creative thinker to generate innovative new ideas. The mindset is crucial; it determines whether time spent generating solutions will be fruitful or barren.

As discussed in Chapter 7, in a group environment, the combined experience of all individuals present can exponentially increase the number of creative ideas brought forth. A group will ideally consist of both "left-brain" dominant people—those with strong analytical, logical, numerical and verbal skills—and "right-brain" dominant people—those who are imaginative, intuitive and have good visualization skills. A well-balanced team also has people with a combination of extensive experience and limited experience, and a broad cross-section of functional/technical skills.

Sandy Hahn of IBM recognized this when she put together a team that was charged with simplifying the international tax reconciliation process while also increasing customer satisfaction. Hahn identified the strongest cortical skills within each team member, and harnessed their diverse backgrounds to generate creativity and innovation. At the completion of the project, Hahn's team exceeded all existing performance targets and attained all its goals—a zero backlog of tax reconciliations, 100 per cent attainment of settlements, and customer satisfaction scores of better than 90 per cent.

A rich diversity of experience and attitude can create a synergy which makes the group a fountain of creative ideas. If poorly managed, however, the diversity becomes divisive, with the group arguing over whose viewpoint is "right." This is most likely to occur when a team has a diversity of opinion about guiding principles, such as moral beliefs or ethics systems.

PROACTIVE LEADERSHIP MEETS GRASS ROOTS TEAMWORK

Paul Casey, a senior manager whose Grass Roots teams attended a Grass Roots workshop, understands the value of process innovation, teams and Mind Maps. In particular, he believes in the value of studying tasks at the granular level:

By "granular" I mean something that is at the very lowest level of a process. For example, in making a phone call, the steps are: first you think about it, then you look up the number, then you put your finger on the button of the phone, and so on. We trained people to think at a detailed level about what they were doing.

In an effective process analysis effort, Casey notes that employees learned to work in a team environment:

After identifying failure tasks, we put action plans in place—names, dates, steps, places that we would use to put a fix in. We tracked savings from the changes. The savings were usually in terms of hours. We generated a lot of savings because of the reduction of hours in particular processes. You can then take those hours and use them for whatever you want—reduction of overtime, freeing people up for other projects, freeing people up to do other parts of their job.

Casey reports that one particular change saved 93 hours a month:

Through the process work, we got people to think literally about what they were doing—not to make assumptions about what they thought they were doing.

But Casey's words say more than might be apparent at first glance. They reflect his application of Brain Principles and the proactive management system techniques discussed in this book. He has helped his employees tap the enormous potential of the human brain to become more effective and to help create a more efficient, competitive operation.

In short: "We get people to think. Could a company—could a manager—ask for anything more?"

Casey was working with an accounting group within the company when he participated in a three-Grass Roots workshop—a workshop that changed his organization.

Management wanted to find out where resources were *actually* being expended, rather than where the management team *thought* they were—this difference between perception and reality is called the "Gap." The results highlighted the need for improvement and suggested some new directions for this 500-person organisation. Casey said:

We have experienced that all business can be helped by process analysis, but that such analysis is absolutely critical in organizations where there has been substantial personnel turnover, downsizing, changes in executive leadership, and changes in information systems, all of which were happening at the company. Management wanted to avoid the common fad of "business change through buzzwords." Instead, we chose to teach people skills which they could use immediately on their jobs to solve problems that they were experiencing. Two aspects of the program particularly intrigued me. The first was being able to quantify dollar savings from specific process improvements. The second was learning a powerful tool—Mind Mapping.

GRASS ROOTS
LEADERS—THE
BRAINSMART
REVOLUTION IN
BUSINESS

194

During the workshop, participants worked on actual failures related to their jobs, using Mind Maps to help identify the root cause of those failures and to generate solutions.

The workshop included five teams of five persons each. Some teams were composed of workers from only one department; others were made up of workers from several departments.

Casey's team's first problem was caused by incomplete data records that were transmitted to the payment system's database from many different sources. Each data record contained the sale price and product numbers from a specific sale. However, certain items were often missing. The defective records were either rejected from the automatic processing routine or "suspended." The aggregate dollar amount due to each vendor was calculated accurately, but fixing the suspended records to arrive at the correct payment was very labor-intensive.

The team drew up a Mind Map starting with the "suspend" report as its central image. They drew branches representing the input for the company's geographical regions, the system used to process the data, the processing analysts, and the contract between the company and the software vendor. When the Mind Map was complete, it was obvious that the problem activity could be traced to one specific source. With the root cause of the problem determined, a solution could be devised.

The action plan involved working with programmers to develop a routine that would compare the data from the problem source with data containing information on installation dates. Defective data would be immediately detected and modified. The net result was a large reduction in the staff time required for the comparison process.

The Mind Map allowed everyone to see the big picture. When the components of the process were seen together, the failure point became obvious to everyone. The Mind Map in this instance was not complex, but it enabled the team to identify the problem immediately. Many other Mind Maps were subsequently used on other processes.

The workshop was intended to provide employees with new tools and help them learn to work as a team. It achieved those goals, plus additional benefits. The number of worker-hours saved was measurable—and substantial. Resources could be managed more efficiently, and overtime decreased. The workshops continued, and the program expanded into other areas of the company. Casey said:

> I believe in the power of teams, Mind Maps, and Activity Analysis, because the results are irrefutable. These are powerful tools for employees in their jobs, careers and even their personal lives.

CONCLUSION

Organizations have been extremely successful at harnessing the energy and creativity that comes from Grass Roots teams using process analysis skills in a proactive management system. Mind Maps and other tools developed through an understanding of how the brain works bring a new level of thinking to daily work actions.

WHAT'S NEXT?

This chapter provided the last piece to the big picture of a Grass Roots Revolution. In the final chapter all the pieces are sequenced into a workshop that has consistently produced excellent results, The Three Day Miracle.

The chapter is closed with lessons for leadership and the answer to Anne Kelly's question to finding a method that is sustainable in changing a culture.

ACTIVITIES

1a. List six activities that you perform as part of your current job. An activity must contain an action verb and an object noun so that the reader would clearly picture the physical action in which you are engaged. For example, an activity could be "I am processing (action verb) a customer order (noun) into the scheduling system."

1b In looking at your activity list, note if there are any activities which are 50 per cent or more related to working on failures/ corrections/ errors.

2 Show your activity list to another person and ask them to describe back to you their understanding of your activities.

3 Meet with a customer (internal or external) on an activity and ask them how they use the output of the activity.

4 Take an activity from Exercise 1a and construct a Mind Map showing the reasons for any failure task that may exist within it.

5 List all the benefits you have realized from conducting the exercise to this stage.

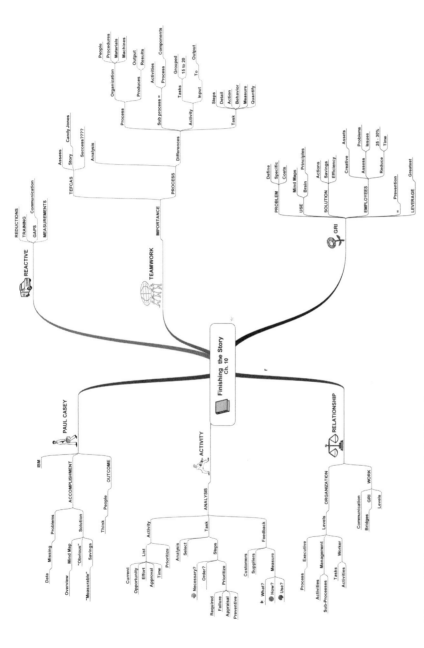

Figure 10.8   Mind Map—finishing the story

The 3 Day Miracle— Finishing the Story

OVERVIEW

Now that the authors have examined many of the latest advances in our understanding of how the brain works, and shown how that understanding can help us be more efficient and effective in our daily lives, this chapter will show how all that information has been integrated into a comprehensive program that helps Grass Roots employees achieve remarkable results.

This is the method behind the Grass Roots profiles in each chapter of this book. You will see the outcomes of the work that Anne Kelly led at Station 11 and answer her most important question, **Can this be sustainable?**

THE STORY ON DAY 1...

A unit of 24 nurses, many of whom had expressed their intention to resign in the near future, attended a Grass Roots Innovation (GRI) Workshop. They came to the workshop feeling extremely skeptical, convinced that things at the hospital would never change.

From their perspective, things could not get much worse. Unplanned absences were rampant, turnover had reached an all time high and morale was at the lowest in the company's history. No one wanted to join the nursing unit, and current staff were leaving for opportunities outside the hospital. Paperwork was overwhelming; equipment was not always available for the nurses to perform their job and nurses regularly skipped lunch and dinner to deliver quality care. Because of pressure to keep costs within budget, overtime was not allowed, so many of the staff clocked out and returned to complete patient charting on their own time.

Mary, the Chief Nursing Officer (CNO), for this organization realized the situation had reached a critical point, and had scheduled the Grass Roots workshop.

At the opening session, she experienced a group of angry, frustrated, stressed and unhappy employees. Mary had no idea what to expect when she returned for Day 3 but viewed the workshop as their last hope.

DAY 2—THE TEAMS SHIFT TO 3RD GEAR

In the workshop, the nursing unit felt that they had permission to bring their experience, intuition and creative ideas to the problems they faced.

They broke into four GRI teams and each team began using what they had learned to create a business vocabulary that helped them speak and listen to each other in a new way. The walls and barriers were suddenly taken away.

The usual 1st Gear (right/wrong, good/bad, possible/impossible) and 2nd Gear (bottom line, competition and power-politics) rules and mindsets were gone. In 3rd Gear they were now a team which was focused on making their workplace more effective, efficient and outcome oriented.

As the workshop generated new knowledge their brains created new links and associations. Each team experienced their "Eurekas and Ahas" and identified creative ways to use Grass Roots tools to improve their lives and the lives of those they worked with and served.

By the end of the second day, each team had a defined achievable goal, a timetable, a plan and the tools needed to achieve it. Each group developed camaraderie and enthusiasm, and recognized that this was just the beginning. A new door had opened. The issues once viewed as problems were now seen as opportunities. The teams had the power to communicate openly with each other, to understand the whole picture and to create solutions that benefited their patients and the organization. The nurses were excited because they now felt that they could provide the best patient care possible.

DAY 3—WERE THESE THE SAME PEOPLE?

When the CNO returned on the last day to hear the team presentations, she was stunned. The hostility, negativity and stress had disappeared. The participants were excited, creative and determined to make a difference. Their presentation provided practical solutions to intractable problems. Their plans were actionable and achievable.

Mary smiled as she rose to speak to the GRI teams. What she saw had far exceeded her most optimistic expectations. She thanked them for their effort and persistence. Mary promised unflinching support for their projects, and an open door whenever her assistance would be useful.

The CNO wrapped up the session by saying,

> *I have just witnessed a 3 DAY MIRACLE. Your energy, passion, and enthusiasm are contagious as a leader, I am committed to supporting the plans you have presented. Your ideas will make a significant difference in hospital operations and provide improved service levels for our patients. I will be proud to champion the change.*

Does this seem like a unique situation? No, the fact is the "Three Day Miracle" is happening over and over. It can take place in your organization too. The Miracle is simply the power of shifting into 3rd Gear to think of creative ways to do business successfully and profitably.

SUCCESSFUL GRASS ROOTS STRATEGY

A successful Grass Roots Innovation Workshop uses time-tested process analytical methods and cognitive science research that have been introduced in the first 10 chapters, to inspire new pathways of thinking among managers and employees. This workshop will reduce the 25–30 per cent of time employees spend making adjustments and correcting errors. After "funding the bubble" (Chapter 2), the savings are reinvested to sustain the momentum for shifting from Reactive Management to Proactive Leadership.

By raising relevant questions, Grass Roots employees find their own solutions and develop action plans with metrics to track progress. Their Grass Roots leadership skills are enhanced by making presentations to the executive/management team to establish commitment and buy-in across all levels.

The objective of the GRI workshop is to generate enthusiasm and passion focused on:

1 Building stronger and more trusting relationships.
2 Creating a common language which enhances the integrity of communications across all levels.
3 Utilizing the inherent creativity of the Grass Roots workers to meet organizational goals.
4 Developing leadership skills which lead to producing measurable and sustainable results.

One of the key features of a GRI workshop is that it uses participants' own work situations as the vehicle for applying new skills and creating change. Employees learn a set of analytical skills and tools that enable them to size up business issues and look for the opportunities to make continuous innovation the standard. These tools turn employees into creative assets of the company.

GRI FUNDAMENTALS

The GRI program uses a blend of theoretical and practical knowledge to drive long-term results. Tony Dottino suggests that the selected teams should have a diversity of functional skills, which include finance, human resources, organizational development and process leadership.

A GRI champion, for instance, Anne Kelly, becomes knowledgeable about the large pool of research available on the human brain, and is focused on finding practical business applications. GRI implementation grounded in the findings of brain research will lead to sustainable change.

Dottino has found that an effective GRI workshop must be pragmatic, and the instructors not lecture, give answers or provide solutions. They need to understand and be able to use all three gears of Success and Leadership. Since people are being encouraged to think, leaders need to be able to shift into 3rd Gear to support employees as they explore new pathways of thinking. This requires new lessons and actions for GRI leaders and their GRI team members, and buy-in is critical for achieving new attitudes and expectations of behavior.

The leadership team must understand that Grass Roots and leadership thinking is constantly shifting up and down. In 1st Gear, it is rule and safety oriented. In 2nd Gear, it is production, time and profit oriented. Only in 3rd Gear is creative, problem-solving thinking encouraged and supported. Like the CNO in this case above, it is the leader's primary responsibility to create focus on creating the right outcomes.

When leaders shift into Gear 3 and synchronize the targets with "moments of new insight," there is an energizing experience that overcomes the old forces of resistance. Since people's emotions are so critical to long-term success, their gear-shifting understanding facilitates change and innovation.

An executive sponsor of a GRI program drives the development of a compelling vision and fully utilizes his team's creative ability by reaching down to his employees to gain commitment and alignment. This creates a bubbling up from employees who are fully engaged and passionate about meeting the organization's vision and achieving its goals.

DEVELOPING LEADERS THROUGH GRASS ROOTS INNOVATION—WHAT HAPPENS EACH DAY

Workshop overview

The most effective way to introduce a GRI Workshop is for managers to group between 20 and 25 employees into four or five work-related teams.

The workshop uses the materials the authors have covered in this book to create process innovation breakthroughs. Interactive exercises are provided to maximize the impact of both individual and team cohesiveness. Executive/management must be involved during sections of the workshops (kickoff, presentations and wrap-up), and participants must know why they were selected and what the reason is for attending the session.

To provide you with a better perspective of how the material in this book is integrated into the GRI workshop Tony Dottino has provided a high level breakdown of the various activities that take place each day. The respective chapters are noted by section.

Day 1

8.00—8.30 a.m.
Executive sponsor kicks off session:

Chapter 8

- Shares challenges
- Obtains group perspective of challenges and feedback
- Explains to attendees how and why they were selected to attend
- Sets expectations of workshop

Creating a consistent message

Debbie Hunt of the Florida Department of Transportation has a passion for her Grass Roots employees.

Hunt is the Director of Transportation Operations for District One in Central and Southwest Florida. Though her office is located in Bartow, she spends much of her time at satellite locations around the district. It is not unusual to dial her cell phone at 7.30 p.m. and find her in the middle of a 2-hour drive home.

Debbie learned about Grass Roots from a presentation Anne Kelly gave at a Leadership Conference. She had always been a strong proponent of leadership education, but timing is everything. She was at the point where she knew if her team was to continue achieving its goals, she needed to provide the tools to improve analytical and interpersonal skills of her Grass Roots employees, including their ability to communicate at a higher level.

Though her employees have varying levels of education, Debbie has faith in their ability to help fix many of the problems the Florida Department of Transportation faces. She realizes there is value in the organization utilizing employees' knowledge and skills gained through years of hands-on experience. A majority of them have worked there more than 20 years. If she could find some tools to help them improve communications with management, they could become an integral part of the decision-making process.

The employees know where the problems are. If they could trust that they would get support from their local management team, they could increase productivity and the quality of work. Grass Roots Innovation seemed like a perfect fit.

To start a Grass Roots Revolution, Debbie believed management needed to learn the tools and serve as a model in using them. No one could begin this process better than Debbie herself. At the first Grass Roots session she wanted to provide clear communication which would remain consistent over time. To help her do this, she created a Mind Map of her vision for this initiative. Her main branches explained why she feels Grass Roots innovation is important, what its value would be to each employee and to the organization, what they could expect in return for their commitment, and the long term returns she is expecting.

Debbie has just begun the journey with her Grass Roots teams and with her leadership, District One Operations will set the standard for others to follow.

8.30—9.30 a.m.
Exercise—Reactive vs Proactive

Chapters 1 and 2

An assessment of existing management system is done by attendees that is used to establish the baseline of progress.
- Answer the question: "Does management provide the time and resources when a problem occurs to investigate the source and provide the necessary resources to permanently modify the process? If not, what does this cost?"

Result:
Momentum is generated to move towards a Proactive system by gaining each participant's "buy-in" and commitment. In a Proactive system, time is invested to understand why problems occur. Accountability is given to the Grass Roots level to discover the root cause of problems so the team can take corrective action at the source.

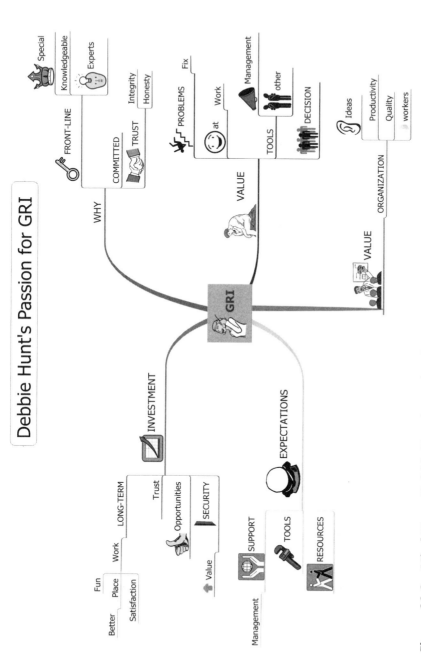

Debbie Hunt's Passion for GRI

Figure 11.1 Mind Map—Debbie Hunt's passion for GRI

THE 3 DAY
MIRACLE

9.45 a.m—3.00 p.m.
So What?
Chapters 3–6

Most of the first day is spent sharing cognitive science lessons focused on teamwork, communications, creativity, and building trust and confidence so that each participant can become a leader of change. At the end of each cognitive science module, we do the "SO WHAT?" exercise to spur the participants to link the theory to practical applications.

Exercise for each chapter

So what does this information/research mean? What does it provide to improve relationships, teamwork, communications and creativity? What change in actions does this trigger as it relates to customers/clients?

Result:
New thinking and perspectives about relationships, creativity, communications, teamwork and Grass Roots Leadership are inspired. A process for employees to communicate with candor and focus is established and practiced. These topics are related to the participant's ability to solve problems and innovate.

3.15 p.m—5.00 p.m.
Feedback is Lifeline
Chapter 7

There are several role plays that utilize the process for giving and receiving feedback, so leaders and employees know what work needs to be done to build trust and integrity in communications.

Result:
A process is established for spontaneous communications which are candid and focused on outcomes. An environment is built that recognizes FEEDBACK is the "LIFELINE TO SUCCESS."

RESULTS, DAY 1:
New behavior is created to foster a safe environment that encourages "straight talk" within the organization. Stronger team relationships and respect for diversity of experiences and perspectives are built. New mental maps are developed which initiate a change in attitude and behavior that generates an energy surge. This enables the team to maximize inherent skills when creating innovative action plans in solving work issues.

GRASS ROOTS STORY—WHO ME?

Joe, a maintenance worker for a state Department of Transportation for 22 years, was a member of a road crew team that attended a Grass Roots Workshop. His team was able to identify five activities that could be improved.

Initially they addressed the problem of responding to late-night emergencies. Since they have more than 250 of them per year, it was an issue that needed attention.

Upon receipt of an emergency call, three workers would report to the yard and do what was necessary to respond. A task analysis revealed that it was taking 25 minutes longer than necessary because keys and equipment were not left in proper places at end of the day shift, and trucks were often left with only partially filled gas tanks.

Their Mind Map pointed to two major problems which could be quickly solved. The first problem stemmed from the fact that operators had their favorite vehicles for work everyday; and many times at the end of their shift they just forgot to put keys on the key rack. Joe's Grass Roots team did an inventory of the key rack and measured the percentage of missing keys by vehicle each day. The truck log would allow them to trace this back to individuals.

The second problem involved the unfueled trucks. To solve it, they created a check-list which tracked the number and driver of trucks not fueled at the end of day.

The team shared their project goal—reducing the time it took to respond to emergencies—at the weekly yard meeting and showed the initial metrics for each. They explained that if a particular truck was needed, in addition to searching for keys, the night crew needed to stop at the gas pumps to fuel. This combination cost 25 minutes for each occurrence. Additional time would be wasted obtaining needed tools and supplies.

With everyone's help the team felt they could totally eliminate the extra time and be able to arrive, get keys, materials and a truck with a full tank of gas. Their measurements helped them to focus on workers who had the poorest memories of proper protocols. Where necessary, Joe's team members used a bit of persuasion and met one on one with individuals to achieve personal commitments in complying with procedures.

In 6 weeks they had taken missing keys from 35 per cent compliance to 100 per cent and trucks not fueled from 60 per cent to 0 per cent. Bottom line, the emergency crew leaves the yard 25 minutes faster. Everyone knew their responsibility and was holding each other accountable to follow the process.

Workers who had not spoken to each other in years were beginning to communicate to achieve a common goal.

Joe was then asked to take this story and share it with two other DOT yards. He did so with tremendous energy and enthusiasm, which helped those locations improve their operations.

He was presenting the results of his Grass Roots teams success to a number of executives when he mentioned this was the first time in 22 years that his ideas for making changes were valued. He had never been asked to make a management presentation. The fact he was then asked to visit two other yards and share his team's actions to fix this system-wide problem was beyond anything he had previously imagined.

At first he was nervous, and worried about how he was going to do this and not look like a bundle of nerves. But with Grass Roots workers, miracles happen. Joe did a great job in sharing the lessons he had learned with his peers, and built his confidence and presentations skills. This led to improvements in their operations which are helping the whole DOT system be much more efficient.

But wait, the story continues. Not only has Joe brought these new-found skills to work everyday, but he has taken them back to his personal life. He is currently working with a theater group and is on stage in front of hundreds of people.

Joe's message to his peers at the other DOT locations:

> *I never thought I was good enough to talk in front of people or share my ideas. I was shaking the first time I had to get up, but this GRI workshop gave me the skills, tools and confidence to do it. The whole experience is a miracle. I was totally skeptical in coming to the workshop. If you had told me prior to the workshop that I would be doing what I am now doing, I never would have come. This has transformed my life and made me both a more effective employee and a better human being.*

Joe is an excellent example of an organization utilizing the assets available to it.

Day 2

The fundamentals of process analysis are integrated with Day 1 lessons.

We learned in Chapter 7 about the advantages of applying the TEFCAS model to our own work. We will now apply this approach to the work of the company as a whole, and to its processes.

You will remember that TEFCAS is an approach to working at maximum efficiency. TEFCAS stands for Try-all, Event, Feedback, Check, Adjust and Success. We started our discussion of TEFCAS with the final letter, "S," which stands for Success in achieving a goal.

Here we'll let "S" represent the end product or service that will be provided to the customer. If we view it that way, it's immediately clear that for the whole process to work optimally, every employee should know what the customer's requirements are—every employee, from trainees to top executives.

In too many companies, however, most employees have only a vague idea of how their work really fits into the big picture. As a result, much of the work that they do is misdirected and inefficient. Since the brain craves completeness, it strives to fill in any knowledge gaps (blanks) with assumptions, as we learned in Chapter 6. Unfortunately, those assumptions can be very far off the mark. When you hear people saying things like "I think ...," "I believe ...," "I assume ...," you know they are just filling in the blanks. If they were confident that had a complete, accurate picture, they would instead be saying, "I know ...." If they did know, they would be able to add detail to enrich the picture, as happens in teams working with Mind Maps.

8.00 a.m.—5.00 p.m.
Exercises—The Importance of The Teams' "S."

Chapters 6 and 7
Create various analysis
described in Chapter 10   Each Grass Roots team:

- Selects a real life work project for improvement and explains how it will help team reach the company's "BIG S."
- Follows sequence in Chapter 10
- Identifies the value created for the customer; and the approach for keeping current.
- Defines the critical questions that must be answered to have a clear focus of what's important to the customer.

Result:
A common language is established to break down complex work assignments into definable pieces that can be managed by Grass Roots teams. Participants learn to think and recognize all three gears of problems and solutions.

RESULT, DAY 2:
An analysis is completed that: 1) lists specific activities that need improvement; 2) measures the amount of waste within the activity selected; 3) identifies the root causes of the inefficiences; 4) relates the activity to enhancing customer value and reaching company goals.

A shared commitment is made that creates a mind shift from "MY JOB" to "OUR CUSTOMERS" focused on creating better outcomes for the customer.

GRASS ROOTS STORY—NURSE PRACTICE COUNCIL

They began the workshop with Sue Eager's opening remark, "This workshop better be worth giving up shift premium overtime" and left with a plan. Today, their results are being recognized at the National Level.

Cindee Jones, Chair of the Nurse Practice Council, Linda Taylor, Susan Ricket, Jean Morrison and Sue Eager are Registered Nurses in the Cardio Vascular Intensive Care Unit at Florida Hospital in Orlando. They are highly skilled critical care nurses who went through a lot of specialized training to get to where they are. Their unit has beds for 30 patients.

They are members of the Nursing Practice Council (NPC) a group which works to share decision making among all nursing staff that are involved in patient care. The Chief Nursing Officer doesn't simply dictate, but gets inputs from the nurses working directly with the patients, for they are most aware of what is actually going on.

The nurses came to GRI a bit skeptical but excited about the possibility of being empowered. Eager to learn new skills to put their ideas into action, but wanting to know that their time would be invested wisely.

They learned to take small steps, build momentum, analyze work activities, gain experience in presenting to management and peers, and strengthened their team. Empowerment and success were just a few months away.

The first project was something they had previously worked on but hadn't successfully accomplished.

The problem involved the time it took to review the Kardex (paperwork) for every patient when shifts changed. It took a lot of time for every patient, and only about 10 per cent was immediately useful. That raised overtime costs.

The nurses decided to modify the Kardex System which involved nurse to nurse communication, nurse to doctor communication and nurse to family communication. They redesigned the form, taking into account everything about the patient's hospitalization—his past history, doctors' orders, proper medication and so on, and integrated all this information into a plan of care.

The skills learned in the workshop enabled them to sell their ideas to the unit nurses. Rather than go back to their unit and mandate, they learned how to unify everyone to the units goals, then test several alternatives and collect the metrics to make their case.

The new Kardex was set up to be read easily and quickly. The change reduced the time it took nurses at change of shift to gather the critical information needed to ensure a smooth transition in patient care. Instead of taking 20 minutes for every patient, the nurses were able to do it in 5 minutes. And did it without compromising patient care. In fact it allowed the nurses to spend more time with each patient and reduce overtime by 10 per cent.

Another problem involved broken and missing cables for monitoring equipment. Cables that connected to monitors could get broken or lost when the monitoring equipment was set up for a new patient. That meant the nurses could spend up to 45 minutes or more to get all the necessary cables arranged. The teams came up with an innovative way to secure the cables so they couldn't be pulled from monitors.

Sue Eager took the problem home to her dad. He created a device, the Eager Lock, that would secure the cables to a monitor, thus eliminating the problem of missing cables and reducing the cost for replacement cables at $50–$200 each.

The teams successes have been shared with other hospital locations and their proposal to present has been accepted at the National Teaching Institute for their annual conference that is attended by more than 6K people from all over the United States.

What does this team want for all this success? Cindee Jones puts in best, "We wanted the administration to fully appreciate the skills and professionalism of the unit nurses!"

Day 3

8.00—11.30 a.m.
Putting It All Together
Chapters 1–3
Exercise   Action plans, metrics for tracking progress
                                and the benefits to meeting the organization's
                                goals are developed.

12.30—5.00 p.m.
Presentations delivered
Chapter 9

Presentations are made to the management team to:

- Have managers learn about issues important to their Grass Roots teams
- Obtain management inputs and feedback
- Confirm benefits of team projects
- Gain management commitment to help teams in their implementation if needed

Result:
Each group has an energy and enthusiasm which can be felt as they make their presentations. An assessment of GRI skills and executive support is made to evaluate the ability to sustain behaviors for creating permanent change in the way work is accomplished.

RESULTS, DAY 3:
Build confidence of Grass Roots teams that "they can make a difference."

GRASS ROOTS STORY—THE TURTLE AND THE STICK

Jim Snook was a supervisor of an overhead construction team for Con Edison's Brooklyn location when he and a team of union and management employees attended a Grass Roots workshop.

Though you may see construction workers on a regular basis, most people notice them when they are climbing poles after a storm. They are the Grass Roots workers fixing power lines and making sure your electricity is working.

At the initial workshop his team made a memorable presentation using the principles we have written about in this book that begins to answer Anne Kelly's question about the GRI tools and skills being utilized over and over.

1 KV GLOVES

The 1 KV glove project was the Grass Root team's first win in getting management to hear what the workers were saying. The task was to convince upper management and the safety department that the use of 1 KV gloves was safe and beneficial to the company and the union employees. These are the gloves they wear to protect themselves from electrical shocks and the higher the number, the thicker, bigger, less flexible and more insulated the gloves.

GRASS ROOTS
LEADERS—THE
BRAINSMART
REVOLUTION IN
BUSINESS

212

The company policy was that overhead workers had to use 15 KV gloves to work on live secondary (110v) wires in confined spaces like homes and not the smaller, lighter more flexible 1 KV gloves. When a worker was on a pole they had to wear the 15KV gloves for safety. When a worker would leave the pole and enter into a residence to work in a confined area, the 15KV gloves were cumbersome. But at the time, the safety committee was concerned that if the workers changed to the lighter 1 KV gloves, they would not stop to change to the heavier ones after they left the residence to go back to the pole.

That problem is what this team decided to tackle as their first project.

At the Grass Roots workshop, the team identified the best approach to get the executives and managers who would be attending the workshop to hear and see what was happening. A demonstration would do it, so they created a mock customer installation in the classroom, got a pair of 15 KV gloves and invited the management team to put on the gloves and work with the wiring. If safety wasn't such a concern the management demo would have been hilarious.

The team was able to make their point without compromising employee safety and then link their results to being more productive by using the 1 KV gloves. They met with the safety committee after the workshop and were able to convince them that the line workers would actually be safer by having both 1KV and 15KV gloves on the truck. Until this point, safety didn't trust the employees to be using both.

This win energized the team and when they realized that management was willing to listen to their ideas, they took off like a rocket. Their manager, Rich Bagwell, gave them the time to meet regularly, and over the course of 18 months they took on more than 17 Grass Roots projects that helped their territory improve.

They were able to change ground cables from 8' to 12' and meet OSHA standards. This helped to reduce lost time cutting and rolling cables saving more than $80k per year. Another project helped reduce injuries due to linemen climbing new poles that were much harder and more difficult to climb, thus saving more than $40k in related time off. The team found a better naileater bit that would penetrate poles more efficiently, saving several thousand dollars on supplies.

Each of their projects had dollar savings and productivity improvements. But most important was the impact on relationships between union workers and management. Since the improvements benefited the workers and made the company more efficient, the team had everyone working toward the same goal.

But it was the roadblocks and how they learned to deal with them that made each successive project easier to accomplish.

Two no's

The team had discovered that the first two times they presented their idea to someone, they would always hear NO, it's not going to work. Their lesson, listen to the feedback and objections, analyze them and correct for issues brought up, the second time the NO will be softer. The third time, it will be YES!

The cork in the bottle

When no clear flow of information from top to bottom or vice versa exists, it creates ill informed managers and employees who show no initiative, direction or ability to solve common problems. Their lesson, always get the facts from the source before finalizing decisions. Otherwise you risk making assumptions that may only make matters worse.

The customer loses—open communication

Customer service and the line operations communications are critical to achieving system wide success. If solutions are found in one area and aren't shared, then the customers of the whole system lose out. Find a way to share your region's problems with others that have the same issue. Make communications a priority or the company loses, that means employees, stockholders, managers and the customer.

The turtle and the stick

The TURTLE AND THE STICK is an analogy the team used to bring management and union employees together. When management resorts to harsh treatment of union employees, workers turn into TURTLES, pull in their arms and legs and let you beat on their hardened shell. This type of management only ends up causing a stalemate where there are "NO WINNERS."

Their advice, leadership should continue working towards a more collaborative environment to create "WIN-WIN" situations. Results where union and management gain something means stockholders, executives and the customers all benefit.

Jim summarizes the workshop in the following comment, "The workshop has given us the skills and tools that create the reality of teamwork—management and union members working together as equals to find the best solutions to the problems we face."

Results of the 3 Day Miracle: The process they have followed allows them to integrate the lessons on teamwork, communication, gear shifting and creativity to transform workers into leaders of a real change effort.

GRASS ROOTS
LEADERS—THE
BRAINSMART
REVOLUTION IN
BUSINESS

214

A high performance, three-gear culture is being established, with empowered managers and employees who can now unleash the full potential of their thinking to solve problems and generate innovative solutions.

FROM INNOVATION TO REVOLUTION

Leadership fundamentals for a BrainSmart Revolution

1　Executives and managers are aligned to organizational goals.
2　The team is committed to proactive leadership.
3　Conversations have integrity of information, and there is no retaliation for speaking the truth.
4　Leadership invests their time listening, coaching and supporting Grass Roots teams. In other words, Leadership "shows up."
5　Teams publicly make commitments to improve processes, and management makes commitments to support the teams in any way necessary to ensure success.
6　Benchmarks are established to measure progress towards GRI team commitments.
7　Everyone is held accountable for their commitments.

As Tony Dottino listens to the team presentations at the follow-up session, he analyzes their results to see what lessons made a difference in sustaining the revolution. He uses the Brain Principles as the way of formatting what he hears most frequently.

Brain Principle 1: The brain synergizes information, so that 1 plus 1 is 2 or more

To tackle problems, generate solutions or formulate policy, the best Grass Roots teams often assemble people drawn from diverse disciplines and departments and then shift into 3rd gear together. They find that equality and "cross-pollination" generates more creativity. For example, an accountant may generate a good idea for one of the sales reps, or vice versa, despite their initial unfamiliarity with each other's work activities.

The creativity that results from getting departments such as Human Resources, Information Technology, Sales and Finance together is just amazing. A much broader range of thinking is generated and stronger relationships are built. Team members learn to respect diversity and recognizes it as the best method for creating a high performance team.

Brain Principle 2: The brain is a success-driven mechanism

Every small success a team experiences drives them to larger and larger successes. The successes accumulate as they build upon each other. There is a confidence that comes from "WE DID IT!"

Brain Principle 3: The brain has the ability to mimic actions perfectly

Grass Roots teams fully utilize the concept of taking best practices from others and copying what is useful. GRI teams become the model that their managers want others to follow.

A Grass Roots student was being interviewed for a key management position and commented to his director, "Having experience with Grass Roots Innovation has given me such an advantage. Thank you."

The director replied, "It was because of your leadership during the implementation of the Grass Roots projects that we observed you tackling some tough issues. This 3rd Gear thinking got you on to our short list of candidates. *Leaders Emerge Through Results.*"

Brain Principle 4: The brain craves completeness—it needs to fill in the blanks

Everyone wants to understand how all the pieces of any puzzle fit together. By looking for an end-to-end process definition of work, including the input and output of every activity, each team member sees the whole picture. This enables their own creativity.

Brain Principle 5: The brain constantly seeks new information and knowledge

It is imperative that people use the tools available to them. It is just as imperative that leaders constantly expose their teams to educational offerings that build relationship and leadership skills. Having a great idea with no support to implement it doesn't lead to success. In today's global world, it's the only way to stay on top of the game.

Brain Principle 6: The brain is truth-seeking

Teams must know the important facts. Organizations cannot consistently make the best decisions when working with incomplete or inaccurate information. Even when the information is accurate, when it is taken out of context it can lead to inaccurate conclusions. To make the best decisions, you must focus on the right details, from process flows through metrics.

GRASS ROOTS
LEADERS—THE
BRAINSMART
REVOLUTION IN
BUSINESS

216

Brain Principle 7: The brain is persistent

The Grass Roots people in this book are persistent. They will not take "no" for an answer unless given a thorough explanation that influences them to take another path. If they are not sure someone is telling them the complete story, they keep pushing the person involved until the story makes sense. They also have a very clear definition of success (Chapter 7), and won't give up until all the work is done to achieve it.

As a finance executive shared with the authors after seeing the results of his Grass Roots teams, "Today, successful companies recognize that the only constant is 'change.'" We established the foundation to quickly adapt and implement changes to our processes. Our employees have powerful tools that allow them not only to *cope* with change, but to *promote* change. To lead the pack, you must innovate and perform better than anyone else. It is not rocket science, it's just a straightforward way of approaching today's challenges."

LESSONS FOR LEADERS

During the GRI workshops Tony Dottino conducts, he has learned critical lessons that are a differentiator in transforming an organization's culture. It comes from listening to what the Grass Roots people are saying.

Leadership summary:

1   Efforts to change the way work gets done, and building a culture of agility are most effective when they include the people who actually do the work. Innovation is more likely to be sustainable than mandates coming from management, task forces or consultants. Buy-in is quickly achieved, and the front-line employees see the benefits of the improvements.
    Result: A model which promotes cultural renewal and drives performance is what keeps it alive. A model of using all three Gears of Success and Leadership at the appropriate time empowers everyone in an organization to handle more complex issues more quickly and profitably.
2   Leaders must invest time to listen to crucial information from their employees and customers; only then will real change occur because a new level of trust and confidence has been built. When employees do not fear retaliation, the stage is set to transform the culture. Workers know that executives and managers are there for coaching and support. Workers recognize that their leaders are operating in all three gears along with them.
    Result: Leveraging the knowledge within the organization equals sustainable performance.

3   Leaders and managers in 3rd Gear are aligned on the organization's goals, and these goals are consistently and clearly communicated throughout the organization. The context of real work provides the forum to evaluate and modify relevant behaviors tied to business results. This leads to an inspired workforce that provides cutting edge outcomes.

    Result: Management and employees have a shared sense of urgency, one that is focused on business outcomes. Everyone matters in making a difference.

4   An intervention should develop synergies between employees (bubbling up) and leaders (reaching down). Leaders who know how to tap into the innovative ideas of their talent pool are the ones that succeed in today's environment.

    Result: Transformed behavior patterns are initiated that reinforce the principles of Proactive leadership.

5   Achieving early victories quickly builds confidence and enthusiasm in the work force. They learn thinking skills they will use everyday and discover that their leadership team will listen to them. Workers recognize that they can make real changes in their work and they expect success with future efforts. Employees are empowered to take on bigger challenges.

    Result: Sustainable implementation of measurable changes by leveraging the knowledge within the organization and changing minds.

The GRI Workshop helps teams solve a common problem in many organizations—focusing so much on 2nd Gear profits, deadlines and timeframes that everyone loses sight of the big picture.

Despite discrete boxes in an organizational chart, every company is really a collection of individuals, each possessing personal strengths. Imagine the power generated by an organization which recognizes the uniqueness of each individual and has the capacity to focus everyone on common goals with the precision of a laser beam. To excel in today's business environment, a company must harness the creative potential of all its employees in a way which aligns them with executive leadership.

An organization's ability to successfully negotiate a permanent change in culture must close the loop for the pioneers of the effort. An article in *Science* (April 1, 2005) suggests that to build trust in people, there must be reward and recognition given to the pioneers of the effort to change culture. The challenge is that each individual is unique in how they associate and connect the words "reward" and "recognition." During our workshops, we conduct an exercise where the Grass Roots Team defines to their manager, "What does reward and recognition look like to you?"

The most eye-opening part of this exercise is that the majority of Grass Roots people, many whom have done some incredible work, do not have money at the top of their list as a reward. The number one item most people request is, "More time with my leaders so I can understand even more how I can make a difference."

STATION 11– ANNE KELLEY (PART 2)

We left Anne in Chapter 1 with her and Tony building a plan. The plan began with information gathering by Anne and her consultant team. She conducted an in-depth 2- day listening and learning session with leadership both from Washington and from Station 11. The session included a reaffirmation of what success (Chapter 7) would look like, an overview of operations and conditions at Station 11, the union's role in the process, the crafting of questions that would be used in on-site focus session, logistics and a communication strategy. Participants at this session included the leadership mentioned above plus union representatives and other managers from the field who had contact with this facility.

Plans were made, and Kelly was off to Station 11. Just seeing its dusty location on a scorching July afternoon brought to life in a dramatic fashion everything that she had previously heard. The physical facility and mood of the employees were equally foreboding and she knew this greening would take more than just some good technical methodologies. The Station didn't have fancy conference rooms, and for a woman from DC the environment was very intimidating. Anne knew that something good needed to happen at the initial session, or her team would not be welcomed back (Chapters 6 and 11).

The initial intervention consisted of interviewing every employee at the facility. The interviews were conducted as focus sessions with groups of 20 employees per session. They were asked a series of structured questions designed to let employees know that someone wanted to listen to what they had to say and to define solutions. It was critical to have DC executive participation at these sessions. These were the questions used in the focus sessions:

- What knowledge existed of the bureau's vision, mission, values and goal?
- How did the work performed support the bureau's mission?
- What things could be done to help better perform the mission?
- What suggestions were there to improve work processes and help achieve cost savings?
- What could be done to further personal/professional development?
- What could be done to improve the quality of the work life?
- What aspects about the work and working conditions/environment are the most stressful?

The results were consistent; all were painfully negative and showed the lack of enterprise, hope or engagement by both management and employees. They spoke the truth, and the truth was ugly. The challenge was great, but so too was the opportunity to make a significant, permanent difference. When an organization is that far down, it is hard to see a ray of hope (Chapter 1).

The data was analyzed and consolidated into mind maps (Chapters 4 and 5) to clearly communicate the true state of things to leadership at both Station 11 and at headquarters. With data in hand, Kelly began the greening process.

The leadership team sorted the maps into two categories. The first was defined as leadership actions; those where local and headquarters would need to take steps to help improving operations.

To everyone's initial surprise, the majority of items fell onto the second map. It represented those issues that leadership felt employees would be best able to address with management support. After all, they were closest to the work. The Station Chief put it best, "I cannot possibly deal with everything coming at me on a daily basis. I need to find a set of skills and tools which will engage the front-line men and women at the camp." The Grass Roots Revolution at Station 11 was about to begin (Chapters 2 and 7).

Planting the seed

The project began in December. Part of Anne's HQ GRI team traveled to Station 11 and conducted a 2 day *BrainSmart Leader* workshop for all managers and supervisors (*BrainSmart Leader*, Gower 1999). The purpose of the workshop was to educate leaders about the Grass Roots process, gain their buy-in and support, and prepare them for their role in deploying GRI to the workforce ("Shifting Gears," Chapter 3). At least on the surface the workshop was a success. More on this to come later in Anne's story on p. 221.

Over the following months, Kelly and Dottino conducted a series of GRI workshops (Chapter 11) with employees and supervisors. In the first two sessions, the employees were "compelled attendees," nominated by their supervisors. These first groups were not happy to be there and considered themselves to be guinea pigs (at least for the first hours of the workshop). After learning about the brain principles, however, they became very interested and engaged in the learning, and genuinely began to have fun. Word spread about how much participants were learning and the impact they could have on their own work environment. Before long, a waiting list of attendees for future sessions existed.

Following each workshop, Kelly met with the participants from the previous workshop to assess the progress they had made in their projects. That is how she learned a valuable lesson—the mid-level management trap. Like a strangling weed, this trap almost destroyed the tiny seedlings of hope that were being sown.

Although the senior leadership at the station saw the value of GRI and were supportive, it became apparent that the mid-level and first line supervisors were not encouraging their employees. They did not provide them with time to meet as a team to work on their projects, and most importantly were thwarting the employees desire to be engaged, creative and take ownership for their work. In short, the mid-level managers felt threatened that this process would render them obsolete and they would lose their jobs. They thought empowered employees would no longer need supervision. How wrong is that?

Kelly and her team faced the problem and determined that the best way to counter this resistance was to focus attention on the supervisors (Chapter 9). Every time the team went to Station 11, a half-day was devoted to a workshop with the entire management team. They had an opportunity to hear the employees who had just completed a GRI workshop describe the projects they were tackling and see their enthusiasm. Then, Kelly and her team reviewed the GRI principles, and asked the managers to also identify processes that needed improvement. They were tasked with devising an improvement plan, and to report on their progress on Kelly's return visit. This procedure was habitually repeated throughout the time that the team was at Station 11, and it worked. The supervisors overcame their fears, became proponents of GRI and used the process themselves to solve some of the overwhelming challenges they faced.

Kelly also saw potential in some members of the management team to identify new workshop participants and projects that the GRI teams would work on. Among this team of inside consultants was Raul.

The son of a Mexican father and American mother, Raul began his career at the station as a janitor. Through determination, intelligence and resiliency, Raul had risen to the ranks of a mid-level manager. It was remarkable to see him in action, even with his "Spanglish." When he spoke, everyone listened because he commanded the respect of his peers, subordinates and superiors. He immediately understood the potential of GRI and helped Anne sell its value to the participants who were unsure if this workshop would be useful to them.

Along with Raul, there were two remarkable women who were champions of the process and of the team. They gave invaluable support by encouraging participation, holding the participants accountable to complete their projects and acting like cheerleaders for the project.

Rosa and Jesse were the two most senior women at the Station, serving as managers in two separate areas but having worked together over the years on various projects. Station 11 was a hard place for women, since most of the employees and detainees were male. Coming up through the ranks, Rosa and Jesse endured chauvinism and sexism and became tough, street-wise ladies. They developed growth and confidence because of the nurturing and encouragement by Anne, and it helped them blossom to become great leaders (Chapter 9).

Nurturing the plants

Bringing GRI to Station 11 resulted in both tangible and intangible results. The employees became engaged in their work, took ownership and gained self-esteem and pride. They learned skills they could apply both at their job and in their personal life. Most important of all, they developed confidence in themselves that they had the power to improve their workplace. They gained a sense of purpose and coming to work added meaning to their lives (Chapter 10).

The employees' projects resulted in improved processes, efficiencies and cost savings. They gained skills that simplified their work and enabled them to find solutions to the myriad of problems that they faced every day.

On the first day that Kelly toured Station 11, she immediately spotted one huge bottle neck that needed attention: the in-and-out processing of aliens.

The facility was receiving and releasing detainees at the same time each day, at 4 p.m. This resulted in a completely chaotic situation. It also created a real vulnerability, as any of the aliens who were arriving could potentially escape among the group being released. A Grass Roots team tackled this issue and come up with a winning solution. They established a space in a separate building to release the detainees who were ready to be deported to their home country.

A second team did a complete analysis of the rules regarding legal hearings. They identified which detainees had the legal right to seek a hearing with a Department of Justice judge, and which detainees could waive this process and immediately return to their homeland. This was a major victory for Station 11, because within 1 month of implementation they increased the out processing of detainees by 46 per cent.

Another efficiency improvement involved the transportation of detainees to an airport. By making a few changes in the process, that team realized a savings of $130 000 annually.

Despite these successes, the most important outcome of the GRI intervention was the attention focused on the facility's preparation for the American Correctional Association (ACA) review. Through accreditation, a facility demonstrates it is able to maintain a balance between protecting the public and providing an environment that safeguards the life, health and safety of staff and detainees.

The ACA audit is a rigorous process that identifies strengths and weaknesses. It includes assessments that cover administration and management, the physical plant, institutional operations and services, and inmate programs. It assesses staff training, adequacy of medical services, sanitation, use of proper detention techniques and crowding. It even evaluates offender activity levels, programs, and provisions of basic services that may impact the life, safety and health of inmates and staff.

In the second year of the Station 11 project, Raul (who was in charge of preparing the facility for its ACA audit) realized that GRI could be used to prepare for the audit. Raul and his devoted ACA team of three other officers had the grueling task of documenting all the procedures and processes at the Station.

The GRI process was used to involve many of the employees. They became responsible for areas that would be audited and developed action plans and tactics to ensure the Station would be in compliance.

A good audit provides the organization with many benefits, including establishment of measurable criteria for upgrading operations, improved staff morale and professionalism, and a safer environment for staff and offenders. How remarkable that the very things that Kelly had been advocating as reasons to use GRI were in perfect alignment with what ACA assessed. Preparation for the audit provided an additional benefit by motivating employees to collaborate and do what was needed to ensure that the facility was in the best possible condition for the audit.

It was a high priority for headquarters that Station 11 pass the audit and get an outstanding rating. The implications for not getting a good audit were dire. A failing audit score would result in added scrutiny from field operations and headquarters, and the Station would have to continue scrubbing its operations since they would be re-audited within the year.

The results came in, and the improvement was amazing. Every employee at Station 11 was overjoyed when the formal audit findings arrived and the score was a close to perfect 95. They finally had achieved something on a large scale that gave them pride in their facility and in their own ability to do good work.

The garden in bloom

The 1.5 years that Anne and her team worked at Station 11 brought phenomenal changes. Despair, lethargy, mediocre performance and lack of accountability were replaced by teamwork, creativity, pride and leadership at all levels. The employees and management gained a sense of self-respect as they reflected on all that they had accomplished on that long journey. Not only had they improved their processes and operations, but they had made improvements that saved the division and ultimately the federal government money. Because of GRI, leadership is in place that understands the principles of effective management and the benefits of engaging employees. Front-line Station 11 workers provide their input and use their own ideas for making improvements. Here is what one of the employees said about Kelly's work:

> *You have helped us through so much difficulty, provided us so much guidance and encouragement and you are a Godsend. I was a skeptic and you and your team proved me wrong—I initially thought you were just passing through. You have made a huge difference in lives here. We are on the right track and I hope things will continue to get better and better*

Anne's question is answered!

Although Kelly's work there has ended, the flourishing of Station 11 continues. Even as their front-line work protecting the US southern border increases, the skills and techniques of GRI are helping the employees meet the challenges and dangers they face. The employees continue to use the skills of analysis, mind mapping and effective communication to eliminate re-work and poor quality. The techniques and strategies they learned are embedded at the Station and the promises that Tony Dottino made at that long ago briefing are being realized.

GRASS ROOTS LEADERS

Hierarchical organizations that once flourished during the industrial revolution increasingly finds themselves out-of-place today. The BrainSmart Revolution is not about terminating middle-managers or evicting executives from plush office suites. Rather, it's a radical new way of looking at line employees—from compliant functionaries to savvy experts of the everyday world. People at the Grass Roots yearn for someone to discover their genius of knowing what works where it counts most—at the front line. A BrainSmart Leader documents a way to make this radical change in perspective a reality in *your* organization.

In this book, we have described people we consider to be Grass Roots Leaders who are leading a BrainSmart Revolution, the new agents of organizational change. They generate an energy that propels them to go above and beyond, knocking out obstacles along the journey.

By the time the GRI process is complete, participants know the brain has unlimited thinking capacity that provides infinite creativity to solve problems and implement innovative plans to make the organization's vision a reality. As everyone learns to better manage and communicate even complex issues clearly, GRI teams build relationships and skills necessary to become a WORLD CLASS team! They win respect, commitment, integrity and loyalty from their managers and peers. Grass Roots Leaders will powerfully lead an organization into the future.

GRASS ROOTS
LEADERS—THE
BRAINSMART
REVOLUTION IN
BUSINESS

224

You can achieve all these results as you now have the tools in your hands—the techniques to develop an aligned workforce, focused on your company's goals and the skills to make it happen. These energized, self-motivated, three-gear teams will show constant improvements and a great return on investment.

We wish you well on this exciting journey. Please communicate your stories to us, and remember to invite us to the celebration of your SUCCESS!

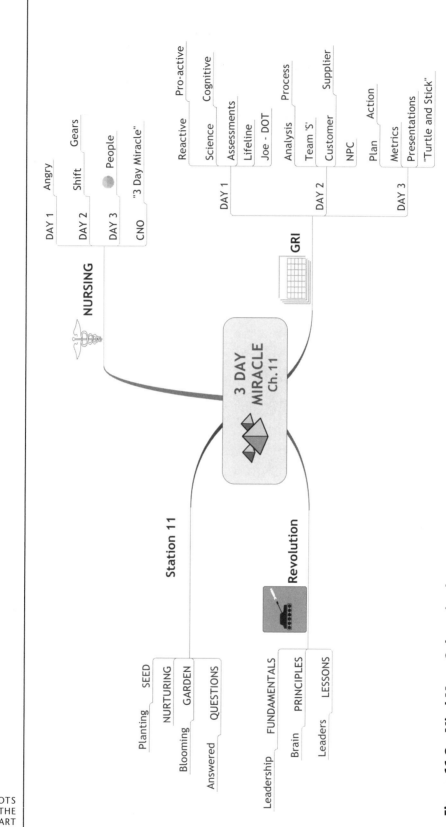

Figure 11.2 Mind Map—3 day miracle

GRASS ROOTS
LEADERS—THE
BRAINSMART
REVOLUTION IN
BUSINESS

226

Further Reading

Embracing Change, Tony Buzan, BBC Active 2005

The Ultimate Book of Mind Maps, Tony Buzan, Harper Thorsons 2006

Brain Sell, Tony Buzan and Richard Israel, Second edition, Gower 2004

The Mind Map Book, Tony Buzan, BBC Active 2003

Use Both Sides of Your Brain, Tony Buzan, Third edition, Plume 1991

Age Proof Your Brain, Tony Buzan, Harper Thorsons 2007

How to THINK Creatively, Conni Gordon and Richard Israel, Conni Gordon Inc. 2002

Shifting Gears, Susan Ford Collins and Richard Israel, Technology of Success 2004

Sales Genius, Tony Buzan and Richard Israel, Gower 2000

Your Mind at Work, Richard Israel, Cliff Shaffran and Hellen Whitten, Kogan Page 2000

About the Authors

TONY BUZAN

Tony Buzan, inventor of the now world-famous Mind Maps®, has achieved an astonishing series of accomplishments.

- The world's leading author on the brain and learning (over 84 authored and co-authored books to date, with sales totalling three million (and accelerating!)).
- The world's top lecturer on the brain and learning. Tony Buzan has lectured to audiences ranging from 5-year-old children through disadvantaged students to first-class Oxbridge graduates, to the world's top business directors, and to the leading organisations and governments.
- Named in 1994 by Forbes magazine as one of five top international lecturers along with Mikhail Gorbachev, Henry Kissinger and Margaret Thatcher.
- Founder of the World Memory Championships.
- Founder of the World Speed Reading Championships.
- Buzan's books and other products have achieved massive success in more than 100 countries and 30 languages, generating revenues in excess of £100 million.
- Inventor of Mind Maps®, the thinking tool described as "the Swiss army knife of the brain," now used by over 250 million people worldwide.
- Previous editor of the international journal of MENSA (the high IQ society).
- International business consultant to major multinationals including BP, Barclays International, General Motors, Walt Disney, Oracle, Microsoft, HSBC, British Telecom, IBM, British Airways, etc.
- Consultant and adviser to governments and government organisations including: England, Singapore, Mexico, Australia, the Gulf States and Liechtenstein.
- A global media personality, having appeared on over 100 hours of national and global television, and over 1,000 hours of national and international radio. He has been seen and heard by an estimated three billion-plus people!
- Waterstones book shops and the Express Newspaper group and their advisers have recently selected one of Tony's books, *Use Your Head*, as one of the 1,000 greatest books of the past millennium. They are simultaneously recommending it as an essential part of the 1,000-book library for the current millennium—the Millennium of the Mind.

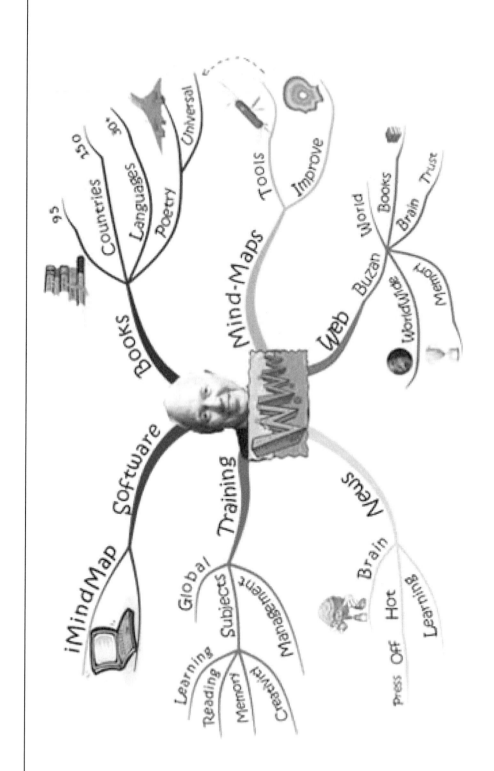

TONY DOTTINO

Dottino Consulting Group, Inc., a privately-owned company led by its principal, Tony Dottino, and Vice President of Innovative Solutions, Evelyn Walker, serves clients in both the public and private sectors.

Its mission: **Provide skills and tools to leaders and their employees that consistently enhance their abilities to promote change, execute strategy and deliver results.**

The demand for finding new ways to lead, inspire a workforce, tap into their creativity and generate new value for customers is fierce. The need for a new approach for mining human resources led Tony into immersing himself in the vast pool of research available on the human brain and applying it to business problems. In many instances, this research explained why many management approaches attempting to improve communication, increase workers' creativity and build strong teams have failed.

The lessons learned have helped him put together several pragmatic workshops which do not lecture, give answers or provide solutions. If people are being asked to think, then DCG's most pressing task is to help them to do so in ways that inspire new pathways of thinking. This requires some new lessons and actions for leaders to engage their supervisors and employees into changing attitudes and expectations of work actions.

Two workshops are the core of their client work. The BrainSmart Leader, helps executive and management teams to learn how to maximize the growth of the organizations most important asset—its people. They develop a compelling vision and desire to fully utilize their team's creative ability by reaching out to employees to gain commitment and buy-in. This creates the first step for a bubbling up from employees who are fully engaged and passionate about using their experience and creative abilities to solve problems.

This is complemented with a bottom up (Developing Leaders through Grass Roots Innovation—GRI) for supervisors and front line workers to provide them with the abilities needed to achieve organizational goals. Utilizing **real work examples** chosen by the participants, the skills and tools taught in the workshop are immediately integrated into participant day-to-day activities. The participants develop their own solution that leads to actions taken with metrics to track progress. Because there is IMMEDIATE feedback and action taken, participants gain the confidence and commitment to deliver even more. Through this process we promote, reinforce and sustain the transformation of an organization's culture.

Permanent changes in the way people communicate across all levels, a systematic problem-solving approach with necessary skills for implementation of action plans, and development of cohesive teams working together to achieve the organization's goals are the results these workshops achieve.

Clients have included Florida Hospital, Florida Department of Transportation, the US Department of Homeland Security, the New York Transit Authority, IBM, JP Morgan Chase and Con Edison. They have found the blend of brain research and business acumen to be a critical ingredient in bringing their leadership teams and workers together.

The *New York Times* article, "Can 'NEUROBICS' do for the Brain what Aerobics do for Lungs?" stated, "IBM, Con Edison, British Airways, and Johnson and Johnson have sought Mr. Dottino's help with business application of brain research. He is a convincing and passionate speaker whose clients speak with satisfaction of the results DCG has helped them achieve, including a comprehensive mental literacy program and cognitive calisthenics to help employees unleash their creative energies." Aside from the *New York Times*, Tony has been featured in *Investor's Business Daily*, *Business News*, *USA Today*, numerous magazines, as well as appearing on a number of television and radio programs.

In 1997, Tony founded the United States Memory Championship. The championship has been featured on CNN, FOX, CBS, NBC, ABC, in People Magazine, the NY Times, Sports Illustrated as well as numerous radio stations across the country. Tony hosted the first national broadcast of the 2006 event on HDNet Television.

Before creating DCG he had a distinguished career with IBM receiving numerous awards that included the "Chairman's Award for Management Excellence" and the "President's Award for Innovation and Teaching Excellence."

Contact information:
Dottino Consulting Group
14 Lafayette Rd
Larchmont, New York 10538
1-201-446-1808
Web: www.dottinoconsulting.com
E-mail: adottino@aol.com

RICHARD ISRAEL

The Technology of Success is a privately-owned US company led by its principals Richard Israel and Susan Ford Collins. The mission of The Technology of Success is to bring the latest information on success, leadership,

GRASS ROOTS
LEADERS – THE
BRAINSMART
REVOLUTION IN
BUSINESS

232

sales and information management to business people around the world. In short, to advance career development.

In the early 1970s, Richard Israel took sales training to the next level. His extraordinary results were acknowledged by *Business Week* and documented in his book with Friedland and Lynch, *People Productivity in Retail* (Lebar Friedman, NY, 1980).

Confident the next business wave would be based on breakthroughs on the human brain, when Richard read Tony Buzan's ground-breaking book, *Use Both Sides of Your Brain*, he asked him how they could apply Buzan's mental literacy concepts to selling. Together they wrote *BrainSell* (Buzan and Israel, Gower, second edition). It rapidly became an international bestseller available in 21 languages. Gower, their publisher, urged them to write sequels: *Supersellf*, 1997, *The BrainSmart Leader* (with Tony Dottino), 1995, and *Sales Genius*, 2000.

Since then, Richard has trained sales teams around the world. His clients include Turner Broadcasting (Asia), BMW (Republic of South Africa), Hertie (Germany), Myer (Australia), Nakamichi (Japan), Barney's and Macy's (New York), International Distillers & Vinters (United Kingdom) and ICBC International (China). Richard's speaking and training has been acclaimed by critics from *The South China Morning Post* to the *New York Times*.

SUSAN FORD COLLINS

While Richard focused on selling skills, Susan was exploring what makes people successful. For two decades, she studied top people in business, entertainment and science and discovered they were using 10 skills consistently but unconsciously. Most people use most of these Success Skills but they fail to use them all, at the right time. Since 1983, Susan has taught The Technology of Success at American Express, Florida Power & Light, The Upjohn Company, Kimberly Clark, Ryder System, IBM, the University of Chicago Graduate School of Business and Jepson School of Leadership Studies. After two appearances on CNN, Lou Dobbs asked Susan to train his startup Financial News Team.

Corporate leaders asked Susan to teach The Technology of Success to parents and teachers so their kids will already be using these skills when they enter the workplace. In 1995, Susan wrote *Our Children Are Watching: Ten Skills for Leading the Next Generation to Success*.

In 2003, to make The Technology of Success skill set available worldwide, Susan wrote *The Joy of Success: 10 Essential Skills for Getting the Success YOU Want*. It was published in English by HarperCollins and, through its subsidiaries, in Chinese, French, Polish and Indonesian. Jack Canfield, co-author of bestselling *Chicken*

Soup for the Soul, says, "This is one of the most sophisticated and useful success books I have ever read. I highly recommend it."

Next, Susan and Richard co-authored *Shifting Gears: How YOU Can Succeed and Lead in the NEW Workplace* (Technology of Success, 2005). In it, they share case studies on the 23 most challenging success and leadership problems business people face today, and 23 solutions you can use immediately. George Naddaff, founder of Boston Market, said *Shifting Gears* is, "A book ALL present and future business executives should make required reading for ALL their department heads."

In 2006, business leaders asked Susan and Richard to help them solve a problem that is stressing people everywhere, Information Overload. How can they help employees increase reading speeds, use e-mail more efficiently and make meetings worth the time and money they invest in them?

This time Susan and Richard developed Managing Information Overload, a training program which took off the very day it was launched. "To say you guys were a hit would be an understatement," Jesus Diaz, Publisher, The Miami Herald. "I only wish I had learned this 30 years ago!," Blas Moros, former Director, Microsoft Latin America and Asia.

Susan Ford Collins and Richard Israel deliver Managing Information Overload face to face. And now, in response to thousands of requests, it is available online 24/7.

Contact information:
The Technology of Success
12040 NE Fifth Avenue
Miami, Florida 33161 USA
305-892-2702
Web: www.technologyofsuccess.com
E-mail: brainsell@aol.com or susanfordcollins@msn.com

Richard Israel and Susan Ford Collins

Index